The Book Against Death

T0253089

THE BOOK
AGAINST DEATH

Elias Canetti

translated from the German by Peter Filkins
foreword by Joshua Cohen

A NEW DIRECTIONS PAPERBOOK ORIGINAL

Copyright © 2014 by the heirs of Elias Canetti
Copyright © 2014 by Carl Hanser Verlag & C. KG, München
Translation copyright © 2024 by Peter Filkins
Foreword copyright © 2024 by Joshua Cohen

Edited from the Estate of Canetti by Sven Hanuschek, Peter von Matt, and Kristian Washinger, assisted by Laura Schütz.

Originally published in German in 2014 as *Das Buch gegen den Tod* by Carl Hanser Verlag. Originally published in English translation by Fitzcarraldo Editions in Great Britain in 2024.

All rights reserved.
Except for brief passages quoted in a newspaper, magazine, radio, television, or website review, no part of this book may be reproduced in any form or by any means, electronic or mechanical, including photocopying and recording, or by any information storage and retrieval system, or be used to train generative artificial intelligence (AI) technologies or develop machine-learning language models, without permission in writing from the Publisher.

Lines by Luis Buñuel from *My Last Sigh: The Autobiography of Luis Buñuel*, translated by Abigail Israel, translation copyright © 1983 by Penguin Random House LLC. Used by permission of Alfred A. Knopf, an imprint of the Knopf Doubleday Publishing Group, a division of Penguin Random House LLC. All rights reserved.

Lines by Robert Walser from *Berlin Stories*, New York Review Books. Copyright © Suhrkamp Verlag Zürich 1978 and 1985. Translation copyright © 2012 by Susan Bernofsky.

First published as New Directions Paperbook 1595 in 2024
Manufactured in the United States of America

Library of Congress Control Number: 2024004634

10 9 8 7 6 5 4 3 2 1

New Directions Books are published for James Laughlin
by New Directions Publishing Corporation
80 Eighth Avenue, New York 10011

Contents

Foreword by Joshua Cohen   vii

THE BOOK AGAINST DEATH   3

Afterword by Peter Filkins   295

Acknowledgments   303

Notes   305

Foreword

"Quixotic" is a word that comes to mind when thinking of Elias Canetti, not just because Cervantes's novel was his favorite novel, but because Canetti too was a man from La Mancha. His paternal family hailed from Cañete, a Moorish-fortified village in modern-day Cuenca Province, Castile–La Mancha, from which they were scattered in the mass expulsion of Jews from Spain in 1492. Having fared better under Muslim rule than Catholic, the Cañetes passed through Italy, where their name was respelled, and settled in Adrianople—today's Edirne, Turkey, near the Greek and Bulgarian borders—before moving on to Rusçuk, a port town on the Danube known in Bulgarian as Ruse, whose thriving Sephardic colony supported itself by trading between two empires, the Ottoman and the Austro-Hungarian. Elias, the first of three boys, was born to Jacques Canetti and Mathilde Arditti in Ruse in 1905 and in childhood was whisked away to England, where Jacques took over the local office of the import-export firm established by Mathilde's brothers. In 1912, a year after the family's arrival in Manchester, Jacques died suddenly of a heart attack and Mathilde took her brood to neutral Lausanne and, once the First World War was concluded, to Vienna. There Canetti acquired, or was acquired by, the German language, which would become his primary language, though it was already his fifth, after—in chronological order—Ladino, Bulgarian, English, and French. Following a haphazard education in Zurich, Frankfurt, and Berlin, Canetti returned to Vienna to study chemistry and medicine, but spent most of his energies on literature, especially on writing plays that were never produced, though he often read them aloud, doing all the voices. At the time, his primary influence was journalistic—the feuilletons of Karl Kraus—which might have been a way of giving himself the necessary distance from the German-language novels of the Viennese generation preceding his own, the doorstops of Hermann Broch and Robert Musil, both of whom were known to him personally. His own contribution to fiction—his sole contribution to that quixotic art—came in 1935 with *Die Blendung* (The Blinding), which concerns a Viennese bibliophile and Sinologist who winds up being immolated along with his library. *Die Blendung* was translated into English as *Auto da Fé*—a preferred punishment of the Inquisition—though Elias's original suggestion for the English-language title was *Holocaust*. In nearly all the brief biographical notes on Canetti, this is where the break comes: when he abandons the theater, publishes his only fiction, and escapes the Nazis by leaving the continent. Exile brought him to England again, and to nonfiction, specifically to *Masse und Macht* (*Crowds and Power*), a study of "the crowd," be that in the form of an audience, a protest movement or political demonstration, or a rowdy group threatening to riot—any assemblage in which constituent individuality has been dissolved and rebonded into a mass, as in the chemical reactions in which Canetti was schooled, or as in the atomic reactions that threaten planetary existence. Canetti's singular study of collective behavior, published in 1960, stands at the center of his corpus, along with his remarkable series of memoirs, each named for a single sense: *The Tongue Set Free, The Torch in My Ear, The Play of the Eyes.* Five volumes were projected, but the series went unfinished: no volume connected to smell or touch was ever completed and the final year of his life covered in the memoirs is 1937, the year Canetti's mother died and he began to conceive of a book "against" death, a version of which—the only available version of which—can be found on the pages that follow.

Five years ago today my mother died. Since then my world has turned inside out. To me it is as if it happened just yesterday. Have I really lived five years, and she knows nothing of it? I want to undo each screw of her coffin's lid with my lips and haul her out. I know that she is dead. I know that she has rotted away. But I can never accept it as true. I want to bring her to life again. Where do I find parts of her? Mostly in my brothers and me. But that is not enough. I need to find every person whom she knew. I need to retrieve every word she ever said. I need to walk in her steps and smell the flowers she smelled, the great-grandchild of every blossom that she held up to her powerful nostrils. I need to piece back together the mirrors that once reflected her image. I want to know every syllable she could have possibly said in any language. Where is her shadow? Where is her fury? I will loan her my breath. She should walk on my own two legs.

Note the date: a week or so after the Battle of Midway, not to mention the United States declaring war on Bulgaria (along with Romania and Hungary), and the Black Saturday when British and South African forces evacuated the Gazala Line. This isn't quite Kafka's remark on a summer day twenty-eight years earlier: "Germany has declared war on Russia. Swimming in the afternoon," but it's close. Canetti clings to his mother's demise as generalized Thanatos mobilizes all around him. An estimated fifty to fifty-six million soldiers and civilians died in the Second World War, along with an additional twenty-some million deaths from war-related diseases and famine, and yet Canetti appears to hold with Kurt Tucholsky: a single death is a tragedy, a million a statistic.

"It begins with the fact that we count the dead. Through death each should become a single entity, like God." Those are the opening sentences of Canetti's posthumous *Das Buch gegen* den Tod (*The Book Against Death*), and no one has any idea whether he would have approved of them. Having apprenticed under the sign of the unfinished, unfinishable work—Kafka again—Canetti was disturbed to find that, when it came to his death book, he couldn't even start: he couldn't even find the first lines that would enable a start, so he resigned himself to the accumulation of pensées, aphorisms, notes to self, and notes to others, which he intended to later rearrange into what he was certain would be his masterwork, a capstone and a headstone. Sixty-five years later, nearly two thousand pages of material later, Canetti succumbed to his subject, dying in Switzerland in 1994, and leaving behind a manuscript that he sometimes referred to as drafts toward a book and sometimes referred to as the book itself, a contradiction that was embraced by his German editors (a team that included his daughter and his German-language biographer) who put together this present abridgment, published in German in 2014.

If I suggest that this book is itself "a survivor," it's only to moot the term and assess Canetti's strange, almost profane employment of it. To Canetti, a survivor is not the person who has managed to escape death in a ghetto, concentration camp, or gulag, so much as he is the person who runs the ghetto, concentration camp, or gulag; a person who sentences people to death in pursuit of social or societal control and to maintain a hold on power. Counterintuitively, a classic Canettian survivor is a Hitler, a Stalin, a Hussein, a Putin; a dictator without limits, who stoops to every deceit and act of violence to perpetuate his reign, slaughtering his fellow man as a means—and increasingly as the only means—of forestalling his own inevitable mortality.

A survivor lives only because others have died for him (parenthetically, has there even been a better definition of an Antichrist?), and it's that contingency that guilted Canetti for having passed the war in the relative safety of Hampstead. As if to justify his continued existence, he set out in the shadow of genocide to write daily about his intimate deaths, especially about the deaths of his mother and of his first wife Veza and of his favorite brother Georg; and after the armistice, he extended this diaristic discipline through the headlines of the Vietnam War, the fall of Communism, the Yugoslav and Gulf Wars, and the more private tragedy that was his winning of the Nobel Prize in Literature ("it's a kind of leprosy").

Those seeking a system among these decades of decay-themed entries will find none: Canetti mistrusted systems, from the Hegelian dialectic (where there is death, there can be no synthesis), to the motley Marxisms and Freudianisms that he regarded as ideological "survivors," explanations of the world that remained and sustained only because they'd conquered and consumed all other explanations, along with all nonexplaining art. In this book in particular, all intellectual systems or methods pale beside death, which is the absolute taxon or order-bringing entity whose definitive sorting of humanity into those "present" and those "passed" or "past" must be resisted by the processes of memory, and by reading and writing.

This is Canetti's core heuristic—he has no plan or program, but he has a heuristic—which is implied in the book's very title. *The Book Against Death*, like so much having to do with resting in peace, has its eeriest meaning obscured by the Latin tradition and the plethora of libri contra, such as Augustine's *Contra academicos* and Aquinas's *Contra errores Graecorum* and *Summa contra Gentiles*. Those works are apologetics, correctives whose contrariety—whose "against-ness"—is a matter of rhetoric or polemic: the Emperor Julian writes *contra* the Galileans because he's sure the Galileans are wrong; their Christianity is merely apostate Judaism and they should return to the old ways of the pagan Imperium; Cyril of Alexandria writes *contra* Julian, in response, and calls him the apostate, and so on. Canetti's *liber contra mortem* is different: it is not just "against" death in the sense that it regards death as incorrect ("But no death is natural"), it is also "against" death in the sense that it seeks to "defeat death," to magically, mystically, apotropaically make death die purely through the force of its sentences, presenting its wordings as warding spells to annul the reaper or at least dull his scythe.

This book, in our reading of it as in Canetti's writing of it, is a type of life traveler's talisman or amulet, a prose garlic bulb or rabbit's foot, or a version of the Balsam of Fierabrás, say, that balm used to treat the wounds of the crucified Christ, barrels of which the legendary Saracen giant Fierabrás was said to have filched from Rome, or Jerusalem, and brought back to Spain, where its recipe was passed down to Quixote, who administers it to himself and Sancho Panza. "It's a balm," the original man from La Mancha says, "the formula for which I've memorized, by means of which one needn't fear death, nor worry about dying from any wound."

This book—this powerfully gnomic, mad-sincere book— is a similar vouchsafe for those who consider themselves "Death's Enemy," a character Canetti posits as the ultimate incarnation of the heroic knight-errant. Quixote, who never relents, who abhors surrender, and who believes in himself and his questing more than he believes in any church, is healed and restored by quaffing the concoction, whereas Sancho Panza—precisely because he fears dying, precisely because he worries about suffering—sips and spends the long long night "discharge[ing] from both ends," which is to say barfing and shitting, shitting and barfing.

"Not since I could think on my own have I ever called anyone 'Lord!,' and how easy it is to say 'Lord!' and how great the temptation," Canetti tells us of his own faith, founded in a fundamental contempt, "I have approached a hundred gods, and I looked each straight in the eye, full of hatred for the death of human beings."

JOSHUA COHEN

The Book Against Death

Cemeteries for the Still Born
It begins with the fact that we count the dead. Through death each should become a single entity, like God. One dead person plus another do not make two. It would be better to count the living, given how perishable that number already is.

Entire cities and districts can mourn as if all their men had fallen, all their sons and fathers. But so long as 11,370 have fallen, they will forever seek to have it add up to a million.

Ants and Death
The ant knows nothing of our illnesses and epidemics. You don't even notice when an ant dies, for it so easily lives again. In regards to this, Miss Feld performed some rather cruel, but convincing, experiments. Of seven ants that she kept underwater for eight days, four came alive again. Others she starved, giving them nothing but a little water on a sterilized sponge. Nine *Formica subsericea* lasted between 70 and 106 days. Among the many creatures in the experiment there were indeed only three instances of cannibalism. And on days 20, 35, 62, and 70 of their imposed fast, several half-starved ants managed to share a drop of honey with those whose condition was clearly hopeless. The ants were only sensitive to cold. But even then, they did not die, but rather fell asleep, opting for an economical and practical state of torpor to quietly await the return of the sun.

The knowledge of death appears to be the most consequential experience of human history. It turned into the *acceptance* of death. Deliberate killing *among us* is only possible once we know that the deceased is to a certain degree dead.

The vanishing, the sudden and secret rapture of the great and the holy, *because they are not allowed to die.*

The Grantor of Years — Benefactor

Imagine granting your *own years* to others. Someone gives to others, whose worth he values, a number of his own years in order to prolong theirs. Say that it has been prophesied that he will live a long time, that he knows he will reach his hundredth birthday. Therefore, after making thorough inquiries while traveling around, he decides who needs his years. He parses them out quite thoughtfully, not too many, not too few—a strenuous occupation. In the time that he has left to him, he considers what the best use of what he is sacrificing could be. The news about his extraordinary undertaking spreads fast. He falls prey to speculators who want to make money from his years. They try to convince him of the value of their clients, their general importance and usefulness, even though in truth they are ancient, ridiculous little old ladies who have a lot of money and even more hunger for a couple more ridiculous little years. So, the speculators *manufacture* important people, because for the benefactor, an incorruptible figure, it's just a matter of paying out the money. The reduced number of his years makes them ever more valuable; the fewer of them that remain, the more people desire to savor some for themselves. What develops is a kind of system of stocks that are traded and which reach incredibly high prices. Those who earlier, before speculation began, were granted years are rooted out and pressured to forsake their rights in any way possible. The years are then split into months and weeks. An organization forms among those who acquired their claims by paying for them, complete with an executive committee and elections. They most of all have to keep an eye out for the moment when the benefactor will reach the long-ago fixed limit of his life. Up until that moment what remains belongs to them.

"On the night following the 14th Sha'bán (the eighth month of the Muslim year) special services are held in all the mosques. The traditional reason is that "on this night the lote tree of Paradise, on the leaves of which are inscribed the names of all living persons, is shaken, and the leaf of any mortal who is predestined to die during the ensuing year falls withering to the ground." 1

His knack for doing everything at the *worst of all* times. The depressing messiness of time, which causes him to feel as if he cannot tolerate its irreversibility. If he were able to execute matters in the correct sequence, he fears that he would accept death, toward which any series of events leads.

Chinese Seamen "Reincarnated"
"Fifty-four Chinese seamen, threatened with deportation from Canada for refusing to go to sea again after they had been torpedoed, claimed they were Canadian by reincarnation. They said that they died in the Atlantic, after their ship was torpedoed, and were reincarnated in a Canadian vessel that picked them up. The Canadian authorities disputed this claim and the Chinese must go to sea again." 2

"Certainly, animals are conscious of a very real uneasiness in the presence of the death of one of their own kind. None of them, however, make any pretense of burying their dead ceremonially. The first recorded examples of the latter come from the age of the so-called Neanderthal men, some fifty to one hundred thousand years, BC." 3

The Last Words of Bourignon (1680)
"If I die, I die against the will of God ..." 4

Numerals in the margins refer to endnotes, which begin on p. 305.

"The sun and death are two things we cannot stare into the eye
of."   *La Rochefoucauld*

August 26, 1942

Stalingrad
"The last day's fighting has been largely hand-to-hand with
tommy guns and bayonets. The dead are so thick upon the
ground that there has been no time to bury even a tenth of
them.

"Reports from the front have described how the German
armies solved this problem using field incinerators, not unlike
large camp cookers in appearance."

The story of a man who does not want anyone to survive him.

Died going to shelter
"Hearing the sirens on Monday night, Charles Stephens Ev-
ans, a 67-year-old laborer, of Newport Street, Lambeth, got
out of bed, and was on his way to a shelter when he collapsed
and died in the street."

Stalingrad
"They had time to bury their own dead in a brotherly grave."

"What is certain about death is made a bit more palatable
through what is uncertain about it; the uncertainty of just
when it will occur gives rise to the feeling of unending, and
from that what one calls eternity."   *La Bruyère*

Death of an Australian
"A man had been found dying of spear wounds out in the bush,
and [was] carried to the Mission as he was breathing his last. I
watched two of the lay brothers bearing the stretcher to one of
the huts, a horde of natives following. I noticed that they held

their burden curiously high in the air. Suddenly, as the dying man was lowered for entry to a doorway, the natives crowding round, to my horror, fell upon the body, and put their lips to his in brutal eagerness to inhale the last breath. They believed that in doing so they were absorbing his strength and virtue, and his very vital spark, and all the warnings of the 'white father' would not keep them from it. The man was of course dead when we extricated him, and it was a ghostly sight to see the lucky 'breath catcher' scoop in his cheeks as he swallowed the 'spirit breath' that gave him double hunting power."

D. Bates, The Passing of the Aborigines 10

The Death of Thomas More
More "laying his head upon the block, bade the executioners stay until he had removed aside his beard, saying that that had never committed any treason." 11

The Dead are Married to One Another
"When one man has had a son, and another man a daughter, although both may have been dead for many years, they have a practice of contracting a marriage between their deceased children, and of bestowing the girl upon the youth. They at the same time paint upon pieces of paper human figures to represent attendants with horses and other animals, dresses of all kinds, money, and every article of furniture; and all these, together with the marriage contract, which is regularly drawn up, they commit to the flames, so that through the medium of the smoke (as they believe) these things may be conveyed to their children in the other world, and that they may become husband and wife in due form. After this ceremony, the fathers and mothers consider themselves mutually related, in the same manner, as if a real connection had taken place between their living children." *Marco Polo* 12

From Grillparzer's Diary
The only entry for the year 1839

"Fröhlich's maid spoke about her father, whom she 'loved so much,' and how she helped with the washing and dressing of his body when he died, the stark coldness of it, how unbearable it was to her. So then she thought: if a 'young and healthy person' were to lie down next to him, perhaps the warmth could revive him. That night, when everyone was asleep, she lay down next to her father in his bed and stayed with him the entire night. The next morning others didn't know where she was and looked for her everywhere until she was finally found half-numb next to the corpse. A vigorous beating was the reward for this allopathic attempt to heal. There is something grisly, but also heroic in such tender folly."

13

1942

In order to manifest death entirely, she looks for insects to kill.

He wants to die in secret, so that no one feels triumphant, and for his last meal he'll eat his will.

The urgency of the dead: they want to get away as fast as possible from the explosions.

No one will survive him; anyone who could stand him is dead.

Too little attention is paid to what remains alive of the dead and is dispersed among others; no method has been conceived to nourish these dispersed remains and to keep them alive for as long as possible.

The friends of a dead man gather together on appointed days and talk only about him. They make him even more dead when they only say good things about him. They should quarrel instead, take sides for or against him, talk about his secret escapades. So long as there is something surprising to say about him, he changes in their view and is not dead. The piety involved in preserving a fixed notion of him is not at all kind. It rises out of fear and will only keep him somewhere harmless, such as in the coffin and in the ground. So that the dead man, by the slimmest of margins, can continue to live, he must be allowed to move. He should be angry, as before, and in anger should require an unexpected curse word that is known only to the one who reports it. He should become tender; those who knew him as hard-hearted and uncaring should suddenly learn how loving he could be. One almost wishes that each friend will have a different role to play for the dead man, and out of all of them together he will then exist. One could also allow the younger and uninitiated to take part in these gatherings, so that they can learn as much as possible about someone who was unknown to them. Certain objects associated with him should be passed from hand to hand, and it would be lovely when, at each annual gathering, a new and unfamiliar object is brought along that holds a story.

The word "freedom" gives rise to an important enticement, perhaps the most important enticement that can be expressed. We always wish to get away, and when there is no name for where we want to get to, when we do not know and there is no border in between, then we call it "freedom."

The spatial sense of this enticement is the deep wish to step across a border as if it were not there. The freedom of flight stretches back to the ancient, mythic urge to reach the sun. The freedom of time involves the conquering of death, and one is indeed happy the farther and farther it can be pushed off. The freedom in relation to *things* is the disappearance of prices, and the ideal prodigal, a very free man, wishes for nothing so much as to be uninfluenced by and not needing to worry about constantly changing prices, which always go up and down, much like the weather, and for no good reason. There is no such thing as a "bit" of freedom, for its grace and happiness entices the man who wants to break through whatever holds him back, and he always wishes for this in order to free himself from the worst restraints. Anyone who wants to kill has to deal with the awful consequences that come with the law against killing, and if these consequences weren't such a threat, he would certainly embrace even more satisfying enticements. However the source of freedom lies in breathing.

You can breathe any air, and the freedom to breathe is the only freedom that to this day has not really been destroyed.

Molière's death: He cannot stop acting. The great roles that he plays, and the applause which the theater showers upon him, means too much to him. His friends urge him again and again to give up acting, but he resists their well-meaning suggestions. Even on the day of his death he said he could not deny his fellow actors the chance to earn a living. In reality it was about the applause, for it appears he could not live without it. So it is curious that on the day of his funeral a hostile crowd gathered before his house, the very opposite of the crowds he encountered in the theater. They were there out of religious conviction, but as if knowing that they were secretly linked with the clapping crowds of the theater, they dispersed when money was tossed to them—namely the ticket sales that were returned.

The dead are nourished on judgment, the living on love.

The "slain"—how grand that sounds, how expansive, how embracing and brave; the "suffocated," the "crushed," the "charred," the "exploded": how cheap they all sound, as if no price had been paid!

There is no longer any way to measure anything once the length of a human life is no longer the measure.

He wants to return to the lush, splendid world in which no one dies and people have their wars fought by ants, which are very human.

Human beings are eternal to the degree that they care for the eternal—unless of course they drown in it.

It's too easy to die. It should be much harder to die.

The promise of immortality is all that is needed to set up a religion. The simple command to kill is all that is needed to wipe out three-fourths of humanity. What do people want—to live or to die? They want to live and to kill, and as long as they want that, they will have to be satisfied with various promises about immortality.

Revenge is a curse, and should they slay my dearest brother, I will have nothing to do with revenge. Instead, I want different human beings.

Wars are fought for their own sake. So long as people don't admit that, there will never actually be any way to oppose them.

He hopes, without God noticing, to live a long time.

Above all, you are afraid of what does *not* come after death.

Immortality is hardest for the miser.

O, if only I had died ten thousand years ago, and already lived again three times since.

He loves the wind and lets himself be incinerated to at last be carried off by it.

On each of his birthdays he holds a little funeral celebration for himself, for isn't it possible that he could have died already?

He never wants to die again.

Today I decided that I will record thoughts against death as they occur to me, without any kind of structure and without submitting them to any tyrannical plan. I cannot let this war pass without hammering out a weapon within my heart that will conquer death. It will be tortuous and insidious, perfectly suited to it. In better times I would wield it as a joke or a brazen threat. I think of the act of bagging death as a masquerade. Employing fifty disguises and numerous plots is how I'd do it. But now death has switched masks yet again. No longer content with its ongoing daily victory, death grabs whatever it can. It riddles the air and the seas; whether the smallest or the largest, it doesn't matter, for it wants it all, and it has no time for anything else. Nor do I have any time. I have to nab it wherever I can, nail it here and there in first-rate sentences. At the moment, I cannot house it in any coffins, much less embalm it, much less lay the embalmed to rest in a gated mausoleum.

Pascal was thirty-nine years old when he died, I will soon be thirty-seven. That means I have barely two years left, which isn't much time! He left behind his scattered defense of Christianity. I want to gather my thoughts on the defense of the human in the face of death.

He longs for the Sirens: as if death could be withstood if it were announced loudly enough.

You shall not die (*the First Commandment*).

Someone who lives a long time to put off seeing again the dead father whom he fears. *The definition of the lost son.*

He would rather have died than be dead—that's how much he thinks about every nuance.

No, said my friend, as he chewed on the barrel of his revolver, I still want to die.

The Sirens' only art was that of *moaning*. It sounded as if they lay dying of love. Therefore, out of love, someone wished to save their lives. Yet they outlived the one who wished to save them and continued writhing in their death throes out of love.

A prize competition for who gets a long life.

His last wish: one last sneeze.

Dying caught him in the act.

It is certainly annoying, that in our relation to death two opposing concerns are involved: the death of others and one's own death. It is difficult to separate the two, and we often mean ourselves when yammering on about others. Nevertheless, we cannot let ourselves be discouraged. The keening of simple folk is such a meaningful experience; it sinks so indelibly into the consciousness of any who get caught up in it, that one cannot doubt the continued need for such a ritual even among ourselves. We prefer our funerals as cold as the stones found in our cemeteries, and the dead like to be dressed so lightly and gathered into heaven as soft as angels. It won't be long until keening once again has the power of incantation and then, as opposed to earlier, the dead will really rise from their graves.

He could not die before he'd read all his obituaries and corrected them.

Five years ago today my mother died. Since then my world has turned inside out. To me it is as if it happened just yesterday. Have I really lived five years, and she knows nothing of it? I want to undo each screw of her coffin's lid with my lips and haul her out. I know that she is dead. I know that she has rotted away. But I can never accept it as true. I want to bring her to life again. Where do I find parts of her? Mostly in my brothers and me. But that is not enough. I need to find every person whom she knew. I need to retrieve every word she ever said. I need to walk in her steps and smell the flowers she smelled, the great-grandchild of every blossom that she held up to her powerful nostrils. I need to piece back together the mirrors that once reflected her image. I want to know every syllable she could have possibly said in any language. Where is her shadow? Where is her fury? I will loan her my breath. She should walk on my own two legs.

I fear *living* historians. If they're dead, I read them gladly.

He hid under the bed so she would not die, for he had heard so much about deathbeds.

"Very necessary qualifications" for a good Persian storyteller
"In addition to having read all the known books on love and heroism, the teller of stories must have suffered greatly for love, have lost his beloved, drunk much good wine, wept with many in their sorrow, have looked often upon death and have learned much about birds and beasts. He must also be able to change himself into a beggar or a caliph in the twinkling of an eye."

14

He lay there comfortably at death's door.

We are more *serious* than animals are. What do animals know about death!

Mosquitos eat him alive: gobbled up by the swarm, he dances about in the sun.

Today, anyone who says anything against *death* is ridiculous. It's like someone who doesn't drink milk, but eats rats and worms instead. Death is in fashion. People go looking for it. It shows up on its own. It is honorable. It is on the side of the Fatherland, and what could be more holy than combining the father and the land? It rolls on like a tank. It explodes. It is faster than anything. It outdoes everyone. It fights on all sides. It knows only Fatherlanders, it isn't biased. God has an old alliance with it. He calls him now and then to serve, as an angel. Death is dutiful. It follows orders. It issued them earlier itself. It is punctual, it has a pact with the clock. It only seems corrupt: whoever looks more closely must admit that it always ends the same way. It yields like rubber. But does it yield at all? A heart held in its grip can sometimes be sewn back together. But eventually it comes after the one wielding the needle. It is amusing, because all fear it, even the Fatherlanders. There is nothing more amusing than being feared; out of fear it will rise up, like love from the sea. It is opposed to terror; when it steps forth in terror it is only to reduce terror to fear. It inures people to life and teaches them to love that which terrifies them. It is also pleased to cost nothing. Moreover, everything about it is sensible. It wears brightly checked pants to make constant change more familiar. It plays the nose flute, because it is for the most part silent and sometimes has to lure someone in. It has very long toes, but they have no nails, because they have all been ripped out by others during their death throes. Its heels consist of splayed hooves; on its elbows are finger-long teeth. It eats both forward and backward, and on both sides, and takes no pleasure from wolfing down anything. It shits nothing, O death, where are your bowels! Kinsman await the droppings. Whatever comes out would be received, welcomed, nourished and cherished and cosseted. Yet it is stingy and leaves no stool. It only hears out of one ear, the other remains deaf. Its eyes flutter softly, accompanying the nose flute. Its hair is always singed and falls out in rotten, stinking clumps.

And God looks on as one person after another dies.

1943

Renounce anyone who tolerates death. Who does that leave?

The dead are afraid of the living. However, the living who do not know this are afraid of the dead.

Science betrayed itself by becoming an end in itself. It has now become a religion, a religion of killing, and it wishes us to believe that in evolving from the traditional religion of dying to the religion of killing progress has been made. Very soon science will have to be brought under the sway of a higher power that will press it into service without destroying it. There's not much time left for this subjugation to occur. It likes being treated as a religion and is anxious to exterminate human beings before someone has the courage to depose it. Thus, knowledge really is power, but runaway power that is shamelessly worshipped. Its worshippers are content to receive locks of hair or flakes of dandruff, as there is nothing else to snatch up while pressed down by the weight of its heavy, artificial feet.

We should also not ignore the worst things done by death, for they feel it is vital that they live on in *any* way possible.

The most audacious thing about life is that it hates death, and the religions that obliterate this hate are contemptible and desperate.

If any advice, any technical advice, I were to give led to the death of a single person, I could not claim any further right to my own life.

"Culture" is concocted out of the vanities of its promoters. It is a dangerous love potion that distracts us from death. The purest expression of culture is an Egyptian tomb, where everything that is vain lies about—utensils, jewelry, nourishment, paintings, sculpture, prayers—and yet the dead person is still not alive.

What strategies, what subterfuges, what pretexts and deceits would we not employ if only to have the deceased be alive again.

To live at least long enough to know all human customs and events; to retrieve all of life that has passed, since we are denied that which will come; to pull yourself together before you disappear; to be worthy of your own birth; to think of the sacrifices made at the expense of others' every breath; to not glorify suffering, even though you are alive because of it; to only keep for yourself that which cannot be given away until it is ripe for others and hands itself on; to hate every person's death as if it were your own, and to at last be at peace with everything, but never with death.

And what is the original sin of the animals? Why do animals suffer death?

In war people act as if they have to avenge the deaths of all of their ancestors, and as if not one died a natural death.

It's nice to think of the gods as the precursors of our own human immortality. It is less pleasant to think of the One God and how He appropriates everything.

O, the animals, beloved, savage, dying animals; flailing about, gobbled up, digested and consumed; digested and rotting in their own blood; fleeing, conjoined, lonely, spotted, hounded, shattered; uncreated, robbed by God, abandoned to an illusory life like foundlings!

The curse of *having* to die should be turned into a blessing. That we *can* still die, even when it is unbearable to live.

We should not be terrified of those who feel melancholic. They suffer from a type of hereditary indigestion. They complain as if they were being eaten alive and trapped in a stranger's stomach. Jonah would rather be Jeremiah. What they say is in fact what they have in their own stomachs; the voice of assassinated prey only renders death enticing. "Come to me," it says. "Where I am is decay. Don't you see how much I love decay?" But decay itself dies, and the melancholic, suddenly recuperated, leaves quietly and abruptly for the hunt.

For many years nothing has moved or consumed me more than thoughts of death. The totally concrete and sincere, constant goal of my life is the attainment of immortality for every human. There were times when I wanted to make this the central figure of a novel that I would call "Death's Enemy." During this war it became clear to me that one must speak directly and openly of one's convictions about such important matters, which are tantamount to a religion. Thus I note down everything I can about death that I would want to share with others, leaving behind "Death's Enemy" entirely for now. I can't say that this will remain the case; it could be that he will be resurrected in the coming years in a different form than I had imagined earlier. In the novel he should fail at his extensive undertakings. I planned a noble death for him: he would be hit by a meteor. Maybe what bothers me most today is the idea that he should fail. He can't fail. But I cannot allow him to be victorious while people die in the millions. In both cases what is intended as bitterly serious would seem merely ironic. I would look ridiculous. Nothing will be accomplished with the cowardly depiction of a character in a novel. I have to fall on this field of honor, even if they bury me like a nameless mutt, denounce me as a raving lunatic, and shun me as a bitter, hardheaded, unappeasable thorn in their side.

How many will think it worthwhile to live once we no longer die.

It is exhilarating to see how each makes up his own tradition. We must bring to the new, which tugs at everyone, many old counterbalances. We run to people and times of the past as if we could grab them by the horns, and then run away in terror when they resist with manic fury. India, we say seriously and knowingly, as soon as we bolt from Buddha. Egypt, we say, as soon as we have finished "Isis and Osiris" in the third chapter of Plutarch. It is indeed good that we now know for sure that people with these names lived in the flesh, and that hardly have we named them before they run furiously to us. How much they wish to live again! How they beg and glare and threaten! How they believe we mean them because we call their names, and how they forget what they themselves did to the ancients! Did Thales and Solon not travel to Egypt? Was the white Chinese pilgrim not at the court of Harsha in India? Did Cortez not cheat Montezuma out of his empire and his very life? Someone discovered the cross but they them-selves brought it. The ancients should breathe so that we see them for real, but they should also remain beyond, among the shades. They should doze but await our beckoning, and the next moment present themselves before us. They should think nothing of themselves, for they have no blood. They should flutter, not stomp; leave their horns among the shades; not bare powerful teeth, make themselves fearful and appeal for leniency. Because there is no empty space for them, their air has long been used up. Like thieves they must slip off into dreams and there be apprehended.

To present death as if it did not exist. A community in which it seems no one has any idea of death. In the language of this people there is no word for death, nor is there ever any conscious euphemism for it. Even if someone thought to break the laws, and especially the first unwritten and unspoken commandment against speaking of death, he would find no word for it that other people could understand. No one is buried and no one is cremated. No one has ever seen a corpse. People disappear, no one knows where to. A feeling of shame suddenly drives them away. Since to be alone is sinful, no one speaks of those who are absent. Often they come back to the living, and we are happy when they return. The time of withdrawal and loneliness is regarded as a bad dream we should not feel compelled to discuss. From such journeys into oblivion, pregnant women bring back children, giving birth to them alone, and sometimes even die at home during childbirth. Tiny little children suddenly wander off and away.

It will one day become obvious that with each death people take a turn for the worse.

If life became much longer, would death no longer seem an escape?

The convulsive tenderness we feel for people when we know they soon could die; the disdain for what we once thought or did not think was good or bad about them, this irresponsible love for their lives, for their body, their eyes, their breath! And once they are fully recovered, how much more we love them, how we beg them to never again die!

Sometimes I think as soon as I acknowledge death, the world will dissolve into nothingness.

Even the rational consequences of a world without death have never been fully thought through.

It is not possible to foresee what people would be capable of believing as soon as they remove death from the world.

All of the dying are martyrs of a future world religion.

To think that you must still plead for death, as if it didn't already overwhelmingly hold the upper hand! The "deepest" spirits treat death like a card trick.

Knowledge can lose its deadliness only with the founding of a new religion that does not accept death.

Christianity is a step backward from the beliefs of the ancient Egyptians. It admits the body decays and in imagining that decay makes the body contemptible. Embalming is the true glory of the deceased, so long as he is not revived.

Ethnology, the study of "simple" people, is the most melancholy of all sciences. How painfully and precise, how rigorously, how strenuously have people held on to their ancient institutions and yet still died out.

The most monstrous of all sentences: someone died "at the right time."

Is anyone too good to die? We cannot say. First the person would have to live longer.

The tears of joy the dead will shed over the first person who will no longer die.

I want death to be serious, I want death to be frightful, and feared most when only Nothingness is to be feared.

It would be even harder to die if you were told that you will remain, but are sworn to silence.

Once again, now for the second or third time, I have thought of death as my salvation. I fear that I may altogether change my view of it. Perhaps I will soon belong to those who praise it, to those who in their old age pray to it. Thus I wish to set down here once and for all that that second future phase of my life, should it come to pass, is not valid. I don't want to become something I've never been in order to invalidate everything for which I stood. One should think of me as two people, one who is strong, the other weak, and to the voice of the strong one should listen, for the weak is of no help to anyone. I don't want the words of an old man to erase those of the young man. Better that I break off somewhere in the middle. Better that I don't live half so long.

One can only stand the erudition of those who do not venerate death.

Death is silent about nothing.

The despair of heroes over the abolition of death.

The two general views of death:
    Better to croak than to die.
    Better to die than to croak.

Death is born of God and has gobbled up its Father.

Freedom hates death most of all, but love is a close second.

After he dies he would like to be turned into grains of sand. To him the stars are too vain and the sea too wet.

He senses that with every destroyed city a piece of his own life falls away.

Am I Nuremberg? Am I Munich? I am every building in which children sleep. I am every open square across which feet scurry. Disgust wells up in me whenever I see the new tools of torture, the much improved, the best of all. As soon as it ends it will begin again. They love to blow things up. They like to fly around the world in half a day's time just to wipe out cities. But what will happen when there are no more cities? What will they blow up then? Which schools, which children? The murderers will escape to the moon, and the sun must never again be eclipsed. Before their eyes cities are flattened like forests and mountains. The rivers rear up as they flow, exploded by a new type of lightning. There are no more birds. Wax figures are scattered across the snowy fields, but captured generals do not so much as glance at them. The noble have developed a nervous twitch, orders go awry, and despairing, they wish to be heard, but it is dangerous, all they can do is twitch. Men hang from balcony rails, no longer so noble. Who will cut them down? To where do they fall? How will they be resurrected? Burial only for the privileged, there is no more room in the earth. Whoever fights back leads the way. Whoever does not fight back, spit in their face. Ah, how many spit and how many fight back. Flies will not have a hair on their head harmed, they are too small and don't understand a word. But babies are large and clever, much too large and clever to live.

Heirs receive something *different* than what the dying leave them.

It would be easier to die if *absolutely nothing* of one remained behind, not even a memory someone else might have of you, nor your name or last will and testament, *nor a corpse.*

He wants to be eaten by ants rather than worms.

The execution of the law of "the seven deaths." Each person has seven lives and uses them up one after another. At the start, thinking that he'll never use them all up, he goes about his business and wastes them. Then there are ever fewer left, and amid his last two or three lives he becomes political and miserly.

To gather together all the poems that ridicule death.

He tells himself not to think too much about what is happening to the Jews in Europe. These thoughts have saddened him. When he read a report about the gassing of Jews in the gas chambers, he suddenly felt satisfaction about the destruction of German cities. He hated himself for feeling this despicable, base, hopeless combination of personal fear and personal hate. What the Germans have done is such that it must awaken the lowest form of fear for one's life. You feel physical waves of disgust while trembling for them all, those you are related to, the distant, near, and the entire branch, the family, and yourself. You hate the Germans like you hate your own murderer. You call them "Germans," just as they call us "Jews." You curse their cities, their children, their land. You hang your heart on the English bombers, which level ten thousand of their buildings in a single night. You no longer say to yourself, "The curse of destruction! If it would only stop! Stop!" You say instead, "It shall be! Night after night, destruction, destruction!"

But I don't want my heart to be gobbled up by Moloch. I don't want to hate. Hate is what I hate. Hate is what I hate more than anything. I am afraid of hate. There should only be the guilty and the innocent, and the guilty should die. Every part of every human being should be marked off, and the better parts should speak freely about the bad ones. No storm of vengeance! No more Yahweh! Nothing sent into the jaws of death. Death is nothing!

To kill emigrants, this war came up with its own method: kill all of their relatives on the continent.

We lament the dead. But how very much we must first lament those who must die!

His home consists of all the places where he has eaten; his friends are all the people who gave him something to eat. He feels good will toward all the people who were present as he ate, and despises the dead, because they no longer can eat.

I am filled with a deep reluctance against every form of cultural criticism. It only increases the closer it gets to my own sphere. I cannot tolerate it when it comes off as entirely cold and righteous. An example of this in modern English literature is Eliot, whose essays on poetry I occasionally encountered. I don't quite understand why they so quickly give rise to pointed revulsion within me. And yet I still feel it, even after one or two pages, and with mounting disgust, attentive to every word that increases it, I read to the end what I should put down, and for days afterward I feel as if I am in an ancient and awful torture chamber.

These essays always take up the question of *rank*. The ranking of names is earnestly taken up like a carefully considered transaction. Does this one or that deserve his place in the anthology? Does he take up too much or too little space? It's clearly understood that writers live and die most of all through anthologies. The humble judgment of a somewhat animated and self-satisfied persona is posed at the start. It must be a genuine pleasure to knock down the dead like bowling pins. Indeed the judgment of the living is a very precarious undertaking, and there are those who would rather have their tongue cut out than to use it to lower judgment on others. But then one comes along who is not at all afraid to do it *to* the dead. He fetches ten pins, preferably those who have slumbered a good while in anthologies, stands them up and bowls his ball. He can then explain why he knocks down six, while those left standing are summed up and their fates precisely approved. The four that remain he praises with restraint. For if he has thrown a good ball, he knows very well that the four will be grateful for their placement, though it would be just as easy for him to also kill them off.

This undertaking is repulsive for many reasons. It betrays how little the bowler thinks of them as poets, something he purports to be himself. For otherwise how could he so coldly go about the business of organizing their posthumous reputations. Why battle over how many lines one gets in anthologies! If his stroke was truly strong then he would leave the bowling lanes and torment living human beings or the gods. But he sits there in his shirt sleeves and takes measure of the dead, whom he stands up and knocks down himself. If he has a heart, it's not in these paragraphs written for hire. But he became a poet, simply because his heart beats less than others, and through clarity he wishes to offset what he lacks in obsession. But if clarity were important enough to him, then he would turn it toward making sense of the real world: he would think rather than just examine, and he would be ashamed most of all to always be ranking reputations simply because he feels it important to do so. He does not think; clarity is for him only a means. Among those who are possessed he plays the clearheaded one, among the clearheaded the possessed.

Who could hold against him the urge to make discoveries in the realm of letters? He only needs to follow his curiosity; to present the material itself, to content himself with what impresses him; to feel joy and annoyance; to grab hold and to shove away, to kiss and discuss; and not to hold court.

Guillotine Bombed
"The French executioner Desfourneaux lost both his guillotines when his home was destroyed in the last Paris raid."
Daily Telegraph, September 22 15

1944

He wants to leave behind scattered footnotes as a corrective to the closed system of his claims.

It is no shame at all, it is not self-absorbed, but rather right and good and conscionable that we are filled with nothing more than the thought of immortality. Do we not see how people are shipped by the carload to death? Do they not laugh, joke, and bluster in order to mutually hold on to their false courage? And then there flies off twenty, thirty, a hundred, multitudes of airplanes above you, loaded with bombs, every quarter of an hour, every couple of minutes, and later you joyfully see them return, shimmering in the sun like flowers, like fish, after they have leveled entire cities. One can no longer say "God," for he is marked now forever, the mark of Cain on his forehead; one can think only of a single thing, the only Savior: Immortality! If only we had it, if only it were already ushered in, how different everything would be! Who then would want to murder, who could lower themselves to murder *when there would be nothing to kill?*

Someone from Egypt meets someone from China and exchanges a mummy for an ancestor.

Dear God, let them all live! Let all who are already dead return! Let us all joyfully see those whom we have never yet known!

Sometime I want to find sentences that will make God stand ashamed before me. Then no one else will die.

The greatest and the deadliest idea was that of zero. Was it spawned by death?

The fable of the man who was too hideous to die.

Earth, the sad fatherland of death.

It was the stars
That chilled him inside,
He died for their sake
Every second night.

He grabbed a star
And made it brighter.
Then he gave away
Yet another.

He threw at people
The light he took.
They ate it and hauled him
Away like a crook.

It was the stars
That chilled him inside.
He died for their sake
Every second night.

In order not to become more understandable, simply don't die.

In recent years the feeling that I could really turn into an animal has become a mighty passion, and sometimes it feels to me just as vital as the need to not die.

1945

The fact that the gods can die has only made death more brazen.

Everything that happens in the world today shifts between two basic views of humankind:
1. Each person is still too good to be claimed by death.
2. Each person is already good enough to be claimed by death.

Between these two opinions there is no reconciliation. One or the other will win out. There is no saying which will be victorious.

The cities die, and people bury themselves deeper.

No one forces me to remain alive. That's why I love it so. It's true, future humans, for whom death will be taboo, will no longer know this great tension, and they will somewhat begrudge what we would have renounced with glee.

The souls of the dead are in others, namely those left behind, and there they slowly die out entirely.

Whatever you have thought about death is no longer valid. In a single monstrous leap it has attained the power of contagion like never before. Now it is really all-powerful, now it is the true God.

Now is the time, Dante, for an accurate Last Judgment.

I have just turned forty, but hardly a day passes in which I do not learn of the death of someone I have known. With each passing year this will become more frequent each day. Death will creep into every single hour. How can one not finally succumb to it!

War has advanced into outer space; the Earth sighs in the face of its demise.

One who, while dying, still learns new words.

The woman who peddles last words door to door, swindling everyone.

A world in which people die as often as they wish, but only for a limited time.

She jumps into eternity ahead of him; he brings along her bags, yet never reaches her.

One can rot away throughout the length of a life, and it can be a long life.

It is so hard for me, for I love to be alive.

Cologne's cathedral still stands. This means that we can spare what we wish to. Thus there *is* something that we wish to spare. The value of tourists and printed guides.

I know well that this generous belief that each will live forever is monstrous, but I will always hold to it, even if it kills me.

When the chickens chop the heroes into pieces.

He cannot stand this, he cannot stand that, he cannot stand anyone, he cannot stand himself, he cannot stand death, so what can he stand?

Life's last meadows.

These English folk feel so obliged to remain stuffy, as if they think it will perpetually save their lives.

Squirrels shot in different years, hung from a scrawny tree in the middle of a thriving cherry orchard.

Every Nazi is the opposite of every animal.

The dead are reborn as machines, made equal through their shadow existence in the underworld.

The happiness of *never* seeing again a tender, beloved person: as if he will live on eternally.

The last death would once again be pleasurable, but only the last.

God, as a paranoid, who destroys human beings because he feels persecuted by them.

The story of a court painter in the Han Dynasty
Emperor Yuan (48–32 BCE) had so many concubines, he did not know all of them. He ordered the court painter Mao-Jen-shou to paint their portraits. In order to be portrayed more beautifully, the concubines bribed the painter. However, Chao Chun, the beauty of the harem, refused to do so; therefore she was portrayed hideously. When it later became necessary to

send a bride to the Great Khan of the Huns as a gift from the emperor, Chao Chun was chosen because of how hideous her portrait looked. The emperor saw her for the first time when it was already too late and fell hopelessly in love with her. To win her return, he sent the king of the Huns a camel loaded with gold. Khan refused to give her up and she became his queen. When she died some years later, he refused to allow her corpse to be returned to China. Her grave site remained forever green, even when everything around it was dry.

Mao-Jen-shou, however, was condemned to death for his betrayal and executed. 16

Above the shattered world there stretches a pure blue heaven, which continues to hold it together.

For the Germans, the six million murdered Jews have been transformed into flesh and blood: there never will again be a German who is not also a Jew.

1946

The dispute between two who covet immortality: one wants continuity, the other wants now and then to return.

That which is expedient would not be so dangerous were it not so reliably expedient. It must be frequently suspended. It must remain unpredictable, much like life. It must turn against us more often and more strongly. By way of the expedient, people have turned themselves into gods, even though they still must die. Through their power over the expedient they fall for this ridiculous folly. Thus they become ever weaker through their delusion. If the useful were more rarely expedient, then there would be no opportunity to figure when something is expedient and when it is not. If there were fissures, caprices, and whims, then no one would become its slave. We would think more, prepare ourselves more, anticipate more. The lines between death and one's death would not be blurred, we would not *blindly* succumb to death. It could not mock our feelings of safety, as if we were animals. Thus the expedient and the belief in it have reduced us to animals. This will increasingly be so, and we are all the more helpless.

Humankind's forms of belief formulate themselves as circles or straight lines. Progress, say the heartless and clever, and they think of everything as an arrow (escaping death through murder). Recurrence, say the tenderhearted and persevering, and they weigh themselves down with guilt (making death boring through repetition). Then, inside the spiral, we try to fuse them together and in doing so combine both attitudes toward death, the murderous and the repetitive. Death then stands a thousand times more powerful than before, and whoever stands up to it as the one-time event it really is, they are defeated with arrows, lines, and spirals.

Only the dead have lost one another completely.

My hatred for death spurs an incessant awareness of it. I am amazed how I can live this way.

It is said that to many people death is a release, and there is scarcely a person who has not at some point wished for it. It is the ultimate symbol of failure: whoever fails to accomplish something great, he comforts himself by thinking that more failure is possible, and he reaches for that monstrous dark cloak that covers us all equally. But if death did not exist, then one could not fail at anything; every new effort could rectify weaknesses, shortcomings, and sins. Limitless time would lead to limitless courage. From an early age we are all taught that everything ends, at least here in the known world. Limits and narrow straits everywhere, and soon a last, painful strait we ourselves cannot extend. Everyone looks down this narrow strait; whatever might come after is seen as inevitable. All must bow to it, independent of our plans or means. A soul wants to feel as expansive as it likes, that is until it is choked, until it suffocates at some point it cannot foresee. Who determines that point is a matter for prevailing opinion and not the individual soul itself. The slavery of death is the core of all slavery, and if this slavery were not accepted, no one could wish for it.

I want anything to do with fewer and fewer people, mainly so that I can never get over the pain of losing them.

The shortness of life makes us behave badly. Now it remains to be seen whether possibly the length of life might not make us behave badly as well.

I stoked her ambitions so that she no longer wants to die, and now she wants to kill me out of her own ambition.

A slain room.

To invent a new history, an entirely new history, one never seen before. Whoever could do that will have lived, and must no longer blame himself for his own death.

I am off to pursue a Great Perhaps!—the dying words of Rabelais.

17

I would like to be able to not think of death at all for an entire week, not even of the word, as if it were something made up, something interjected into the language, one of those monstrous creations composed of the letters, D.E.A.T.H., no one knowing any longer what the letters stand for, and no one who cares at all for language lowering themselves to utter it.

Only the stupid can hope for grace, for there is none to be had, but rather only gods who like to kill.

To some death is like a sea, to others it is hard as a rock.

In the past there were only a few things that came to be prized above all others. However, names are something especially prized. It is as if the immortality of one person were only attainable through the mortality of others and their ability to be forgotten. Names in whose nature lies the ability to conquer all languages prefer to do so quite early to gain an advantage. There are names that constantly grow, like trees, and there are names that only increase through *rapture*. There are some names that disappear after initial rapture, but if they are discovered now and again, then their future is more certain. That everything depends on *names* is amazing; it appears to still be the only form of survival through which humankind can attain some kind of knowledge and certainty. But the names live on names. They nourish themselves with other names which they consume and digest like big fish do little fish. They are unbelievably voracious. They require a constant flow of victims and they refuse anything other than names. They have their henchman, who bring them victims, and who hope to make their own name. This leads to a lot of talk about judgment and reassessment, but in reality just involves ordinary fodder.

One thing is clear: the *Book Against Death* will never come into being if the word "death" is avoided within it.

1947

Everyone is charged with protecting the lives of others, and woe to those who do not find lives that must be protected. Woe to those who fail to protect those they find.

To be incessantly aware of death without any of the comforting religions, what a gamble, what a dreadful gamble!

Even if today it were possible not to die physiologically, it could be that no one would have the moral strength to evade one's death, simply because there are so many dead.

Death has its own way of creeping into its enemies to demoralize them and undermine their will to fight. It continues to present itself as a radical solution, reminding us that, except for death, there is not a single real solution. Whoever lives with the blank stare of hate directed at death gets used to it as the only ground zero. But how this zero grows! How one so quickly trusts it, because there is nothing else to trust! How we tell ourselves: at least that remains, when nothing else remains. It thrashes around, lashing out at anything close to you, and when you're nearly done with suffering, it smiles and says: You are really not as powerless as you think you are, you can overcome yourself and your suffering. It then prepares for you the suffering from which *it* will release you. Which torturer/ judge has ever understood his position better?

Whenever I read about sacred things, I recall them only because they were sacred, and as long as they breathe within me,

I am at peace. O the peace they must have had before they were doubted, those luscious golden apples, strongly fragrant and round. I seek out all that is sacred, and it breaks my heart, for it is all now gone. There is nothing left for later. Naked, I have called out death. Woe to those who, naked, have called it out. All that was sacred amounted to its garments; as long as it was so dressed, human beings, those eternal murderers, could live in peace, and nothing would happen to them as long as they did not rip off its garments, those plunderers, those thieves, as if they did not have enough of murder already. I myself was one of the worst. I wanted to be audacious, so I said: "Death, death, and yet nothing more than death." What good is audacity or even temerity. Yet we have become powerful, having brought it forth, having hauled death out of its every hideout, there being none now that we do not know about. We vilify Hell, but it at least came *after* death. What pain could be better than nothing. Audacity, O stupid audacity, we have fallen into the clutches of your vanity, nothing, nothing can remain intact, and nobody dying any longer knows where they are headed.

One who, by a millimeter, is immortal.

The resurrected suddenly complain to God in all languages: that would be the true Last Judgment.

There is nothing more dreadful than the gaze of a dying enemy; that all the enmity in the world has not ceased for that very reason, I will never understand.—We see the face of the dying, but we don't see where we ourselves struck him. And yet you feel, how you feel the tiniest pinprick you gave him, and how you feel that without this pinprick perhaps he would have lived three full moments longer.

The most significant thing about asceticism is that it encourages compassion. Those who eat their fill have less and less compassion and eventually none.

A person who would not need to eat, and yet thrives, who remains intellectually and emotionally sound as a person, even though he never eats—that would have to be the highest moral experiment thinkable. Only upon its successful completion could one seriously think of conquering death.

Whatever you, another, or anyone ever does is useless. O the vanity of all efforts as victims continue to fall by the thousands, the millions. This life whose sanctity you wish to conjure is sacred to no one. No secret power wishes to maintain it. Perhaps no secret power wishes to destroy it, but it destroys itself. How can any life that is laid out like an intestine have value. No doubt plants are most likely far better constituted—but what do you really know about the agony of being strangled to death?

To think that there might be another life behind this one, and ours still might be the restful one in which all recuperate!

I would love to study the faces in heaven. Otherwise I'd know of no reason to want to show up there. The faces in hell I already know well, as I wear them all at various times myself.

It is the hours in which one is alone that amount to the difference between death and life.

From "The Vision of Tnugdalus"
The Prince of Darkness: He is immense, black as a raven's feathers, a thousand arms writhing in the darkness, each with iron claws ... He twists and turns, seething with pain and fury, his thousand hands reaching through the dark air, which is full

of clutching souls, and when he has grabbed enough, he shoves them into his burning mouth like a thirsty farmer swallowing a bunch of grapes, after which he sighs and belches them out. When he takes another breath, he sucks them in again.

18

At a funeral today a woman showed up who thirty-five years ago was the one who reported to me that my father had died. Back then I was seven years old. It seems there are people that one only sees at funerals, most of all *relatives*. In the future there will be just as many left of the tribe or clan. You will never get to know them or see them. You will hardly hear anything about each other. Only at funerals will you suddenly bump into those with whom you share the same blood and who walk about with the same, but differently mixed features.

That letters still mean something, that they still have their form and weight and the power to manifest something in this destroyed landscape of faith rife with bodies; that they still remain signs rather than having disintegrated like life itself; that they have not grown invisible out of shame, and every good sentence which you use them to compose still holds potential; that an innocent man does not hang the moment any are crossed out on this page — or could it be that they are even more damned than we are and haven't a clue?

When the famous journalist died, they found among his things twelve boxes full of lead articles for the next eighty years.

A people made up of individuals who have kangaroo-like pouches, into which they stuff their shriveled dead and carry them around with them.

Someone hits his head on a gravestone and dies.

If the entire ocean were poisoned, as well as all other bodies of water, and humans were to avoid any contact with water, as it would be *deadly* to do so, then, and only then, would we be able to fully grasp what it means to live in this world today.

With advancing age you move less and less. Early on you run around the entire world. Then you settle down in your city. After some time your world shrinks to that of your house, and then a room. The room becomes a chair. The oldest of all no longer get up from their chairs and simply sleep there.

A man who retains others *so that they die before he does*. Is that not the essential nature of the despot?

Adam strangles God; Eve looks on.

1948

If Ananda had made a plea at the right moment, he could have extended Buddha's life. But it didn't come to pass, and Buddha decided to enter Nirvana in the course of three months. When I learned of the last days of the Buddha nothing impressed me more than this missed opportunity. In the hands of the disciple lay the life of the Master. If Ananda had loved him more, if his love had been more attentive, Buddha would not have died then. This only shows how much depends on the precision of love. In its precision this feeling first becomes meaningful and saves or sustains the life of the loved one.   19

In a religion like Buddhism, in which death is accepted, discussed and manifested in so many different ways, as well as transformed into a multifaceted *Überdeath*, nothing touches one more deeply than the life impulse that in essence runs *counter* to the teachings, a spontaneous flame, especially since everything eventually is extinguished. In this, and in exactly this, life contains something inextinguishable. The eighty-year-old Buddha, having recovered from a grave illness, speaks about the beauty of the realms through which he had wandered; he calls out their names in the hope that the disciple will attempt to keep him alive. He repeats his words three times, but the young man doesn't take note, and the mute sadness with which the Buddha relinquishes his life is more eloquent than any sermon.

How many plausible expressions of hope and goodness would we have to find to counter those of bitterness and doubt which we have tossed about so freely! Who dares think of death, knowing he has only increased the sum of bitterness, even if out of the best of motives? Had he remained ever silent, at least he could die. But he wished to be heard, and so he screamed loudly. Which means that now other things must be said and indeed must be heard, since they cannot be screamed.

Nietzsche never seems dangerous to me: for besides all morals there is in me an immensely strong, a supremely powerful feeling for the sanctity of each person, but also really the sanctity of each life. And that thwarts all attacks, from the rawest to the most refined. I would rather lay down my own life entirely than sacrifice that of another, even in principle. No other feeling approaches the intensity and unshakable nature of this one. I accept *no* death. Thus all who have died remain genuinely alive to me, not because they have claims upon me, not because I fear them, not because I feel that something of them is still alive, but rather because they never should have died. All of the deaths that have occurred thus far are a multithousand-pronged form of judicial murder that I cannot deem legal. Why I am concerned about a massive amount of such precedents, why they concern me, is because not one survives! Nietzsche's attacks are like poisonous air, but one which cannot touch me. I breathe it in with pride and exhale it with contempt, and resent him for the immortality that awaits him.

The Eaters

For some people the physical proximity of others is unbearable, as if there were only one type of closeness, namely that which leads to engulfment.

Megalomania and paranoia probably are closely related: one wants to become immense, to increase in size, to *entrance* others, as if there were no better way to snatch them up than to be *taller* than them. The tallest, whose head rises above all others, would then be the least endangered. The hunted saves himself amid *vastness* by running, in the *heights* by climbing higher, in the *depths* by hiding.

The heaven that you enter after your death is the place where nothing bothers you anymore. Nothing tries to snatch you, there nobody is snatched any longer.

In such empowerment there is also always *mercy*, for you live on, you have indeed been chewed to bits. To drink is so much less culpable than chewing something to bits, for the teeth do nothing and there is nothing to chew.

What, what can a human being do in the face of his fear of stronger *beasts*. They all bare their various teeth on a single day.

The universal burial of teeth.

A café full of dead heroes who sit around drinking coffee and eating cake.

God's immortality is really that of the Devil.

The story of the turkey that was murdered by my own beloved at Christmas was told to me in minute detail some hours before I sat down to a festive Christmas dinner. I had known him since I was little. I was amazed at his increasing girth, his proud strut, his beauty. In total I probably saw him five or six times, but he was as familiar to me as if I had raised him in my own room. Everyone ate him, and I also ate. If I had not been so ashamed before the others caught up in the spirit of the moment, I would have choked on it. And yet I controlled myself and reined in that shameful gagging reflex that is always at the ready, and even let myself be served a second portion. I wasn't sick at all, but rather took part in all the conversation and the good company, and only today, three or four days afterward, thoughts of it suddenly sicken me, as if I had eaten human flesh.

1949

Not since I could think on my own have I ever called anyone "Lord!," and how easy it is to say "Lord!" and how great the temptation. I have approached a hundred gods, and I looked each straight in the eye, full of hatred for the death of human beings.

The thought torments him that perhaps everyone died *too late*, and that our death really is death only when it is delayed, and that each has the chance to live on if he were to die *at the right moment*, though nobody knows when that might be.

All lovers of death end up the same, namely they deny it.

"*During a terrible famine in Cairo* citizens used gigantic fish-hooks to fish for men from roofs. Victims were hoisted up, murdered, and eaten raw."

The butcher's girl who kisses the cleaned head of a pig.

Aboriginal Australians, people of the Stone Age, believe in an eternal dreamtime, the time of myths from whence they come and to which they return again. From it they have not come to something; they have just been taken away from something. Their belief is the greatest of all, the only one that I sometimes share, and if I were an Aboriginal person, I would hold to it always. But since I have the doubtful luck to be a modern person and live in London, for the most part I don't believe it at all. Only to the extent that I am a writer am I aboriginal.

God endures until the last blow.

The days when he stands frozen with fear in the face of his own evil. There is then nothing left for him but to stand there dead to himself.

These conversations, these conversations with old friends! He is dead, and that one is dead, as well as that one, really every other one now dead. They had already crumbled away from you years ago, and you just didn't know it. Anyone whose death you do not actually *experience* you still believe is alive. How tenaciously we hold on to the lives of others, as tenaciously as you do your own, for there is no difference.

1950

A smile, which *holds off* death.

It seems to me that, without a new attitude toward death, there is really not much to say about life.

Existence wishes to exist in general, otherwise it's not existence.

I do not accept a single death. That gnats and flies die does not make death more understandable to me than the dreadful story of Original Sin.

It makes no difference whether something of us lives on somewhere else or not. We don't live here fully enough. We have no time to fully prove ourselves. And by accepting death, we engage it.

Why shouldn't there be murderers as long as human beings *compliantly* die, so long as we are not ashamed to, so long as death is *built into* our institutions, as if it were the inmost secure, best, and sensible foundation?

I swear that my life does not matter to me. I swear that the life of the one I love does not matter to me. I swear that even my work does not matter to me. I swear that I am prepared to disappear without a trace, such that nobody would even know, if only it would mean there would be no war. I am prepared for this bargain. To which authority do I make my appeal? Is God not even available for this?

It's not the dead we fear, it's all those who will come after us.

The name of the first, but entirely secret death.

All artists are cannibals of their ancestors.

Joking feels like trying to do in death with *pinches*. That which is truly funny *treats* death as *fodder* to be swallowed whole.

One who *fears* flowers because they wither.

The Boy
The only one who is forgotten by death entirely, and forever. A very simple man who never changes and after many hundreds of years *eats* exactly the same things he did at twenty. He speaks exactly the same words and doesn't dress any differently. His memory, which was never all that good, also doesn't get any worse. He remains single, has no luck with women, and thus no children. He is very humble and is just happy to have something to eat. He loves to have visitors, but not too many. He looks at the rain as if the drops were years. Sometimes the sun is too much for him. He breathes easily and is not afraid. Sometimes he stretches out his feet, like tree branches, close to the fire until they sizzle. He has forgotten his name, and so he doesn't have one, but instead he is referred to simply as "The Boy." He thinks of children as his peers; he understands right off what they want. Adults think him a bit slow. The boy sleeps on a mat spread out on a dirt floor. When it's not raining or freezing, he's happy to sleep outside his hut. His dog looks as old as he does, but there is always a different one. He never calls to him. The dog comes by itself whenever its master wants him near. The boy's hair no longer grows at all. It looks a bit odd, but anyone expecting it to be a tangled mess will be disappointed. Nor can it be described as white;

its color is somewhat mellow and hard to describe, as if one were asked to describe a victim's wounds to the victim. It's this aspect of his hair that causes the sick to approach him. For anyone who saw him earlier, and who has been hit with their first serious illness, still recalls the look of his hair many years later, as if it were a remedy, and talks quite heatedly about it. There is no doubt whatsoever that at the sight of his hair the sick are healed, but whether the power to heal exists within it is hard to determine. He alienates women somewhat; they expect nothing from him and the sight of him rarely heals them.

As to where he lives, there are a great many differing opinions. Some assume that he has lived for hundreds of years in the same place. Others attest to traces of him in far-off places. His hair supposedly has been found in Africa, and his footprints in Australia. It's entirely possible that he could have wandered far and wide; there was enough time to do so, and the fact that he has lived in one place so long does not preclude the possibility that the same person could have managed to live in vastly different and far-off places. Those who insist upon his time in Africa scoff at the idea of him having come from Australia. No one has ever managed to walk on dry feet across that ocean, and if he had used a ship, well then its remains would have turned up somewhere. But this question need not be decided here. However, it would be foolish to simply dismiss such doubts. "The Boy" could have been brought from Australia by others. That he has always lived alone seems true. But who can maintain that he was never *pirated off*? He was probably enslaved as a rower at first, and then his masters, because of the peculiar sense of loneliness he radiated, became annoyed and perhaps a bit spooked. Rather than just throw him into the sea, they set him on the coast of Asia once they reached it, understandably with enough provisions to last him a while. Thus he remained alone, just as they supposedly found him, and as he made evident during the long voyage, though now returned to a different continent. His modest needs and the particular talents of his age he also brought to his life here.

But it would be going much too far to take up all the possibilities that an existence such as this entails. We should perhaps not ask for too much at once and instead be satisfied with considering and contemplating what "The Boy" is now. The description of his person, only if true and unbiased, must go further than just speculation about his past. The reverence that such a creature deserves is a great deal more reasonable.

1951

You are always asked what you *mean* when you berate death. They only want cheap hopes doled out by religions ad nauseam. But I know nothing. I have nothing to say about it. My character, my pride stems from the fact that I have never *flattered* death. Like anyone I have sometimes, very rarely, wished for it, but there is no one who has ever heard me offer a single word of praise for death, nor can anyone say that I have bowed to it, or that I have ever accepted or validated it. It seems to me as useless and wicked as ever, the fundamental curse at the heart of existence, the unresolved and incomprehensible, the knot in which everything has always been tied up and captured, and which no one has ever dared slice through.

It is a pity for everyone. No one should ever have had to die. The worst crime did not deserve death, and without the *acceptance* of death, the worst crime would not even exist.

We would have to conceive of a world in which murder never existed. In such a world what would all other crimes look like?

We carry the most important thing around inside ourselves for forty or fifty years before we risk articulating it. Therefore there is no way to measure all that is lost with those who die too early. Everyone dies early.

The behavior of martyrs seems despicable to no one, even though everything they did was done in anticipation of *eternal life*. How despicable would the same martyrs be to Christian believers if they had been concerned about eternal life *here* rather than somewhere else?

Even the idea of transmigration seems more plausible than taking up residence in the hereafter. The proponents of the belief in the hereafter never note that it involves something they never mention, namely the fact that everyone would *remain next to one another* in the beyond, thus creating a crowd that would never shrink. Once gathered there, they will never want to leave one another.

What would a paradise be like in which the Blessed never saw each other face to face, in which each would experience a kind of hermit bliss, cut off from the others, such that not even the voices of others could be heard; a paradise of eternal loneliness, without bodily needs or complaint; a prison without walls, bars, or guards, where there is nowhere to escape from since there would be nowhere to go. Everyone would have to talk to themselves, be their own priest, teacher, comforter, and no one else would hear any of it. A blissful existence which will cause many to prefer the torments of Hell.

I cannot explain why my clear appreciation for the wickedness of this life should go hand in hand with an ever-present passion for life. Maybe I feel that it wouldn't be so bad if it were not arbitrarily severed and cut off. Perhaps I fall victim to the old concept that the *permanent* occupants of paradise are good. Death would be less unjust if it were not a fact imposed *in advance*. For each of us, even the most wicked, there is at least the excuse that nothing we do comes close to this preappointed judgment. We must be bad because we know we will die. How much worse we would be if, from the beginning, we knew when.

Religions are always satisfied with everything. Is there no

religion of perpetual acute despair? I'd like to see someone who *cannot* calmly look death in the eye try looking into his own; someone whose hatred fills his resting place with an ever-present current of dissatisfaction; someone who does not sleep, for during sleep there are those who do not wake up; someone who does not eat, for if he did, during his meal others are eaten; someone who does not love, for while he loves, others are torn limb from limb. I'd like to see someone who has only this feeling, but always feels it; someone who, while others feel joy, trembles for their joy; someone who feels the meaninglessness of "impermanence" as a sharp torment, as the torment of death, and who alone breathes through this torment.

N. wants to retroactively drop all contact once he learns that someone is dead. He fears delayed contagion through death. He believes that one can stay alive by effectively repudiating the dead, even within himself. To avoid death, he kills off his dead entirely.

Sophocles's *Electra* contains death in all its forms.

It begins in the shadow of a murder and leads to two more. It is murder in its most concentrated form, the first being that of a husband, Agamemnon, the second a mother, Clytemnestra. Only the third and last is of a lover who is not a close blood relation. Electra is always full of thoughts of her father's death. Her brother, Orestes, whom she turned into an avenger, lives in a different city; he is always in contact with her. Now, after he finally arrives, he lets the news of his own death spread about. One sees the effect of this news on both Clytemnestra and Electra. The report involves a very detailed account of Orestes having fallen in a chariot race. For the mother, who fears his vengeance, this is above all the death she *wishes for*, while for the daughter, who has set all her hopes on Orestes, it is the death she *fears* the most. He himself appears, after the mother has left Electra, as the bearer of his own ashes. Thus he witnesses his sister's agony over his death, something that is rarely granted anyone who dies, because naturally they are not around to hear such news. Electra's pain is so great, Orestes reveals himself: for her he returns to life. Their reunion is all the more intense because of the false news.

In a previous scene Electra has taken on the role of the avenger, as she believes her brother to be dead. Her sister, whom she tried to get to help her, refused to do so. As soon as Orestes is alive again, *he* becomes the avenger. As the messenger and bearer of his own ashes, he enters the palace in search of his mother and slays her. Outside, Electra helps him to carry out their terrible act.

At the close, the murder of Aegisthus is employed as a new form of death. A bier with a bedecked corpse is brought before him. He believes the dead Orestes lies beneath. He lifts the sheet and sees Clytemnestra's bloody body.

Thus *all* of the elements of death and dying are in this play. The *memory* of the dead daughter that has impassioned Clytemnestra—she avenged the death of Iphigenia at the hands of Agamemnon; the memory of the dead father—in the urge for revenge in Electra and Orestes, as well as the submission to death on the part of her sister, Chrysothemis; the *fear* of death on the part of the guilty, be it in Clytemnestra or, in a different way, Aegisthus, who in the moments right before he is slain is *conscious* of what is about to happen. The *undaunted* spirit of Electra in the face of death and her fascinating effect on others. The murderer who presents himself as a dead man and arrives carrying his own ashes. The bier, the urn full of ashes, the dead victim. The news of his death and its resulting different effects. The shift from a wished-for death of one's own (such as for Clytemnestra), and the same shift, but slower, from a wished-for death to a feared death, and finally one's own death (as with Aegisthus through Orestes, Clytemnestra, and himself). All of these forms, elements, and transformations of death are witnessed by the Chorus. Its function is that of a crystallized mass that parses the proceedings for the larger audience. Orestes appears with a friend who never says a word and functions as a doppelgänger or shadow. The herald, a very old man, is somewhat like an insidious Angel of Death, who through the news of a false death prepares for a true one.

There is an essential difference between the dead in general and one's *own* dead, with which one is well familiar. This is exactly the difference between the masses and the individual.

He asks himself whether he can manage to succeed at composing readable notes in which the following words never appear: God, Death, Crowds, Power, Transformation, Love, and Fear.

He only wants to be kissed by very old ravens.

Finish it, at last finish it, the awful, painful, slow, continually announced, continually unfinished book, and then have done with it all, done, completely done, have nothing to do with anyone you have known, not even yourself, no one, or otherwise: Die.

Slowly, over many years, he has placed death on the same level as God. He sees nothing else, he thinks about nothing else. Will he ever let it go?

God the executioner.

What is more saintly, the clueless or the aware victim, Abraham or Isaac, *every* dying person or Christ, the animal or the soldier? This is the supreme question of every religion, and who dares answer it!

A dead man calls someone up. (An idea for a play.)

The judgment of death lowered upon all at the beginning of Genesis contains essentially everything that can be said about power, and there is nothing that cannot be deduced from it.

A play in which the characters do not differ except for the point at which each one dies. A dramatic, yet very measured piece. But I believe that, when the topic is death, and it is addressed seriously and from all sides, the characters need to be treated with restraint. There is the ancient Dance of Death, in which the victims of death differ from one another only in terms of their social status. It is possible that in the course of the performance everything might change. But certainly at the start I can sense my own strong resistance against masks used for projecting the actors' voices, against any kind of extreme that does not contribute to the handling of the plot alone. I want to be very plain and clear. This play should preserve its entire identity in every language. It should be as good in Bantu as it is in English or Japanese. It should be even more transparent and universal than *Gulliver's Travels* or *Robinson Crusoe*. Through it I wish to find a new classic form so that something classic exists everywhere, in every language and every culture.

I can't decide if this goal frightens me or seems particularly difficult. I believe that the idea itself determines that there can be no other form. The idea is really what contains the form. It's been decades since I have felt so certain of something. With the *Ape Opera* that I wrote last year, I was bound to the music and composers that I knew. If I wished to proceed with restraint, then it had to be in accordance with them. But the idea itself was not at all restrained and could withstand an extreme performance with no trouble at all.

Now in *The Numbered*, it is as if I wish to speak for or act the part of every man. The grievance is one held by all people and aligned with my own belief, which is evidenced within, and in fact completely contains what is left *over* from all religions, be it nothing less, but also nothing more. The idea slumbered inside me for over seven years. It initially occurred to me in 1944, I believe the end of May, when I first met *Gwyneth Bartall*. Someone told me about her before I had even seen her, and the first thing I heard about her was that she only had half a year to live. The certainty of this prognosis horrified me. When I then saw the girl, my heart opened up to her and I loved her very much, but in an entirely different way than I had loved anyone before. I treated her as a poet, which she wanted to become, and perhaps granted her more talent than she had. I read her manuscripts carefully and *immediately*, something I had never done before or since, and spent long hours talking with her about them. I gave her some of my most beautiful books and spent whole afternoons in the unbearable company of her mother and father. Nevertheless, the prognosis was fulfilled. She died roughly six months after I met her. I should have dedicated the play to her. I would have done it if I had ever dedicated a piece to someone else before. But I have never dedicated a work to Veza, nor my mother, nor Georg. It would be inappropriate and *indecent* to put Gwyneth above all the others, and so I must think some more on the issue of the dedication.

In the last several weeks, perhaps since getting back from Paris, I find myself breaking down human activity more and more into gestures, how bodies move in their own distinct ways. I look at the outstretched hand of a salesman as he returns my change; the profile of a mouth as it opens to say a word; I sense my own step exiting a door; the feel of a signature that is still damp; the swaying coat of a stranger; a soup spoon raised halfway above a plate; a chair that is not entirely filled; a single finger; hair that sticks out; an open pocket. I can't make anything out of any of this, except for a momentary dissolution,

21

an isolation from that to which something otherwise belongs.

Whenever this happens, I think of writing a *story* about this gesture, this part of a person, but a general story in which, as in philosophy, the view of this gesture or body part speaks to all humans today, always, and to come. I would not want to *explain* anything in any of these stories, but instead to imply that each unique action alone is also linked to others.

I sense in this everyday "vision" that I am shamefully stirred by the fact that I am alive and that I bear witness to those I observe, and at an age when many others are no longer here.

Today, on All Souls Day, I vow that this play, dedicated to all who have died and all who still must die, will soon be completely finished. This should be understood by all and I will not feel shame before anyone because of it. For if I do not finish this play, my first authoritative statement on death, I will not have lived. Nothing else I could ever do can, by comparison, even come close. To anyone who has ever gotten close to me, I have railed against death, but nobody has understood. Only women liked to see in it excessive power and a religious undertaking which in private and personally they interpreted as an extension of every type of youth, love, and pleasure. The others, the Christians, tried to explain it in their own terms; in other words, to openly recognize it as the views of someone who is secretly a Christian and a believer, but whose pride prevents him from admitting it. All the others, proponents of art, saw it as something unhelpful and perhaps too public a declaration of their own obsession, saying, "He wants to become immortal." God, who does not exist, is my witness that I have not intended any of this: I am neither a lover, nor Christian, nor an artist, but I do *not* accept death, and that is all.

1952

In regard to the premise of *The Numbered*: I don't understand why people are not *more* preoccupied with the fact that we cannot know the span of a life. In essence, all fatalism is tied to this question: is the span of a person's life fated or does it stem from how one lives? Does one arrive in the world with a set quantity of life ahead, let's say sixty years, or does this quantity remain uncertain for some time, such that the same person experiencing the same youth could end up reaching seventy or only forty? And when would the point be reached where the limit is *clear*? Whoever believes the first is naturally a fatalist; whoever doesn't believe it ascribes to human beings an astounding amount of freedom and grants them the ability to influence the length of their lives. Generally, we live in a fog, as if the second assumption were the right one, and one comforts oneself about death with the first. Perhaps both are necessary and must be applied alternatingly so that fainthearted human beings can stand death.

A smile like one from the underworld.

A coffin upon which one dances from time to time. The dead shake and his bones turn to dust: "He will be danced to dust."

He feels as if kissed by the hereafter.

I am waiting for the *sensible* death of a person I have known, and I know that such a thing does not exist. It is always senseless.

I have hung paintings by Grünewald on the walls of my room, as my pain has not yet found its full expression. So *he* expresses my pain for me, and I have also included a Madonna and Child. Perhaps she finally realizes from a distance that it is my child, that I never conceded it was hers. I have hung Grünewald's "Concert of Angels" so that they can continuously play to provide her mercy. Also, the landscape of light is there, so we have our own light for our love. This room is now sacred to me, and I hardly ever dare enter it.

I am not ashamed of this transformation; I have never loved or revered anything more than I do Grünewald. Holy Grünewald, pray for her, Holy Grünewald, pray for her, Holy Grünewald, grant her life.

Imagine, the moment it happens, I will die *out*!

The happy suicide who looked forward to it for thirty years.

He left behind a collection of desks, and on each the first sentence of an immense work.

First death will bash him over the head, then it will be as if he had never existed.

The two words I have needed most often in my life — strangely enough — are God and death. I'm always openly talking about death to others. To myself, in my notes, it's God again and again who slips out of the pencil, most often against my will and in sentences that make no sense at all. I am beginning to believe that both words, God and death, stand for the same thing, that they are the same thing: my philosophy of identity.

We do not die of sadness — out of sadness we live on.

Can any language be made viable that does not know the word "death"?

A person who takes his life is, in my eyes, wicked and clueless, and only a thoroughly monstrous *despair* could possibly justify it. To spend a life for nothing, as we know so well, is ungrateful and shameless. I cannot forgive what Kleist did. His lowest act was his last, and within it one can readily see the kernel of his military ancestry most clearly and shamefully. No psychological explanation (no matter how illuminating it might be) could ever alter in the least my basic feeling about this. Every death is possible, but none is justifiable. Even someone who against his will allows himself to *murder* is also guilty in my eyes. Yet the guilt incurred by the murderer, or for that matter suicide, is to me immeasurable and cannot be forgiven for any reason. I ask myself seriously whether any person who *dies* is not made guilty by that fact alone. If there were a just God, the story of Original Sin would sound a lot different. Adam was *curious* about death and playfully tasted it. The apple of knowledge was from *one* tree. *For that* he was punished by God and cursed: with the sweat brought on by knowledge, humans thereafter had to attempt to *escape* death, to *eradicate* all traces of the apple of death within themselves. No Christ and no shedding of blood can release us from this guilt. Through *knowledge* you must find your own way back to your natural immortality *by yourself*.

Aging amounts to the death of others and nothing else.

"A cotton cloth was wound around his neck and both ends were pulled by two people in opposite directions while the king reached into a gourd full of pebbles and baobab leaves and grabbed as many pebbles as he could: these indicated the number of years of his reign, at the end of which he was strangled." *Monteil, Les Bambara du Segóu*

Reigning heads, separated from their bodies, and impaled on horrible pikes.

My basic fairness toward people is a product of my attitude toward death. I cannot love anyone who accepts death or makes plans for it. I love anyone, no matter who he may be, who abhors death, does not accept it and never and under no circumstances will employ it to accomplish his own ends.

That's why there is no one today whom I can value who is an atomic scientist or a technician in that realm; no one who volunteers for a military career; nor a clergyman who invokes a future life as a comfort for those death has taken, while he himself does not think he might soon be taken; no one who thinks the death of a family member or friend occurs *at the right time*, as if it were a way of completing life's fixed measure; no one who does not feel shame instead of gratification at the death of an enemy; no one who has disowned his heirs. Who then can I value at all, for who does not fall into one or another of these categories sometimes or in relation to this person or that?

Thus I, who affirm life without reservation and without any kind of limitation, must judge others with a moral that is in no way applicable so long as death exists. I am so aware of the basic contradiction of my nature that, again and again, I have to remind myself to approach all circumstances with modesty and careful deliberation whenever I am inclined to again lower the most severe of judgments against any person.

1953

A terrible peacefulness comes over you as more and more die around you. You become totally passive and no longer fight back, becoming a pacifist in the war on death, turning the other cheek toward it and toward others as well. From this, out of this frailty and fatigue, religion mints its coin.

Someone turns into a mass murderer because a cure is found for the illness that kills the person he loves most soon after that person has died.

Assume for the moment the Promised Land is denied to *everyone*, just as it is for you, that no one expects anything further, that at the moment of their death everything comes to an end for everyone, that humans through and through, here and everywhere, and in the future are *time-bound* creatures—what then, what exactly would they change about the way they live with one another?

Would they undertake less or more? Would they be more cunning? more secretive? Would it satisfy them to hide all of their terrible deeds until the last moment, knowing full well that with one blow they can put an end to it all anyway? Or would the memory they leave behind replace the notion of an afterlife entirely?

I believe it is hard to know exactly, for the remains of faith in each still plays a role. Yet I could imagine that the desire to do something good will become a true passion in any faithless person, as if they themselves would stand for a wise supreme power, and for everything one would expect from it.

Is it possible that her death cured me of jealousy? I have become more tolerant of the people I love. I watch over them less, I grant them their freedom. I think to myself: do this, do that, do what makes you happy, just as long as you live, do whatever you have to against me, if it must be, annoy me, betray me, shove me to the side, hate me—I expect nothing, I want nothing, only the one thing: *that you live.*

The paralysis of one death after another: not a free word in between, not a free step. The worst paralysis, this hopeless hope, that it survives it all.

Oh the comforts of those who believe, those who can deny everything, who can take comfort in the idea of seeing their loved ones again, a privilege which in fact will never be granted them! What wouldn't we give to live in this placid, civilized world, where the dead simply *wander off!* Where we have simply to *call* if we are to—at least briefly—see them and hear them, before we are with them once again for good. Where they can be angry with us, such that we try to appease them, where they are hungry and are thirsty and freeze and worry about those left behind. My desire to believe is sometimes so fierce that I can think of nothing else. I see then Odysseus's shades and wish that mine stood among them. I draw their image in empty space, and a subtle voice says straightaway: Believe, and you will have them, whenever you want!—But it is this voice that brings me to my senses. I cannot *ransom* my dead. I cannot allow anyone to negotiate anything between them and me. If they are *captured*, and should they let me know they are, then I will do anything to free them. If they have *resigned themselves*, then I have time to fall into this awful submission/submissiveness, and the time still allotted me, the time of such rebellion, is the most precious thing that I have. If they are *nowhere*, then I do not want any kind of fata morgana to hide them, for here every lie as well as every fiction ceases, since here, and only here, I want the most naked truth.

The emptiness of a restaurant that was just full. The children that have disappeared, the silenced voices. The sudden potency of the hour. The two waitresses who now assert their authority; no one orders anything more and thus they take over the place. Every emptying out of this kind is both soothing and sad at the same time, as if one were in a place that death has not reached, and as if it had already taken everyone else.

Her handwriting, which becomes ever more precious the more that it becomes unreadable; most precious of all when it no longer means anything. The fear that her letters could disappear inside my pocket. When does something *begin* to turn into a relic? When does one tremble before the most trivial object simply because a loved one made it or held it in their hand? When does one begin to guard it as if it were the thing most worth living for, even more than the loved one herself? I cannot grasp what is *delayed* in the process, what you have to experience again and again in order to take it seriously; what you can only experience *singularly*, what you never master, because you can never accept it. In fact, it's quite the opposite, for you think that it is possible to remain by saying to death, "No! No!" Yet why does it matter to death when that is its greatest triumph, when all it leads to is a mere object being suffused with the love of the person one has lost! Whether there is an intention behind that which we call death, we cannot know, but if there is an intention, it can only be this: the reduction and debasement of the living to a trifling object, a trace that amounts to not even a millionth of what the living once amounted to.

A dying immortal man—what else is Christ?

The dead tear us away from the living, and all the more strongly the closer we are to the dead. We cannot stand the bursting forth of the living, the pose they take, the helplessness and powerlessness they feel in relation to the dead who never leave you. It is a barbaric injustice that the living walk the earth, supersede the legacy of the dead and walk all over them. We stand on the side of those fallen and despise the victors. It is so easy to wish that someone would die; it is much harder to keep someone alive. The partisan feeling toward the dead is so strong that we lump together the dead one with everyone else in the race, simply because we are still alive, and we forget that each of them, even when we are the first to lose the race, should be just as important to us as any other.

1954

How clever was the Buddha's father! And how shameful is the legend of the Buddha's first encounter with aging, illness, and death!

Would it all have been different if his father had introduced him to someone who was aging, ill, and dying when he was a boy, such as playmates or pets, such as dancers, women, and musicians?

We always have something for which to reproach the living, whom we know well. However, we are thankful that the dead do not forbid our memory of them.

We never know ahead of time what will be the most precious thing to those who are left behind, meaning that perhaps someone will press some old pair of worn-out shoes to their lips long after all of your papers have been burned.

There are still a number of people who *believe in all gods*. Each person is allotted two thousand gods. The survivors as the pack horses for all past worship.

They do not know that the dead creep into the living and hide there: until one suddenly reveals to you, when you least expect it, a very familiar tongue.

Kierkegaard's father was fifty-seven when his son was born, and his mother was forty-five. He himself died at forty-two.

The Islamic view that the walls of the grave press together to torment the dead is the scariest thing I have ever heard, and were I so inclined, it could spoil any desire for death that I might have.

Veza's Dream (during the night of the 3rd and 4th)
Yesterday morning, when I phoned Veza, she asked me anxiously how I felt. "Good, good," I said. "You know full well that I'm feeling very good." I always tell her that, but yesterday it was indeed true. Then she told me that my mother appeared in a dream to her and said to her that I was in great danger. She had aged a great deal, and Veza didn't recognize her, but she knew it was my mother.

It wasn't hard to calm Veza down. I was a bit surprised that it was so easy, for it's not like her, as she is very superstitious.

That night I was with some friends, and Clement was also with them. I told her about Veza's dream, to which she replied that she had had a similar dream the night *before* (meaning not the same night as Veza). Veza had called her and said, "I need you here, Clement. Canetti is dying." She screamed out loud and heard her true voice for the first time. Francis listened as I told Clement about Veza's dream and she relayed her own. I'm only writing this down because both had similar dreams over the course of two nights. Naturally, I don't believe both are valid, but if indeed they prove true, it will not at all be uninteresting to find them written down here.

We cross ourselves to show that it can't hurt to do so.

1955

He walks among the people wrapped in the thick coat of kindness in order to never be cold. He would rather sacrifice the shirt off his back than give up this coat of kindness. Sometimes, in distress, he imagines there could be a law against doing good. Sweat breaks out on his brow, and he hurries along as if harried among his victims who, thankful and beaming with happiness, receive him. If he does something good for two people who do not know one another, he makes sure that they meet each other. He stands before them as they sit there together and talk about him. Later he reports what was said on both sides, and precisely compares each to the other. Because he is willing to be cheated of anything, but not his goodness.

He is at his most humble when he does the greatest good, for it increases the effect. He loves to look back at his entire life and realize that there never was a time when he was not good. He cannot see a funeral without imagining himself in the place of the deceased, perhaps even envying him a little, because everyone says good things about him. But he is comforted by imagining what will be said about him when he himself is the deceased.

One day he imagines this so fully he spreads word about his death. He subscribes to a wire service and collects all the obituaries that are punctually filed. He passes some pleasant days pasting these clippings in an album. Yet he is fair and does not ignore the obituaries that he thinks are too short. He lays the impressive volume on his bed as a pillow and falls asleep on it. He dreams of his funeral in the next day and, when everyone is done with it, tosses a shovelful of goodness into the grave.

So long as there is death, humility is not possible.

One is sometimes so sad that it feels like one has died and knows that there could be no reason at all for it to happen.

"I haven't seen you for a long time."
"I died."
"How terrible. When did it happen?"
"Two months ago."
"But you are all right now?"
"Not bad, thank you."   24

A nightshirt in which you never again awaken.

Tell stories, tell stories, until no one else dies. A thousand and one nights, a million and one nights.

What does a man want, what drives him to put one foot in front of the other
Along the ridiculous/heartless city streets,
What does a man want, what opens his eyes
Again each morning, what does a man want,
What halts his breath in the middle of a dream,
What does a man want, what opens/offers
Bad/poisoned/wretched food to his mouth, empty books/
     deceptive words offered to the spirit
What does a man want when he curses,
What does a man want when he offers praise,
What does a man want when he never follows any path to its
     end,
What does a man want, when he never leaves his old haunts
     behind.

What does a man want when he falls, and what does he want
    when he rises.
What when he waits for days and weeks, moons and years,
What when he hunts/drives out children and enemies and
    dogs and women,
What does a man want, what does a man want.
What does a man want when he moans,
What does a man want when he dies.
What does a man want when he laughs,
What does a man want when he yells/rampages,
What does a man want, what does a man want.
What does a man want when he grovels,
What does a man want when he flies,
What does a man want when he believes,
What does a man want when he scoffs.
What does a man want, what does a man want.
What does a man want when he lies, what when he cruelly
    speaks the truth,
What when he begs, what when he gives.
What when he gives something away, what when he steals.
What when he spits, what when he swallows,
What when he is silent, what when he sings,
What when he weeps, what when he hits,
What does a man want when he murders.
What does a man want when he loves.
What does a man want, what does a man want.
A man wants,
A man wants to find his dead.

1956

Each year should be one day longer than the previous: a new day on which nothing has ever happened before, a day on which no one has died.

Perhaps it would not be so bad if we died happily, so long as we have never happily experienced the death of another.

Since she died, he turns his head away from every bud.

Thoughts about the dead are attempts at reviving them. We care more about reviving them than *keeping* them alive. The obsession with reviving the dead is the core of every faith. Since people no longer fear the dead, they feel a particularly boundless guilt toward them: the guilt of not succeeding at bringing them back to life. This guilt is greatest on the liveliest and happiest of days.

A play in which all your dead appear on stage. Some of them meet up again, others get to know each other for the first time. None of them are sad, for their happiness at appearing is so immense. (What should you say about the happiness of the one who allows them to appear?)

The power of killing disappears in the face of the power of conjuring. What is the greatest and most fearsome killer in comparison to a man who brings a single dead person back to life?
How ridiculous seem the efforts to fend off death on the part of strongmen, and how magnificent the efforts of the shamans

to conjure the dead. As long as they believe, as long as they are not charlatans, they all deserve veneration.

The priests of all religions who cannot bring back the dead are despicable to me. All they do is strengthen a border which no one can leap across. They hold sway over the lost so that they remain lost. They promise a journey to somewhere to disguise their weakness. They are only too happy that the dead do not return. They keep the dead in the hereafter.

It's often so oppressive and embarrassing to consider the cult of the dead maintained by *others*. A turning away from the world of the living, and since we belong to the world, we feel offended by the cult set up for the deceased by someone else, as if we meant nothing to them whatsoever, nor could anyone else who is alive mean anything.

We should make it a point to not be imprisoned by the deceased; we should allow him to remain free and encourage others to have a connection with him. Without being too bothersome, we should speak about the deceased with others and not let him remain in isolation.

With the growing awareness that we sit atop a heap of dead humans and animals, and that our sense of ourselves is actually nourished by the sum total we have survived, with this rapidly realized awareness it becomes much more difficult to come to any kind of solution about which we do not feel ashamed. It is impossible to turn away from life, whose value and prospects we always feel. But it is also impossible to not live from the death of other creatures whose value and prospects are no less than our own.

The bliss of simply withdrawing into the distance, something that traditional religions feed upon, can no longer be our bliss.

The beyond is within us: a grave realization, but it is trapped within us. This is the great and irreparable fissure of modern humans. For within us is also the mass grave of all creatures.

I understand religion in a way I have never understood it before. A feeling that one can only designate as religious rules me entirely. *Religion* amounts to a feeling of connection with the dead. Perhaps in some people this feeling has been so strong that it even caused them to revive the dead.—Christ, for instance?

Year after year I always return to the figure of Mohammed. I can't let go of it, and it won't let go of me; its dread is seated within me. What of the Greeks, the Jews, the Chinese! Why deceive myself with these true men of culture? No matter how much I yearn for them, I am not them. Mohammed, however, is like a Jew. He swallowed the God of the Jews. He finished off the God of the Jews, brought him into his realm. The only Prophet is Mohammed, all others have misunderstood Yahweh. *I* know exactly what Mohammed wanted; I know exactly how he felt. I know his cemeteries, I know his women, I know the arrogance of his judgment. I know his inclination toward corporeality, I know his disinclination toward souls. I know the fire of repetition, and I know the decline in revelation of what is law. I know that he was the first to experience death, and died a thousand times again, and like him I hunger for all to live again. I, too, want nothing to come between the grave and resurrection. Absent the body, the soul is a mockery, and any belief that speaks of souls is like water slaking off me. I also know fear, the one true worm; but I know that it is not a fear of any judgment, for I know what Mohammed does not know, namely that it is the fear of the judge in me who continually judges others.

1957

Throughout this entire month I have thought about the triumph of killing versus that of survival. It can seem like all that I have managed to accomplish through loudmouthed rebellion is the realization that death empowers others and therefore is loved by them. Don't make such a big deal of the fact that you must die, I seem to be saying, for you will see many others die before you first.

It is as if every single death, no matter whose, were not a crime that would have to be prevented by any means!

The heartbeat of those who have died too early. Thus does his own heart beat, like all of theirs through the night.

"Great" is what we think of someone who escapes a seemingly imminent death. How he manages to bring about the danger itself is his business.

Perutz, now dead, sitting at my table in the café—gentle and kind.

I, the conscious witness to the two greatest wars humankind has ever known, having experienced both as an *onlooker*. I wasn't in any army, nor could I have ever been, nor will I ever be. With all the strength of my soul—and it is a strong and powerful soul—I have opposed war. To make it no longer possible is the acknowledged goal of my entire life, which I cannot abandon. But such an attitude, which pervades humankind entirely, is not meant to lessen my understanding of war from the inside out. Every indictment made from *outside* of it is pointless. Better people than I have failed at this. One must have the strength to shove your hand into war's mouth and gullet entirely and mercilessly yank out its intestines. Whoever is overcome with disgust even before it opens its mouth, it's better that he stand out of the way and sings songs. Oh, I would have loved to sing songs, and far be it from me to condemn those who have yielded to them. But I have decided to oppose war and death, to not kill, to destroy its magic aura, to chase away its priests and to remind people what they can be without war and without death. Everything that I have tried to do thus far was in preparation for this decisive moment. It has opened its mouth before, and I've stuck my fist in it. I cannot pull it back out until I have grabbed hold of its intestines and very marrow.

1958

In an Italian newspaper I read an article about a nun who has just died at the age of one hundred.

She had already died once when she was a seventeen-year-old girl, and the coffin was already nailed shut when her sister insisted that it be opened. She then came to and sat up. This miracle inspired her to become a nun and to dedicate her life to God. Thus she lived another eighty-three years after her first death.

The last thoughts of someone dying influence his next rebirth.

O, such peace and a distant train, the anguish of this year now dead. Meanwhile he would give anything if the anguish were she, and she were still alive.

Then, when she was still alive, a hundred years ago yesterday.

I have always known Kanaimà. God was Kanaimà to me. Ever since I could think for myself, he was inside me, the spirit of enmity, threatening all. Kanaimà—what did the wisest Greek know that is deeper than that? Kanaimà is fear and hate together, the murderer murdered everywhere.

The military campaign of fifteen men from the Taulipang tribe, plus a *single* one from the Arecuna, against many more Pischaukó who gather each night in their big house as the shaman infuses a sick person with health. There they are, men, women, and children, the shaman saying to them: People are coming, the shaman saying: People are here, and already two women toss torches at the house, the threatened residents running out, the enemy pressing down upon them as all are slaughtered. Two young women escape. The children cry, and they are thrown into the fire. One of the Pischaukó men is still alive, so he covers himself in blood and lies among the dead. But each of the dead are hacked in two, and the survivor is discovered as well and hacked to death. The dead chief is hung and shot to pieces. The victorious chief opens the vagina of a dead woman and says to one of his tribesmen: Inside it's good, you can go in, and the happy warriors head for home singing, and dance in their own house. Then they sit on small stools above giant ants that bite them furiously before they stand up and lash one another.

That's all. That's how it is still. But now there are more than fifteen men.

I hasten to add that some of the enemy who live in small outlying houses have escaped to the mountains. There they live to this day, all of them hated like clandestine murderers. Kanaimà.

It is exactly the same. There is nothing to add at all. Then as now you would have to make something of your life to fathom it.

But have you fathomed it? Yesterday you read this account, which was no longer than four pages, and today you read it again, writing it down word for word and then reading it two or three more times. You have not forgotten it for a moment since. You would not have forgotten it had you read it earlier, either. But you have learned a word for it, one that is shorter, better, more correct, more concentrated than all our teachings and tracts. *Kanaimà*. Who would want to look ridiculous while babbling on about aggression when one can say "Kanaimà," and thus say much more!

27

I, however, am addicted to the ancient wisdom of humankind, all its myths.

I love the stupidity of the living.

I hate death.

The trout put the ravens at ease. But it's because the weasel is dead.

1959

On a Pacific atoll, people were recently eaten for the last time in honor of an atomic explosion.

Sometimes it seems to me as if finishing has become an end in itself. I think of the goals with which I began, about the confidence I had that I would achieve something real. As I have worked toward those goals, the world has become weighed down by a thousand-times-greater destruction. This destruction is *contained*, but does that make any difference?

And what is this obsession that drives me to oppose every kind of destruction, as if I was named the world's protector? What am I but a helpless creature who suffers the death of one close friend after another, who cannot keep his own loved ones alive, shipwreck occurring left and right, as well as pitiful screams!

To whom am I of any use, whom do I serve with this unspeakable defiance?

Nothing is left but this defiance. New people slide away, new words and conversations slip one's mind, only the past remains alive, but when will chance destroy it as well? Nothing will be left, and I will still be standing here—a child standing on his own feet for the first time—and with all my might yelling: No!

A face that is composed of many dead.

1960

The lament for the dead is about reviving the dead, *that* is its core passion. The lament should last until it succeeds. Yet it ends too soon: not enough passion.

It might be possible that someone who refuses to kill finally has no choice at all. So he must harden himself to the fact: he shall not kill.

The dead, which everyone has lived off of, are part of every life. Among tender, decent, brutal, and terrible people—the misused dead are everywhere. How can one stand to live when he knows this about himself? Owing his own life to the dead, he never stops feeling them, which makes them eternal.

Grief always leads to something, but it does not help at all to say that.
   My grief involves no kind of release. For I know too well that I haven't done anything against death.

A woman who feels the need to smile at everyone, who smiles herself into the greatest confusion, who cannot stop smiling even when miserable, who smiles on her deathbed and dies smiling to still please all who might see her dead. She smiles in her coffin and under the earth.

Whoever could find out what binds people together would be able to save them from death. The puzzle of life is a social puzzle. No one has a clue how to solve it.

I can only befriend spirits who know death. They indeed make me happy whenever they succeed at saying nothing about death, doing what I cannot.

A restaurant in which everyone is silent. The customers sit speechless, alone or in groups, and drink their drinks. The waitress mutely holds out a list of items and you point at one, at which she nods, brings you what you wish and sets it on the table without a word. Everyone looks at one another without saying a word. The air inside the room where nothing is being said is stagnant. It is as if everything is made of glass. The people look more fragile than the objects around them. It is as if words are what makes everything fluid, for without words all is numb and stiff. Glances are sinister and incomprehensible. It's possible that no one thinks of anything but hatred. Someone stands up. What will he do? Everyone is scared. A child, like in a painting, opens his mouth wide, but no scream is heard. The parents say nothing and shut his mouth for him.

The lights go out, something rattles. It happens again, but no one is smashed to pieces. Coins are counted, familiar as little animals. A cat jumps onto a table and takes command of the restaurant. Nothing can silence it, for up until now it has always been silent.

Now the place is hopping with the dead.

Pavese's journals: How he crystallizes in his own way the thoughts that consume me. What happiness! What liberation!

He prepares to meet his death, but he does not overdo it, allowing no emotion to rise within him. It comes off as natural. But no death is natural. He keeps his death to himself. We learn of it, but it is not idealized. Nobody would kill themselves because he did.

And yet when last night, amid my deepest depression, I

wanted to die, I reached for his journals, and *he died for me.*
Hard to believe: through his death, today I am reborn. This
mysterious process should be studied, but not by me. I will
not touch it. I want to keep it secret.

Someone who escapes death because he has never heard anything about it.

He always anticipates the end: so he need never begin.

What will I do if the doctor says: There's nothing wrong with
you? I will call Veza, then I will walk around the city for a bit
and maybe buy a couple of books. Because the only thing that
sets me at ease is to buy books, much like having a drink does
for others. Then, on this very same night, I will begin to write
like the devil and then produce *daily* a fixed number of pages,
which shouldn't be too small, a minimum of five.

What will I do if the doctor says: You have cancer? I will call
Veza and talk to her in the same way as I would on any other
day. Perhaps I will try to sound a bit cheerier in order to be
more convincing. Rather than go for a walk, I will sit in a café
and have a talk with myself. I won't buy any more books. That
evening, before it even grows dark, I will sit down to work
and begin to write. Each day I will produce at least ten *pages.*
In three months, I'll finish a huge novel. At the same time, I
will travel to Paris in order to speak with my brother. In the
summer I will travel with Veza. I will visit Paris and Zürich,
Munich and Vienna. I will finally live as I should have always
lived, working feverishly, and even if I were to have only one
year to live, I will leave behind the greatest novel of our times,
of which not a word has been written, and much else besides.

Someone who completes his life's work at thirty and then lives until he is a hundred. He has time to experience fame, being forgotten, and then rediscovered.

1961

In every generation only one will die, a deterrent to others.

The victim who in death turns into his own killer and calls for
29   help in his own voice.   *Ramayana*

Learn, at age fifty-five, to speak again, not necessarily a new
language, but to speak. Discard all prejudices, even if nothing else is left. Read the great books again, whether they've
already been read or not. Listen to people without lecturing
them, especially those who have nothing to teach. No longer
validate fear as a means of fulfillment. Battle against death
without constantly having to talk about it. In a single phrase:
courage and righteousness.

The ten suns of the Chinese. The archer who shoots down
nine of them from the sky and saves humankind from the le-
thal heat.

1962

Napoleon dying, miserably, as if he had never known anything about death, as if he were experiencing it for the first time.

There, the dead live on in clouds and inseminate the women as rain.

There, the living fast and feed the dead.

Even from their dearest, the dead disappear, forgetting to invite them to come along in the end.
    It's for the best, as we live so vibrantly that no one thinks he can die.

No one will convince me of the glory of killing, for I know what it feels like, without myself having killed. It's worth less than a single breath of air, be it of the one killed or the killer.
    The hand that forms a single letter is mightier than the hand that kills. And the finger lifted to cause death will turn to dust before it has time to wither. As if it weren't enough that people die, the fact that they help bring it about!

Might not returning be even sadder than disappearing?

I no longer want anything *enough*. I want it somewhat, and hardly have I taken the first step toward it, when I don't want it anymore.
    I am ashamed to seize hold of an opportunity. That it offers itself, that it exists, is nice, therefore how can I just grab it. If

you feel sure of it, you don't. Do so, and you've lost it. But if you don't grab it, you may have lost it, though I never think about that.

I am too old. I hate hardly anything. I have reached the point where one likes everything simply because it is there. I am beginning to grasp for the first time that there are philosophers who say that all that exists is good. It's true, the disciples of death still fill me with disgust. Yet I have found no solution. I am consumed with the same doubt as always. I know that death is horrible. What I do not know is what can replace it.

With every hour spent alone, with every sentence that you draft, you win back a piece of your life. There never was a person who could so easily be made happy. Especially someone who writes without ceasing, and moreover never anyone who has failed so persistently and senselessly amid such happiness.

Write until your eyes close, or the pencil falls from your hand, write without wasting a second or thinking about what and how it should sound; write from a feeling of untapped life that has become so huge that it is like a massive mountain gathering inside of you; write without setting up a hundred different plans and restrictions, and with the danger that it will not last, and the danger that it will fall to pieces; write because you are still breathing and because your heart, which is probably already diseased, still beats; write until *something* from the mighty mountains of your life is carried away, since an entire nation of giants could not carry it *all* away; write until your eyes close forever; write until you choke to death.

Burns Singer (a friend of Gavin's, a zoologist and writer), the young writer who visited me, told me that he first wanted to kill himself when he was nine years old. After a fight between his parents, he and his seven-year-old brother decided that they would strangle each other simultaneously. They grabbed each other's throats and squeezed and squeezed, but nothing happened.

Later, as a student, he came home after having dissected a squid and found his mother hanging in the kitchen. He was twenty-one when it happened. He felt guilty and again wanted to die. His mother was tiny, only 4' 8". The father, a very tall man with an enormous nose, was a real drunk, and the mother had endured a living hell with him for twenty years. When the father was completely drunk, he forced the children to get on their knees and say "Shema Yisrael." It was the only Hebrew phrase, the only prayer that the young B.S. knew, and it was what told him his father was drunk.

The father, who came from an Orthodox family, married three times, and none of his wives was a Jew. That's why he forced his children to pray when he was drunk.

Yesterday I read Djilas's *Conversations with Stalin*, and I could hardly breathe as a result. It didn't help that it confirmed so much of my thinking about power. Whether or not Stalin is still alive does not matter, for it all carries on in similar manner. And by that I don't mean that it occurs only in Russia, for it's in essence the same everywhere. What can be done? What can even be said? Does it make any sense that I continue to grapple with the same issues?

It only makes sense if I believe that I can achieve something. I have never failed to believe that I can. Yet it could be that it involves a belief similar to that held by the despots themselves. What makes me their dangerous enemy? Am I jealous of them, as Nietzsche is of God, or as God is of other gods? That would be so horrible, I cannot think it true. I don't really believe it is so. My deeper instinct is opposed to killing, yet it is through killing that the despot stands and falls.

The true essence of the despot is that he hates his own death, but only his. The deaths of others are not only all the same to him, he also needs them to exist. This tension between his own death and that of others makes him what he is.

My true essence exists in the fact that I repudiate *every* death and hate them all. I do not think it impossible that at some point I could halfway accept *my* death, but never that of another. That is so certain, and I feel it so strongly, I can locate it at the beginning of my thinking and at the center of my world. It is *my* "Cogito ergo sum." I hate death, therefore I am. *Mortem odi ergo sum.* Even though this sentence leaves out the most important part, namely that I hate *every* death.

Anyone who has not killed is not a man: this sentence, which Hemingway fashioned, means nothing at all. It means nothing, and above all is false. For one thing, there is no one who has never killed, and the less someone has killed, the more he is engaged with it unawares. If there is supposedly something "manly" implied through this (and that "something" is indeed to me doubtful), it has to do with a lingering reluctance to kill that has to be overcome. But as soon as a lot of killing occurs, this reluctance disappears, and killing becomes mechanical, therefore becoming less interesting than smoking or typing, requiring neither reluctance nor indecision, but rather becoming an unconscious urge like smoking and as automatic an activity as typing. Killing can mean something the first time, and if it only happens once, it can stay with you for the rest of your life. It was enough for me to experience the sudden death of someone—that of my father. But the hunters, the soldiers, and the murderers must think of nothing. The *danger* for them is actual excitement, and they indeed experience that ever anew, but killing itself is nothing, only its consequences for those who survive amount to something, and only those who talk about the manliness of killing conflate one with the other.

Hemingway's stupidity disgusts me more than I can say. I allow anyone the life they choose, but it seems to me that his was especially shallow and injurious.

I am not afraid of death. I think it is superfluous.

The beauty of ashes, like a sacred vestige of the world. As if out of ashes every destroyed form could be divined.

1963

I call him P, the practical peacock, and for a while I want to see everything through *his* eyes.

P wants to bulldoze all cemeteries, as they take up too much space.

P wants to destroy all records, so that no one knows who lived at an earlier time.

P would get rid of the teaching of history.

P is not sure what to do about family names, as they keep alive the memories of fathers, grandfathers, and similarly deceased.

P has nothing against handing down estates, especially of useful items, but they shouldn't be tied to the names of those who once owned them.

P goes even further than the Chinese philosopher Mozi: he is completely against having any funerals, and not just because of the expense that can be saved.

P wants the Earth to be for the living, and away with the dead; even the bare surface of the moon is too good for them, although it could be used as a transition point rather than a cemetery. Everything that is dead could from time to time be rocketed to the moon. The moon as a rubbish heap and graveyard. Monuments? For what? They take up public squares and streets. P hates the dead, because they take up space and keep spreading.

P only has young lovers. At the first sign of any slack skin, he gets rid of her.

P says, "Fidelity? Fidelity is dangerous, it ends with the dead."

P goes where he can, leading by example and inventing outrageous impieties.

P censors a newspaper. It must be *so*. No death notices. No obituaries.

P, who is very rich, buys up all the mummies and destroys them publicly and single-handedly.

P, however, is not an advocate of killing, only the killing of the dead.

P rewrites the Bible according to his modern aims. He is also interested in other sacred books and cleanses them of notions that don't agree with his way of thinking.

P dresses in a way that never reminds one of the dead.

P does not allow any objects in his home that are known to come from the dead.

P destroys all letters and pictures of people who have died, and does so the moment they die.

P invents an effective art of forgetting.

P only visits the sick when they are once again healthy. He only rejects the fuss made over dead pets and fights against it.

P feels we treat animals properly. He only refuses to deal with the circumstances of dead animals and wants nothing to do with them.

P advocates the need to reeducate doctors.

P's special prayer. There are aspects of God he approves of. Christ he holds for an imposter.

P *walks* unlike others, as if he knows of no dead.

P is convinced that the moment we see a dead person we are contaminated forever and cannot ever recover.

P maintains that he will never age, simply because he takes no notice of the dead.

The year in which the lake froze, the year in which death took its revenge upon him.

When the one struck down lies in a heap on the floor and doesn't know anything, nor does he want anything but the return of this one dead person, when in fact he is ready to sacrifice all living persons for this one thing, only then does he grasp that death has annihilated him, and that it would be better had he never been born.

Those who are unbroken, how do they manage it? Those who remain unshaken, what are they made of? Once it's over, what do they breathe? When it is dead quiet, what do they hear? When the fallen do not rise again, how do they go on? How do they find the words? What wind blows across their lashes? Who penetrates the ear of the dead? Who whispers the frozen name? When the sunlight of their eyes is extinguished, where do they find light?

We are familiar with the one who has died; it's the living we do not recognize.

His darkened eye, which has dined on death.

The nodal ties of existence persist in recognizing the dead in the eyes of the living. We always want the latter simply to *know*, yet we give them nothing. We are unspeakably stingy with the dead.

It is possible that only the unhappiest are capable of truly knowing what happiness is, and that might even seem just to me—but then there are the dead, and it appears that they say nothing about the matter at all.

1964

A society in which people suddenly disappear, but no one knows that they are dead, as there is no death, there is not even a word for it, which pleases them.

Buddhism does not satisfy me, because it gives up too much. It has no answer for death, it just sidesteps it. Christianity has always held dying at its very center: how else to describe the Cross. There is no Indian teaching that really deals with death, for none has opposed it absolutely: the worthlessness of life exonerates death.

It remains to be seen what kind of faith arises in those who see and acknowledge the *enormity* of death and deny it any kind of positive meaning. The incorruptibility that such an appreciation of death inculcates has never existed before. Humankind is too weak and gives up the battle before we even resolve to engage it.

The illusory reparations made to the dead: they do not help, for the dead know nothing of them. Thus everyone lives on with incalculable debts, the burden growing and growing until we suffocate. Perhaps we die because of the growing debts we owe the dead.

There is no relationship stronger than that of two people who meet under the torment of such debts. One can carry the debt of another for a while in order to spare him, release him, for a little while, and even shifting this weight for just a brief moment can save them both.

The door beyond which at night I could hear her breathing.
   I still keep listening.
   The black head of hair on the pillow. Ashes.

His self-glorification, his grave.

Now it is important to block your ears often, especially when matters of power do not change. Because the ancient voices, which are now *interior*, cannot otherwise be heard.

I have constructed a library that will last for a good three hundred years, all I need now are those years.

1965

She likes meat so much that, after she dies, she wants to be torn apart by birds of prey.

The story of a man who conceals the death of his nearest and dearest from others.

Is he ashamed of her death? And how does he manage to hide it from everyone? Does he somehow keep her alive through all who do not know of her death? Where is she? Is she living with him? In what form? He takes care of her, dresses her, feeds her. But she can never leave the apartment, and he never goes anywhere for long, making sure to never be away for more than a few hours.

He receives no visitors. She doesn't want to see anyone. She has withdrawn and can't stand anyone. But sometimes on the phone he speaks like her, and he also writes all her letters for her.

Thus he lives for them both, and *becomes* both. He tells her everything, and he reads to her. He talks to her just like he used to about what he should do, and sometimes he's annoyed by her stubbornness. But in the end he always manages to get an answer out of her.

She is very sad, because she sees no one, and so he must comfort her and cheer her up.

Because of such a secret, he becomes the strangest man in the world, someone who must understand everyone else so that they do not understand him.

The rift among the crowd of mourners in Aeschylus's *The Persians*: those strong enough to bring back the deceased, and those who mourn with the survivor to no avail.

The actual drama begins with Queen Atossa, the king's widow: *her* dream is the first messenger of misfortune, and until the real messenger arrives, this dream is all there is. Then the messenger reveals the true nature of the misfortune. Upset by the news, the chorus turns into a crowd of mourners that invokes the most important casualty of all before his widow. The guilty verdict precedes the appearance of the guilty man, as if the dead seemingly brought along the living, the father the son, and the founder the destroyer.

Thus *The Persians* involves three successive conjurations, dream or vision eliciting reality. Atossa's dream brings the messenger; the visionary message the messenger delivers brings the venerable dead man; and finally, his verdict brings the defeated son.

I know that everything will be *different*, and indeed, because I feel the unstoppable approach of the new, I turn to the old wherever I can find it. It could be that I only wish to save the old and carry it over because I can't stand anything transitory. However, it could also be that I am seeing if I can use it against death, which still remains undefeated.

Others write *memoirs*. I am also interested in memoirs. However, it is still difficult for me to take it all that seriously, especially in the face of death.

Perhaps I am afraid of weakening the seriousness and commitment of my sensibility by revealing its sources in my life. It does not matter if I arrive at something that concerns others just as much as me. I would need to write memoirs in a way that strengthens my convictions in the eyes of others. Yet I still mistrust the selective cleverness of such a young sensibility. Thus I also do not take seriously enough formal speculations about the renewal of an art that was once mine. It seems like a game to me. True, I love games, but I don't wish to sacrifice any of my concerns to them. I could try to tell myself: Give death a rest for a year, and use that year for everything you have missed out on because of it. But can I do that? Can I really?

What do the clever know about how much wiliness and effort it takes for someone who is naturally inclined toward paranoia not to succumb to it! With what hardheadedness he must fight against his own *integrity* the way others must against their dissolution. How artfully and tirelessly he must distract his mind in order not to focus on madness and evil. How he splits himself into a thousand pieces so he has enough breath to take in the world. How he also torments those that he loves because he loves them even more intensely. How he must guard against seeing through things, for it can only lead to seeing everything as nothing. How he cannot let go of death, his enemy, because it alone is universal enough to contain all that he despises.

Our only difficulty in drama these days is that we have no gods and in fact know nothing about the dead. If *one single* dead person were to manifest himself, drama would again be possible.

But since we have none, it is only possible to think of tragedy dressed as comedy.

The sight of countless cars in this city, the relentless stream that eventually ends in a crash.

The car still needs to be invented in which you are protected from every danger. Only when you get out could you potentially die. Safe, absolutely safe cars that people get into to feel immortal for a while.

My pencils are safer vehicles. As long as I write I feel (absolutely) safe. Maybe that's the only reason I write. It does not matter what I write. I simply mustn't stop. It can be anything whatsoever, as long as it's for myself, not a letter, nothing that is imposed or demanded of me. If I have not written *anything* for a day, I am restless, in despair, dismal, vulnerable, mistrustful, threatened by a hundred different dangers.

Prevarications, prevarications, where is everything that you once were? What was it all for, hidden, afraid, the stories that made you who you are, where are they? In the slaughterhouse of years, in the stairwells of the schools, the faces of the boys, the savoring of languages, the blind patriarch, his great-granddaughter that led him along, seething tons of water from the Donau, and sacks full of grain, dust, clay, and melons, children and chickens, the songs of mourning sung by Armenian refugees, wood chopping and the axe, very sharp, with which you wanted to strike your cousin. *Agora vo matar a Laurica! Agora vo matar a Laurica!* An early war anthem, before the slaughter of this century.

The worms congratulate him upon his 160th birthday.

Who would kill another person if the act were to remain secret and unknown forever?

The diplomat who represents murderous politics, and at night manages his diarrhea.

It could indeed be that a powerful hatred of death could have at least *one* virtue: that humans will no longer wish to kill.

But that's not at all utopian, for humankind's continued existence depends on it.

Most people know this already, but they don't see that the solution to this question is not at all technical or legal, but rather requires the creation of a proactive, new way of thinking. Just as we turn away from vomit in disgust, we must also see death for what it is: repulsive as any stench.

For the first time the feeling that there are people who *understand* you. Only a few, but these understand you especially well.

Should I be happy about that? Or should I mistrust thoughts that have become comprehensible to others?

Most of all it surprises me that my attitude toward death is not met with ridicule, but instead is grasped, and yes, even supported. Indeed it was always the most important concern of my life. I never wrote the novel *Death's Enemy*. Hardly anyone knows my play *The Numbered*, which takes up the subject. But the substance of what I have to say against death is here in these notes, and perhaps these point out something quite strongly to many who are unlike myself. If I were to die tomorrow, *this* has been said and can be taken up by others who will learn from it. Thus I feel I have not lived entirely in vain. Thus have I tossed a pebble into the future.

I wanted solitude. Now I have it. But do I want it now?

We feel solitude in relation to the living. In the face of the dead there is no solitude. They are always there.

Perhaps what a critic wrote is true, namely that I have found my form in composing brief "notes." If that's true, then I am not a writer and can hang myself.

1966

There should be a court that could absolve us of death, if only we answered all its questions honestly.

What point is there in the unspeakable victims, the blood of animals, the torment and guilt—is it so that we too should die?

Miserable is he who knows. How miserable God must be in knowing everything.

Even Goethe was not spared his own agonizing death. Yet we tack some peaceful hours on to his final day so that it is more beautiful and more appropriate to his habits.

I very much long to be free of the things which have shaped me and all thinkers of this time, and to thus consider death "impartially," as if I were a person of the past century.

Before dinner Megan, the wife, showed us the temple called "The Chapel." It sits on the farm, a few meters away from the house, which was built in the fourteenth century. The temple is simple and austere, a plaque hanging on the wall dedicated to Megan's great-grandfather, who preached here.

Born 1805.

Born again 1825.

Died 1849.

Just behind the temple there is a small cemetery, the grave-stones having almost all been made out of slate, the immediate and extended family having been buried here for a hundred years.

Thus, the farm encompasses all: the living, the animals, the temple, the dead, and the language used is always that of old.

People I have not seen in a while, I forget that they have died.

He stood before his dearest departed and said: God is good. He repeated it over and over, a thousand, a hundred thousand times. Still the dead did not rise.

God is good, he keeps saying, and the dead never once appear in his dreams.

The fate of someone who hated the idea of surviving: he makes sure that *he* will be the one who is survived.

It could be that writers who love death can never summon the toughness that feeds the hatred of death. Because they do not object to death, their spirits grow soft. Death does not bother them, therefore nothing compels them to mock it.

Of course there are writers who *appear* to accept death as a ploy against it, such as Schopenhauer. Deep inside they remain entirely opposed to it, and that shows up in the way they write.

The first human would be one who never killed and never wished for death.

The suspended animation of larvae in helium. After three years the completely dried-up larvae come alive again: unchanged. One day a person will also be able to withdraw from this existence and leave instructions that he be woken up in three hundred years. In this way, out of the transmigration of the soul will come the transmigration of the body.

Departing for a time yet to come will be much more important and exciting than rocketing into space. What courage will it require, and will you have it? For is it not precisely what you have always wished for above all else? Rather than launching your name into the future, you could launch *all* of yourself, including everything that you are, that you know, what you remember, all of it arriving in the future intact. You can go to sleep and, instead of the next morning, wake up *the same* three hundred years later. A tremendous idea which causes you to tremble, much like a devout Moses trembled once in the presence of God in the burning bush.

The painfulness of the stars since we started trying to actually reach them. They are no longer the same stars.

Now covered with the leprosy of death, they give off a *different* light.

Breath, breath,
How can I find my breath.
Is it my own—
No,
It's the breath of the asphyxiated
I am their ashes
I am their fear
I am the gas
I am their murderer
I cannot take myself apart.
In me hunkers
Their halted breathing.
An old man
His bony finger sticks
In my throat.
I've never seen him before
I've never tried to help him.
As he gasped for breath, where was I.

The most ingenious, the most careful, the most painful, the most patient, the most precise fictional depictions have never once scratched the surface of death.

As soon as they succeed at that and much more, most likely writers will quietly bite the dust.

Since suffering a costly, an unspeakably costly death, I no longer see death everywhere.

Above all, when I am dead, what I will miss: the voices of people in a restaurant.

"A polyphonic, polychromatic, polydeadly life."   32

What interests me the most is the key element of any drama, namely death.

As fodder it is the source of comedy, whereas the *victim* is the source of tragedy. Today, in modern drama, both have become one: indivisible, polysemous death.

Jean Améry puts me to shame like few other people do. He has been tortured and humiliated and does not wish to forget it. His death has looked different than mine, for he saw it being enacted directly upon the body. Mine was met by my dearest loved ones before my very eyes and spared me. Thus I can say: It is their death, not my own, that I hate. But that could mean that I am living a lie that ennobles me. For how can I possibly know that it's not all just about my death? Jean Améry knows better because he experienced it himself. I refer to him by his name, though that is not at all his name. *I* didn't have to give up my name. I have escaped through those who allowed me to do so. He, however, refers to himself by name and knows that is not who he is, and the home he does not have is his lost name.   33

How shameful, shameful that *I* have outlived all the victims. Was I in battered Madrid, was I among those who fled Paris, was I in Auschwitz?

Have I done enough, have I justified the fact that I was only a witness, not a victim, do I *deserve* to live, and will the outcome of this life alter future horrors in the slightest?

Perhaps everything I have thought is inadequate, misguided, perhaps containing only invisible seeds of a new disease sprung from past bloody years.

What shall I do? And have I at least done what I could?

Obsessed with *my* dead, whom I loved, since they were my very life, have I thought enough about those whom I love because I do *not* know them?

How can I find the balance between the close and the distant, how can I be the scale that justly weighs the two? In my heart I know that it is not about me, but rather about everyone else, but is it enough to know that in one's heart, when perhaps each is deceived by his heart?

I am no longer present, I am a thousand pencils, I don't want to know what they write, I want to disappear amid their motion, which I no longer understand.

The dissatisfaction in which I live exists for the simplest reason: I now know for certain that I have not accomplished anything to defeat death. Die, you loudmouth!

Elijah
"To him it was told: There are three keys in heaven. One to the storehouse of rain, the other which bestows new life, and *one which returns to the dead their lives*. But only one key is granted to a single person, so that no one can say: There are two keys in the hand of the Son and only one in the hand of the Father.

Therefore Elijah gave back the key (that for rain) and *held on to the one that woke the dead.*"

"In the second year of Ahaziah's reign Elijah was enraptured and concealed; from then on he was not to be seen until the Messiah arrived. Then he would be seen before disappearing again, until the coming of Gog and Magog.

In the time until then, however, Elijah will write the history of all these races."

The Ascension

"When Elijah was to travel to heaven, the Angel of Death stood in his way. The Lord spoke: 'I have created Heaven only so that Elijah can ascend to it.' However, the Angel replied: '*Now all humans will point to him, wanting not to die.*' The Lord answered in turn: 'Elijah is not like other people; *he can choose to leave the world himself.* His power is not known by you.' Then the Angel of Death said: 'Tell me of it, so that I can ascend to him and understand it.' The Lord replied: 'You may do so.'

And so the killing angel ascended. When Elijah saw him, he pinned him down with his feet. *He thought of expelling him from the world, but that was not allowed him.* So he forced down the Angel of Death, swung himself toward the heights and flew into Heaven."   *The Sayings of the Jewish Fathers*   34

The price of fame is the exalted mistreatment of the famous one after his death. How surprised, even amazed he would be to hear, if only he were able, all he said and thought. For there will be people who will have inhabited his body, be it his lungs, his heart, his kidneys, his bowels. They can reinvent him from the inside out into something he won't even recognize. They will have been there when he embraced his wife and will know how he wooed her. They will have seen him weep and will know why he wept. He will have told everything to each of them alone, having not a single secret among a hundred people. Each will know the truth, and what the others say will be false.

1967

These people who, smiling, employ a death wish in their defense of death. What else are they saying except that any resistance posed against it is in all cases futile?

The one ambition that is always legitimate, to keep people alive longer, has been specialized in the profession that sustains people: medicine. Doctors see the greatest number of deaths and are more used to it than others. Yet their ambition grows stale because of their professional circumstances. They, who always have done the most to counter religious resignation in the face of death, in the end take it as something natural. We can only hope that doctors develop a new attitude against death from their occupation: an unshakable defiance of death, whereby they increasingly detest it the more they witness it. Their defeats could be the seedbed of a new faith.

To write letters to be sent after one dies, for years afterward, addressed to everyone, whether you loved them or hated them.
    Or: a kind of confession to be made after death, an admission doled out in stages over the years.

What often seems boring about Goethe: that he is always so *complete*. The older he gets, the more he mistrusts passionate one-sidedness. But he naturally encompasses so much that he requires a different sort of balance than others do. He does not walk on stilts, instead he rests like a planet of the mind around which one must circle like a little moon to try to understand him, a humiliating role, yet the only suitable one to adopt in his case.

Rather than the strength of bold action, he provides that of longevity, and I know of no other great writer in whose presence death remains concealed for so long.

The greatest struggle in life is to not become inured to death.

The man who says of himself: In my entire life, not a single person I know has died.

This man, this man alone, I envy above all others.

The parasite's dilemma: to be threatened by the death of its host. He does not know what would be better for him. Has he stored up enough to start his own career without being controlled by the one dying? Should he quickly rush after more? Should he do anything he can to keep his host alive a little longer? Should he at least be present at the host's death to report that he is the "sole survivor"? If people refuse to have anything to do with him for a while after the threat of death emerges, he panics. He calls up every day, but no one answers the phone. Will he finally get up the courage to linger in front of someone's house "out of concern"? He only resents the sustenance that is suddenly being withdrawn from him.

And what if God had withdrawn from Creation out of shame for having created death?

A Greek god, hidden in the sea, the last one. Hauled out like a fish and left to die upon the beach.

A More Accommodating Murderer
Someone who makes one sick complains before the court. He is a decent person. He has never murdered anyone. He only murdered because he was ordered to. He only obeyed

out of idealism. Did he get anything out of it? The Reich is in shambles. But he is ready to pay back the wages he earned for his actions in monthly installments. But not the pension, for during those years he did nothing wrong and he can prove it. There were no longer any camps, so whom could he have harmed?

Your wholesale view of life, of every life—on what is it based?

If what lurks behind it all is that you yourself don't wish to die, then it is worthless.

But if it is all sincere and really is directed at life in general—how does it help anyone to live?

The persistently painful roots of this life, these you have recognized more clearly than anyone else, and yet they live on?

I don't know the answer to any of it. I am, as is clear, a *chauvinist* in relation to all of humankind, all animals, perhaps even to all plants. An Indian without the soul's transmigration, a Christian without God. I see, without any hesitation, immense masses swell before me, but every attempt to shrink their size calls on death and so gives rise to my hate and disgust. There is no death, not even of the oldest or most miserable person, that I have ever tolerated or accepted. The image of Egyptian soldiers dead in the deserts of the Sinai torments me as much as the ramps at Auschwitz. I know what these very soldiers would have done had they succeeded at entering the Jews' cities. But now *they* are the dead: now I grieve for *them*. I can make no distinction between the dead. I have no power over myself in this matter, I cannot violate this fundamental belief. I think it would be useful as a general belief and that many ingrained difficulties of our shared common life would disappear by adopting it. I really cannot contemplate anything else; I stand for something that is as important as it appears circumscribed.

I always have hope, but it is no longer the same hope, as death has hit me too hard, and love has made me too happy.

There is much she could savor if she were able to kill death.

"Her life was coming to an end, and let no one try to tell me that battlefields and other horrors are any more terrifying and horrific than the end of any human existence. All endings are cruel, and every human life is a heroic life, and dying—everywhere, and under no matter what circumstances—is equally bleak, cruel, and sad, and every human being must prepare himself for the poorest and worst exigencies, and every room in which a dead person is laid out is a tragic room, and there was never a human life that lacked tragedy of the most sublime sort." *Robert Walser, "Frau Scheer"*

What will happen to the mousetrap in his apartment when he dies?

"... for humans love immortality more than anything." *Plato, The Symposium*

The Symposium, how wonderful, even if it is the last thing that I ever read. *The night of September 24 to 25, 1967*

1968

Most important of all is conversation with strangers. It has to be done in such a way that *they* talk, and everything you do in the process is to get *them* to talk.

Whenever that is not possible, then death enters in.

There is nothing that people and animals have more in common than love.

Death for humans has become something quite different. Humankind has made itself so powerful through death that it now bears it on behalf of all creatures.

However, the link between death and love is aesthetic in nature. That it has elevated the place of death is its sin, and one of the gravest, which nothing can atone for.

I must reread *The Plowman of Bohemia*, which I read as a schoolchild. I need to see whether the hatred and defiance of death which fills that dialogue is truthful or just rhetorical. How little genuine hatred of death there is in literature! But this small amount needs to be found, collected, and mixed together in concentrated form. A Bible against death could supply many with strength when they feel like giving up. It will also separate one's own defiance from hubris, for how is it possible to stare death down on one's own? I'm not looking for allies, rather witnesses. For would it not be awful if my own tough-minded, fearless stance against death is in the end "explained away" as psychological, as if it only springs from special circumstances in my own life, and thus means something to me alone? Wherever such a stance is found in others it belongs to a *different* life, and thus the probability it also belongs to *every* life is far greater.

36

A good man asked me for directions. I'm afraid I can't tell you, was my answer. He looked at me kindly and was astonished. But he said nothing and seemed satisfied with this response. Uncertain, he walked on, and from the way he walked it was clear that he would not ask anyone else. I looked on at him sadly. Should I have told him the truth? I knew that he must die, since no matter what path I might have indicated, death awaited him. If he had known that, he might have remained where he was, for his salvation lay only in staying where he was.

"Don't move," I called after him. He heard me, but since I had dismissed him, he dared not stand still and continued on. "Don't move," I called louder, and he walked faster. Then I bellowed, guilt consuming me, and he began to run.

Save me, Kafka. Will you not save me. Do you despise my weight, my lechery, my stomach? Was Flaubert not as heavy as me, was he any less lecherous?—Where are your writings, I hear you say. Alas, nowhere, nowhere. But could I perhaps not still find them somewhere? I am not dead, for I love with a fire, passion, and commitment that you never attained. Does the road to truth run only over such asceticism? Kierkegaard and Flaubert were never my models. But Stendhal and Gogol and Aristophanes, they are no less than them.

Writing for me is also a form of prayer, the only one that I know. My trial is one involving death, and it is not yet over. Your reckoning happened too early. I have lived longer than you and carry more dead than you. They are what cause me to deny your asceticism. So long as I am hungry, I cannot fob them off. I wanted to survive *no one*, and therefore they all live within me. As for what speech I can grant them, still I have none. But I cannot abandon them, and *that* accounts for my fruitlessness.

I am so full of my dead, no else can die, for there is no more room inside me.

In the center of the city on a high pedestal stood their most sacred monument: a car.

Before this strange car the citizens gathered reverently three times a day: early morning, midday, and in the evening.

At night the car was closely guarded. Too often suicides were found inside.

A man like this Simon Wiesenthal, whose book I have just read, moves me a great deal.

A Michael Kohlhaas, but Jewish and cleverer, for who can deny the justice that he single-handedly promises. There are things in his book that stir one on the deepest levels (instead of doing the work I had planned to do in the past few days, I have instead read his book). He is courageous and just, and the accusation that he has become a hunter of human beings doesn't hold water, for it is not human beings he is after. One cannot help but be amazed that there are not more like him. If I had gone through what he had, I would have become much harder and more obstinate. He is the One-Man Police Force of the Jewish internees. Others who survived it wanted to forget it all, and therefore perhaps the understandable attempt to do that made everything all the worse for them.

In a different way I also became a kind of policeman, but I cannot rest easy in thinking it was for the Jews alone, but rather for all humankind and its entire history. *Crowds and Power* involves nothing less than uncovering all crimes of power, and how often in the many years that I dedicated to this pursuit have I felt disgust over this history and for the people who acted like tyrants and criminals. I did not rest until I found the gruesome source of it all within myself: everything that has happened exists within each of us as both capability and possibility. Perhaps that is what separates me from a man like Wiesenthal. Neither of us can forget, and both of us are convinced that one should not forget. But he searches for the persecutors, I for *the persecutor in ourselves.* It would not be enough for me to bring the worst of these killers to justice, because all the other human beings who could potentially become persecutors would still exist. I cannot feel sorry for anyone who W. himself has exposed after many years. Pity is always out of the question. But more disturbing than everything that has happened, or so it appears to me, is that it was possible then and will always *remain* possible. Human beings must come to know themselves as precisely as their worst enemy, they cannot rely on supposed self-awareness. Each must understand what death has done to him and be done once and for all with his resignation in the face of this "fact of nature."

37

He is dead. But he doesn't like these people who are gathered round his corpse.

Cain murdered Abel: he sank his teeth into his breast. "*And he bit him with his teeth like a serpent.*" (after the *Zohar,* I: 54b.)
 The murder is depicted this way in the New Testament. Abel lies on his back, Cain on top of him as he sinks his teeth into the top of Abel's breast, just below the windpipe, blood spurting out of the wound.

38

He only kisses necks, whereas throats he bites clean through.

You are order itself, for you have learned *nothing* from chaos, as you have cowered in your snail shell, your horns pathetically pulled in. You know nothing, you are nothing, you have never lived. Sometimes you have read a book in the dark. Sometimes you have talked with a shy woman, and then put a thousand miles between you and her. You have not fathered a child. You have not denied death to anyone it went after. Soon you will die and all that will be left of you will be some letters written in an orderly manner.

There is nothing more you can do *against* it, your resistance against time has been reduced to a pose. Even if you are as shrewd, devious, and despicable as others, you still can learn nothing from a person whom you love and who has remained unsullied.

Your misfortune is that you are not terrible enough, just as your misfortune is that you are not good enough, you, modest man haunted by the fear of causing the death of another. Forty years ago, when you were a writer, you had the same fear, but hidden within, unnamed, active, yet unspoken. When you began to give voice to it, it paralyzed you, the wasp of death having stung you and carried you in its stomach, *hoarding* you. Hoarding you for what?

Am I not like that beggar, do I not call out "Death" instead of "Allah," am I not a blind saint of repetition?

One only shrinks from others' repetition; in your own case, you just accommodate it.

1969

The one who, after every announcement of someone's death, *eats* more.

Not to write that someone is marked for death. Even writing it down is a sin.

The one breathing says: I have yet to breathe everything in. The unhappy one says: I still have room within me for someone else's misfortune. The dead one says: I don't know anything yet, how can I be dead?

To find a stronger word for love, a word that would be like the wind, but come from beneath the earth, a word that doesn't need mountains, but dwells in immense caves from whence it travels through the valleys and the plains like water that is not water, like fire that doesn't burn, but shines through and through, like a crystal, which doesn't cut and instead is transparent, pure form, a word like the voices of animals, as if they understand one another, a word like the dead, but all alive again.

The essence of my nature is that I cannot humiliate myself and yet must transform myself.

I cannot be transformed through death. Therefore, with intractable stubbornness, I view it as the end.

I know that I have said *nothing* about death. When will I do so once and for all? Or must I, out of my hatred of it, deny myself the chance?

Three albatrosses flew by as his heart stopped, and together they carried it home, heavy as it was.

Go a month without newspapers, and you could still make something of yourself.

A year without newspapers and you would be dead.

As an officer in the war, Musil got used to seeing dead people. Up until now I have refused to get used to it, and every dead person I see is still for me the first dead person I have seen.

Nevertheless, I can't help admire his ability to say no. He rejects almost everything of his time and *stands* by his rejection. The energy that stems from rejection is the impetus of his book. He creates characters who only exist on an intellectual level so he may precisely and thoroughly attack them. It is a sweeping approach, even if not always a battle advanced with great finesse. He cannot take any opponent seriously, for he is always in a superior position, and after a long while this advantage pleases him no end.

There is nothing of Don Quixote in Musil, and despite the fact Don Quixote is the greatest character forged by the European mind. Musil remains tinged with a vestige of vanity and pettiness. Musil is indeed invincible and the cleverest of all. He was never imprisoned as a slave in the war as was Cervantes, and in *his* war he didn't lose an arm. And yet he was able to take the measure of the most outwardly successful people of his time. That he could outstrip them was both his good fortune and misfortune. The highest prize, even the recognition of his genius, was immaterial to him. The word "genius" haunts his book persistently throughout. He wants to restore its purity and, once purified, reserve it for himself.

Love belongs to his legitimate experiences, and *especially* in the physical sense. It's from the richness of this experience that his tendency toward asceticism arises. I went in the opposite direction. For most of my life, love was not that essential to me, but as an older man, after having rejected it, or more so ignored it for decades because of my obsession with the masses, I gave in to it entirely. It is now in part the crowning aspect of my life, followed by the lesser task granted me, namely the assessment of the masses, which in essence was a success, even though the other, albeit greater challenge, was a frightful failure, namely the foiling of death.

39

She hung herself from her false eyelashes.

And what if your banning of death is nothing more than a dam constructed against your own obsession with destruction?

Perhaps how Fritsch took Thomas Bernhard to task
I got to know both of them in February 1962, at a tea held at the Society for Literature. There were others there also: Herbert Zand, Friedrich Heer, Jeannie Ebner, someone named Adel, and perhaps one or two others whom I don't recall. Fritsch hardly said a thing, while Bernhard made a scene by taking up cantankerous subjects and keeping the focus entirely on himself. He was the only one who stubbornly opposed me, going so far as to explain to me what an order is. Herbert Zand was insulted by his "disrespectful" manner and supported me. However, I was struck by Bernhard's stubbornness and liked him. Fritsch remained noticeably aloof, took no position whatsoever and impressed me not in the slightest.

Fritsch appeared already by then very *brown*, and I always thought of him as "brown."

I am ashamed to have outlived a man who was nearly twenty years younger than me.

The television movie for which Gerhard Fritsch wrote the

text will be broadcast for the first time on June 12. His name will appear next to mine.

I think of my tenderness and concern for Franz Nabl in Graz, who is now eighty-six years old, at exactly the time that Gerhard Fritsch hanged himself in Vienna.

Could I have saved Fritsch, who was half Nabl's age, the same futile, dreadful question again.

Bernhard, without a family, completely free, has no one to worry about, and only himself to think of.

Fritsch, with children from three marriages and yet another on the way. Compliant, and therefore burdened. Not a sharp thinker, and without a strong will, too easily influenced by those obsessed with themselves. Where then does the acuteness of his novel *Fasching* come from? I understand him less and less because I do not understand his death.   40

How does one live with this immense mass of powerful memories?

Is it possible to thin them out and live more freely? The images that one carries within oneself are weakened by nothing. Everything that belongs to the dead is strengthened within us day by day. We become the conservators of their lives. They cannot be suppressed, for what is real is now them. They appear and talk ceaselessly, as if we give them blood to drink. Perhaps it is such that all of one's life is transformed into the lives of the dead. What you see, what you hear, what you smell, they feed on it all. They cannot be fobbed off with insights and viewpoints that have nothing to do with them.

How strange is their power, which for so long was mute. When one observes full of delight young people unaware of their own strength and beauty, one does not think of adopting them as one's own. Yet they are gripped by the dead and serve as *their* life. It is not a greedy, predatory, hideous process, but instead something that is quietly exhilarating, peaceful, natural, and understandable. It runs its course as if it were the only sensible thing to be done. It hinders no one, but rather keeps everyone going and somehow makes them stronger. Any other endeavor only gets in the way, for it is the only legitimate one, and anything else amounts to usurpation.

That which is named remains alive.

A young Arab visited me to tell me that he had nothing against me, and then shot me dead.

Slowly death empties you out. The word is no longer what it was to you. It bores you, it has become a formula. Can you finally put it behind you and live forever?

To the Moon
Perhaps there are still no dead on the moon. After the first person that dies there, after the moon witnesses its first dead, it will be more familiar to us.

A new form of suicide: to disappear into space. The most expensive form of suicide, only for billionaires.

If you were to know, preacher, that tomorrow you will *die*, what would you preach this evening?

Since learning how people have used sociological jargon to describe death, he no longer likes to think about it. It is no longer the same death. It is death turned into gibberish.

Someone puts off finishing his most important work year after year. He knows he cannot die before he has delivered it, and so it seems to him that against death any ruse is allowed.

"We knew when people were dead because their screaming stopped."   *Rudolf Höss*   41

The massacres committed by the Americans: now more than ever it is clear that we are all capable of the same.   42

Even you yourself, and don't think you're not, for there is no respite in the fact that you have never yet been forced to kill. Had you been present, and with your life in danger, if you had the opportunity to *fight back*, then you would have learned something about yourself. But as things stand, you know *nothing* about yourself.

What there is to say can be said about everyone, yourself included. There is no one who is better, there are only those who are horrible, and the truth is that *all* of them *must* change.

There are massacres all over the planet and they can remain hidden for *years*. That means that many of them can remain hidden for good.

What you have said about the survivors is *true*, but *all* are survivors.

Those who live in the safety of London like you, those who enjoy any kind of safe haven, have to know who they really are, and what they are capable of. To say to others—you devils!

And yes, to say it to *themselves* as well!

I am more convinced than ever that the political theories of the nineteenth century—and I mean *all* political theories— are misguided and wrong. But that does not mean that they could be improved or expanded upon: they are wrong at their very base. The most distinctive were the most consequential, those espoused by Hegel. *Absolutely nothing* worthwhile can come from the dialectic as Hegel understood it.

In the final analysis that also has to do with the fact that there is an *irreversible fundamental fact* that undermines all of them: death.

Any philosophy that genuinely and not just superficially deals with death cannot be dialectical.

Death does not contain life, it has nothing to do with life. It is irrefutable, fruitless, and cannot be argued with by any means. The life struck down has nothing to do with death, it knows nothing of it, it does not lead to it. Death is at present only an aspect of all *higher* life. Accordingly, there are *two* different kinds of life, the immortal and the mortal, yet the lesser one is the immortal, and not the other way around.

1970

At the burial the coffin was lost. So the bereaved were shoveled hastily into the grave. The deceased suddenly emerged from this ambush and threw a handful of dirt at everyone in his grave.

Death: "Vadim died in February of 1843. I was there when he passed, and that was the first time I experienced the death of someone I knew well, not to mention the entire and complete horror of it, its entire senseless randomness, its entire stupid, morally bankrupt injustice."   *Alexander Herzen*   43

It's not enough to say that everything is death.
    Of course everything is death.
    But we must also admit that, hopeless as it seems, we firmly and intensely oppose the idea that everything is death. Absent cheap tricks—death shall lose its stature. Death is a fraud. It is our intention to show that it is a fraud.
    Anyone convinced that there is nothing but death only empowers it.

Some of the best writers of our time have, without knowing it, eulogized death through their hatred of it: the remnant of Christianity within them, a misunderstood remnant.

This multifaceted engagement with death, which you are very proud of, has cost you nearly everything in your life. It has raised your vulnerability to the death of your loved ones to such a staggering level, you have to focus exclusively on that, though you yourself have yet to kick the bucket.

It's easier for the others who take notice of death only in conventional ways. That probably seems to you quite despicable, but all of human experience is wrapped up in it nevertheless. What you seek, this open and *unguarded* life in the face of death involves immense hubris, as if you alone with your own hands could lift up this horrid principle of creation, revoke it, and refute it.

Visiting Thomas Bernhard

Prince of his own country court. Three thrones. Twenty pairs of shoes and boots. Empty. Forty little beer mugs. Empty. In one of the upstairs rooms: an engraving of Basel above a picture of his mother, who was born in Basel.

A walk through the fields and forest to a country inn. After the meal we listen to the speech of three mean talking to one another. B. thinks of it as *his* speech, which he then proceeds to demonstrate (he hardly stops to think that it is also "my" speech).

On the way back through the woods he talks about his stay in the hospital in Gmunden, which was located next to the slaughterhouse. The patients heard the screams from the abattoir. His sensitivity to mass slaughter is exactly like mine. But he was also very sick and a hypochondriac. His skin is an ugly red color, breaks out constantly in a rash. He has turned the bare white walls and corridors of his house into his clear skin.

That his country court exists, that he did not just dream it up, both impresses and upsets me. In any case, he has not settled for a middle-class life. Perhaps, says Bernhard, he does not want any animals in his house, because animals are slaughtered.

I believe I do not like B. I believe he wishes death for all.

Death does not allow its story to be told.

Everyone asks me about Thomas Bernhard, everyone wants to know what I think of him. I praise him and explain what he's about, I try to help others better understand him. I elevate him to my disciple, and naturally he is, and in a much deeper sense than someone like Iris Murdoch, who is always so pleasant and light, while underneath it all she has become a brilliant and amusing popular writer. She is not really a disciple of mine, because she is so obsessed with *gender*. However, Thomas Bernhard is obsessed with death.

On the other hand, in recent years he has come under the influence of another, which *conceals* my own, namely that of Beckett. Bernhard's hypochondria makes him susceptible to Beckett. Like him he gives in to death, rather than opposing it. He sees it everywhere and passively damns all to it.

Therefore I think that now, because of his empowerment through Beckett, Bernhard is somewhat overrated, but overrated by the higher-ups: the Germans have found their own Beckett in him.

The entanglement of my influence on Bernhard with that of Beckett is curious and obvious. It's a little too simple to really please me. So, I declare here, for myself, that I have defended him too much out of generosity. I am not entirely sure if it serves him.

44

Young men with funereal faces and voices to go with them. In Hampstead alone I know of three, each looking just like the others, wearing the same clothes and carrying a travel bag, as if ready to attend a funeral after a plane crash.

Ban obituaries. Only allow the news of a death to be carried from house to house, apartment to apartment.

The prophet Elijah defeated the Angel of Death. Making my name feel ever more uncanny.

What is completely missing from my book is a *study of death itself*. This study is what I had once undertook. I even found a way that would have allowed me to drill down on the subject: *Kanaimà*. I wanted to study killing that did *not* result from an order given, but rather is done for its own sake.

I have abandoned the book for at least ten years. Because of the death of people near and dear to me, I was not up to this study. To remain alive, I had to throw myself into a passion, into a love to which I dedicated myself entirely. But since I had never experienced this so powerfully, it turned into an experience that completely consumed seven years of my life. In these seven years I really did nothing else but mourn and love. The time has come for that to change. Nothing is holding me back. I am still strong, or at least think myself so, and I must try to set in motion what I had begun.

While I have been committing to paper proud sentences against death, during these many years people have been tortured to death in the most shameful manner.

The strength of the powerful has led to violence on the part of the powerless. Nothing could be more clear, and I would go so far as to equate one with the other. But this is an aspect of power no one has yet fathomed, and what ultimately cannot help but occur.

1971

What if it turns out that we, perpetual penitents before the future, have lived in the best of all times!

If we were *envied* by the millions of starving Bengalis.

If our dissatisfaction and our miserable conscience were ridiculed as charming Biedermeier affectations!

If again and again and a thousand times over we were to study how we might have managed to achieve so much freedom, so much room to breathe, so many thoughts!

If our cluelessness were declared the pinnacle of humanity and our aversion to death viewed as *harmless* bloodlust!

The Russian cosmonauts were dead when they landed on Earth. They successfully touched down and did not die of any wounds resulting from the landing. If it was a matter of heart failure, it happened to all three hearts simultaneously. An end more gripping than disappearing into space. That's the way they were found, which is a warning. It would be better if a reason for their death is never discovered.

Yet one must still take seriously the collective sorrow of the Russians for their three dead. If such tasks were to assume the function of wars, as a form of collective participation in a life-threatening undertaking, then space travel would be meaningful after all.

So much about the ancient gods has been lost that we might fear something has also been lost of our own simpler God.

But as to the god that brought death into the world, I can never make my way back to it. Nowhere do I see a god of life, only the blind who gloss over their misdeeds with God.

The philosophers who want to *pass along* death to you, as if it was always there in you from the beginning.

They cannot stand to meet it for the first time at the end of their lives. They prefer to extend it all the way back to the beginning, signifying death as the most intimate companion of one's entire life, thereby making it bearable for them in its diluted, familiar form.

They do not realize that as a result they have granted it more power than it deserves. "It doesn't matter that you die," they appear to say, "for you have been dying all your life anyway." They don't sense that they are guilty of one of the most vile and cowardly tricks, for they only cripple the strength of those who could stand guard against death. They prevent the only battle worth fighting. They espouse as wisdom that which is capitulation. They persuade all to follow their own cowardice.

Those among them who claim to be Christian thereby poison the genuine core of their faith which drew its strength from the triumph over death. Any resurrection to which Christ bore witness for the evangelists would be senseless if one were to follow their way of thinking.

"Death, where is your sting?" It is not a sting, they say, because it is already always there, ingrown into life, its Siamese twin.

They deliver human beings to death as if an invisible blood pulses through its veins.

It should be called the blood of acquiescence, the secret shadow blood of the true blood that continually renews itself in order to live.

Freud's notion of a death drive descends from older and more sinister philosophical teachings, but it is much more dangerous because Freud cloaks it in biological terms which garner the respect of the moderns.

This psychology, which is not philosophy, stems from philosophy's worst legacy.

The philosophers of language who ignore death, as if it were something "metaphysical." But relegating death to metaphysics changes nothing about the fact that it is the oldest fact of all, older and more far-reaching than any language.

The Stoics conquer death through death. The death that you impose upon yourself cannot do anything more to you, so there is no need to fear it.

Whoever chops off his own head feels no pain.

We have to ask whether it is reprehensible at an advanced to age to try to sum things up. For it is arguable that under the pressure of all that is dredged up you become unwilling to absorb anything new and therefore absorb nothing.

Perhaps the value of absorbing anything late in life is doubtful. Not everything seeps in, there is a tendency toward the superficial, and you wear an impenetrable cloak that rejects anything new.

On the other hand, the openness toward what is felt *inside* grows so strong that you *must* give in to it, even if its yield only half justifies doing so. The difficulty is that there is a glow to all earlier things simply because they occurred earlier, which is really the glow of the dead. However, you are not allowed to mistrust this glow, for it contains gratitude for what you have lived. It *can* only be what you have lived yourself, that which you have lived alone, while the guilt you feel from time to time in it having nothing to do with the lives of others, because essentially it excludes them, is a presumptuous guilt, for how could you live the life of everyone else for them?

For the most part I mistrust the moral code with which I am obsessed.

But nothing seems to me more despicable than to simply throw it overboard as N. has done.

About the horrible inflation of the ego I can say something.

But I also know that it is *nothing* but a miserable means of deceiving oneself about death, against which it does no good at all.

"Bunin could hardly keep up with the old man, who had started to run and in a rough, wild voice kept repeating: 'There is no death! There is no death!'" (about Tolstoy)

It could indeed come to pass that someday I may *yield* to death. I ask anyone who might hear of it for forgiveness.

What accounts for the *vibrancy* of Buddhism?

Does it come from how far it has spread and the many kinds of people that have engaged with it?

Why is Christianity so much less vibrant?

Is it because its seats of power have been known to us too long and too well? Or is it because it rarely and hardly engages with the life of animals?

This last has much to say for itself. Anything to do with Saint Francis is fascinating. Before a Veronese in the Galleria Borghese titled *Saint Anthony Preaching to the Fishes*, I stood as if before a miracle. No Madonna could possibly mean as much to me.

Christ on the Cross *means* something if his pain is depicted as horrifying. But mostly he appears as a pleasant, handsome man. One could imagine taking him down and hearing him talk as if nothing had happened. He makes death seem less burdensome, by making it seem pleasant.

The watering down of Christianity, when I think of the grandeur of the Sermon on the Mount, the torment of Christ's death, is unbearable for me.

If I lived in a Buddhist country, would I perceive a weakening of Buddhism?

The falling-off cannot be entirely the same, as Christianity is in essence more intense and more violent. It involves killing, and the suffering on the Cross cannot be seen as easy, otherwise it means nothing.

In Buddhism, the death of the founder is gentler. It is lengthy and involves a spiritual process, not the employment of external violence. The ideal nature of this founding figure always astonished me. Even to this day I don't completely understand its effect.

But since its existence is entirely free of force from the start, it can never degenerate to our own capacity for violence.

The vibrancy of Buddhism that I began with has to do with the premise that, eo ipso, turns it into a universal, namely the belief in the transmigration of the soul.

In each existence Buddha was always at home. Compared to the story of his birth, The *Jātaka*, the story of the saints of the church seems somewhat monotone.

The Buddha, who was once *everything*, possesses the most all-encompassing existence ever ascribed to any creature. The essence of this belief has remained vibrant, no matter how much its outward practice has faded or been diluted.

It is impossible to say nothing about a death. You demand a host of howling mourners, and when there aren't any, you attempt to speak to them across distances through letters.

But the force of grief felt for the deceased is so great that you do not just write to those that knew him, but rather you demand of everyone you know to honor his memory. You introduce your dead to them retroactively, saying the best that can be said about the deceased. You make very clear what the person meant to you while also applying a kind of pressure on others to do the same, and woe to him to whom the deceased did not mean so much. Privately your continued friendship with them depends upon their reaction to your death notice. You size them up and observe with suspicion, carefully weighing every word they say, and when one is found to be too light, you shove them away mercilessly, for they can never be a part of you again.

Death disappears amid the play of language.

If I were to be totally honest with myself, I would have to say that I would like to destroy everything that Joyce stood for.

I am against the *vanity* of Dadaism in literature and the elevation of itself *above words*. I worship intact words.

The most vital part of the language involves *names*. I can grab hold of names and haul them down, but I cannot break them into pieces.

That is true as well for the name of the one I hate above all, the founder and guardian of death: God.

The only letters I would like to write are those to my dead.

I would be prepared to do nothing else but write letters to my dead.

How can you know if you will mean anything to future generations. You might bore them to death. You might stir them in the marrow of their bones. You might pet them or whip them. You might inspire the worst in them, or you might become their conscience.

But you can never know how it will be, and the hope that

your life will have meaning is indeed necessary, though also comical.

The only figure who could inspire me would be the defender of death. To stir myself out of the torpor of my hatred of death, I must invent a *friend* of death.

Could it be that you are too proud of your "rejection" of death?
First you rejected God, then Freud, then Marx, and death all the way through. To where are you running in such a hurry, little rabbit?

Your death-kitsch. You must consider whether *The Numbered* in the form you currently have it is not kitsch, your death-kitsch.

Each new massacre creates a new model, and it is as if the rapid growth of humanity only serves its own massacre.
No one, no one at all, can say through what miracle it will be brought to an end.
If we want to think hopefully that the experience and awareness and general consensus brought the American war to an end, it would be just as possible to counter that this war could never be won. Maybe today there is the possibility of converting near defeats into a feeling of disgust; but as for victory, nothing like that is possible.
The victory over the defenseless Jews back then was hard for most to resist, and just as irresistible is the victory over the Bengalis today.
Weapons that kill more easily than ever now kill masses of people, but they have not given up on the methods of killing of individuals of old, *they just integrate them with the rest.*

47

You cannot kill the moths that whir about your clothes for you love their silken wings.

You also cannot trap a mouse who has soiled your provisions. Entranced, you have observed the traces of their teeth on the foil paper wrapped around your butter.

You have watched the fly that wandered into the heat of your lamp and fell to the desk on which you write as if it were badly wounded or burned. It lay there on its side, a wing looking as if it were mutilated, two of its legs stuck together, incapable of moving. It lay there a while and twitched. Slowly it spun itself around, but as if it were in its last throes. I had no idea how I could help it. It appeared to me that it was in great pain, and the only thing I could do was to not cause it any anxiety by disturbing it.

Suddenly it spread its wings as if to fly. I marveled at it and felt that it would take off, and though it didn't do so right away, it tried to, trembling a little as it did. Then it flew away and disappeared, circling past my pencils.

I was overwhelmed with happiness and would have been delighted to let it know how I felt.

He holds the German language close to his heart and begs the dead for their approval.

All the hearts of the world will disappear and be replaced by plastic hearts.

I'd like to see Halley's Comet again when it returns (1986). That seems to me a modest request, for I could wish to see it three more times in all (in 2062 and 2138, as well).

Chewing their cud, they fell from the cliffs to their death below.

The thought of a single person you have lost can lead you to feeling love for all others. Who indeed lost Christ? A blind spot in the Gospels.

Do you wish to renounce the transformation of the dead within us? In their transfiguration you recognize the source of beauty. That which can no longer exist becomes beautiful. That which cannot be attained is transformed. An amazing word—how much must fall away, how much that is trivial and unsettling has to disappear in the process of transformation. The splendor of the dead is that they were once here and are remembered. Do you wish to renounce it all, can you?

I read what an array of philosophers have said about death and am ashamed for them. Am I the only one who has found the path back to the original feeling of primitive humans? Can I be the only one? Is that conceivable? Did my father have to die at such a young age for me to travel this path? Was he the victim sacrificed in order that this vital path be restored?

I have no doubt at all that I would have become an entirely different person if I had stayed in England and if my father had *not* died so young. Most likely I would have become an English writer, but I cannot at all imagine what I would have written without that core experience, probably rubbish, or nothing, and it would have been better if I had become a doctor.— There is no doubt at all that there are central events that change a person from the start.

He Shares the Grace of the Dead
Someone he was close to has died and he writes about him to all. What does he write?

He exalts the deceased, he depicts him and elevates him and calls him—against his better judgment—a saint. He gives the impression that the deceased was very close to him, ever closer and closer, until finally he was the closest one to him of all. That's why he understands the saint so well.

Then he tries to connect everyone he writes to with the saint. "I spoke to him about you, and we talked about you. He knew everything about you." Sometimes this rises to the level of a final message from the deceased to the listener. "I should tell you this and say he meant to tell you it. He asked me to do so."

Such duties are invented. An irresistible power compels him to invent them. They *could* be true, but they are not. Perhaps they should be true. But since it's about the sanctity of the deceased, someone for whom he feels the deepest grief, it is surprising that he presumes to invent such messages. Still, he feels gratified and feels no guilt, for they are good and noble messages. Their intention to help the deceased be remembered in a deeper way and to make others curious about him is a good one. To compel good remembrance, that is certainly the central thrust, for he is so full of the deceased that he turns into him, acting like him as if he were still alive.

There is probably nothing to be done about this. But there is more involved. He presumes to represent the deceased, he takes control and channels a supernatural presence, deciding for himself the messages of the deceased. He feels that he is doing something good for *him*, but in reality he is just elevating his own reputation. He doesn't do anything differently than what priests do when they share the blessings of Christ. He assumes a spiritual body and walks around in it among the living, who tremble before *their* own death.

A window, quite small, into the deathless future.

1972

He shook hands with the dead and joined them as the newly arrived.

The self-hater loves death *more*. He trembles with excitement before death and says: "That is the best thing we have."

Everything that the seventy-five-year-old mouse recalls is false. But no one says a word when she can't remember a thing. So she talks on and holds forth, and if she gets only a few names correct she is allowed to get older, and to know less and less and less.

Finally she is even too small for the last hole and evaporates into thin air.

What one still has plans for at the end is very important. It's the measure of death's injustice.

The "deepest" was the most cowardly. One should not think away the wall that we smash our head against.

To take the unbearable weight upon oneself. To not deny anything. To not just skip away.

Not the loneliness, not the afflictions, not the misery of old age, none of that can convert you. Your mind is quiet and focused as a tiger. Is it self-satisfaction? Can you say anything good about even the slightest piece of history? And yet it will go on.

How will it be any different after this history. Will it be allowed to be buried, denied, revised? Do you have a recipe for how to do it?

Yet it is possible that we see a *false* history. Perhaps the true one can only be made public when death is defeated.

Out of the efforts of a single individual to stave off death the monstrous edifice of power is created.

Countless deaths were ordered up for the sake of the continued life of one individual. The bedlam that followed is called history.

This should be the beginning of the true Enlightenment, one that establishes the right of *every* individual to live on.

When we know how wrong everything is, when we are capable of appreciating the extent of its wrongness, then, and only then, is stubbornness the best approach, the constant pacing of the tiger behind its bars in order not to miss the single brief instant of its release.

Your disdain for all who line up death with birth as if one offsets the other.

Yet now you yourself think about birth and find as a result that death hardly occurs to you anymore, no longer threatening you and worrying you, it suddenly doesn't matter to you, the expected birth being the only thing that matters.

Could it be that you were obsessed with death because it was not until your old age that you looked forward to a birth?

What must be added: even if your own death is made easier through this birth, that changes nothing about the death of others. Indeed, you have really been thinking about them, not yourself.

Your obsession was not self-absorbed, it was what it was, namely for all who had died. How can any birth possibly ease *their* death?

Yet there is a *particular* insight you have gained from your new situation:

The fact that humankind has not seriously rebelled against death has to do with the fact that they were granted the ability to bring new life into the world. It's *that* which has occupied them, *that* which has bought their silence.

The begetting of children is an immense undertaking. The blossoming of a new life causes your own to fade. The hope that the new life will be *better*, especially when you have not been satisfied with your own.

There is much to be said for this continuance of life, for none of us comes to terms with our own. Ascent and descent chafing against one another.

from *Dramas*
V.
The dead are prayed to and carried around like mummies. They enjoy the status of gods, even though there are many of them. They gradually shrivel up and turn into jewels fastened to necklaces.
XIX.
For every death sentence a judge hands down he gets a medal. Soon they are all weighed down by rattling medals like long-serving officers.

I would like to know what constitutes a crime.

Up until now I have only known: is it another form of killing?

There, they line up to die, and each brings an official paper saying that he can.

An arms dealer who gallivants about with a pack of enthralled followers before whom he demonstrates the force of his weapons. He uses his wealth to amass the greatest art collection the world has ever seen, which he then bequeaths to humankind, and thus dies a philanthropist.

So that nothing is lost, he only writes letters that he does not mail, his archive complete.

In 1953, when I first returned to Vienna, people were scandalized by my being a Jew. Whether I felt so or not, to others I was a survivor, and was perceived as such by the guilty as well as by me.

Today I am taken as someone who stood on the sidelines. The carnage has moved on to other parts of the world. Vietnam and Bengal are far from here. The Viennese can proudly point to them. No stranger has a clue what happened here. Vienna's chief export, Hitler, has disappeared. Bandits take over the culture at large.

The most beautiful animal remains unknown. It died out before we came along.

You have pressed yourself to do the most important thing of all: to take stock of matters as a whole. It was too boring to just string things together. A thought was only of value to you when it had the power to murder. You who curse killing and death are a mass murderer in a hundred thousand sentences.

Most Pacific salmon die in the spawning grounds while spawning. Long stretches of a salmon river can be strewn with the bodies of dead salmon on their banks.

My friend asked me to give him the mummy, but I didn't give it to him. I wouldn't give the mummy to any friend. He then asked me for a centimeter of its hair, but I didn't give it to him. I wouldn't give a centimeter of its hair to anyone. My friend said the mummy loved him, that it smiled at him. I slew my friend whom the mummy had smiled upon.

The first Methuselah. What one wouldn't give to know him and question him! Perhaps he is still alive today. Perhaps one could at least give him *orders*.

Sunday, December 24, 1972

I am beginning the year's tally already at Christmas. I have good reason to begin it so early, for the new year has already begun. For the first time someone has been *born* to me. Until now it was year after year of dying, dying, dying.

Perhaps my life will have to proceed as it once did, such that I am sufficiently *aware* of death. But now that it is evident that I have taken notice of death, things can change, and I am allowed to look on as the tiny creature that was born grows and thrives, wriggles and gurgles. Even if I spend all my time gazing at it—of that I could not feel ashamed.

48

145

1973

Why do I resist the notion that death is already present in the living? Is it not in you as well?

It is within me because I need to attack it. For this, and only this, I need it, for this I've let myself be infected.

The collector of last looks: how I lament those who, upon dying, desert all those who live and will live.

Death used three things to bribe Schopenhauer: his father's pension, the hatred for his mother, and Eastern philosophy.

He thinks he is incorruptible because he was not a professor. He will not admit that the most reprehensible, most unredeemable corruption is to accept death's bribes.

In this way he is not a useful enemy. What can be said against him is better said against the Eastern philosophers.

To *rescue* extravagance, one must not die reasonably.

Whoever is obsessed with death is implicated by it.

Whether or not God is dead, it is impossible to say nothing about Him, since He was around for so long.

Whether to cover up or sharpen the focus on the end: the only choice.

You've had your doubts, and yet you must have wanted your fame. But have you not wanted the return of a dead person a thousand times more? And you never managed to achieve that.

Only the pitiful, superficial, shameful wishes are fulfilled, and the great ones worthy of humans remain unfulfillable.

None will come back, none ever returns; those you hated rotted away. Those you loved rotted away as well.

Would it be at all possible to love *more*? To revive a dead person through more love, has no one ever loved enough?

Or would a lie suffice, one as great as Creation itself.

What will become of the images of the dead that you hold within your eyes? How will you leave those behind?

I would no longer know how to count all of them, all my dead. If I tried, I would forget half of them. There are so many, and they are everywhere, for my dead are scattered across the entire Earth. Thus the entire planet is my home. There's hardly a country left for me to acquire, the dead having bought them all for me already.

"When Solon wept over the death of his son and someone said to him: 'It will do no good,' he replied: 'That's why I am weeping, for it can do no good.'"

Perhaps we sense that the dead are still there, but only in a few words, and whoever might know these words will be able to hear the dead.

A survivor of the end of the world — a missionary.

I don't regret these orgies of book buying. It feels like the time when my library expanded while writing *Crowds and Power*. Everything back then also occurred through the adventure of books. Back in Vienna, when I was penniless, I still shelled out money I didn't have for books. In London, in the worst of times, I still managed somehow to buy books from time to time. I have never learned anything systematically, as have others, but instead in sudden bursts. It always began with my eyes falling upon something that I just had to have. The feeling of pulling a book off a shelf, the joy of shelling out money, then taking it home or to a café, gazing at it, sizing it up, thumbing through, tucking it away for years, eventually discovering it anew, when it really mattered—all of it is part of the creative process whose hidden particulars I do not understand. But that's the way it is with me, and until my dying day I must buy books, especially when I know for sure that I will never read them again.

I believe this also has to do with my defiance of death. I never want to know which of these books will remain unread. Right to the very end it's not clear which those will be. I have the freedom to choose, for amid all the books surrounding me I am free at any time to choose and through that choice hold the course of life in *my hands*.

Death is my lead weight, and I take desperate measures not to shed it.

A note from my time in Zurich while living on Scheuchzer-strasse: "I would like to die a hero's death for the sake of my mother."

This I wrote on a note card that I then stuck in a book. What great shame when my mother found this card. I thought of a fire into which I could plunge in order to save her. I imagined carrying her in my arms from the fire. I was then not much older than twelve, small and delicate, but I didn't worry about how I was going to manage to *carry* her. I always saw the fire before me into which I would bravely plunge, always emerging with my mother in my arms. Although I succeeded at saving her, I nevertheless died on the spot, having sacrificed my life for her. I never thought of either burns or pain, for it was only important that I die for her.

I cannot imagine that writing my *De la mort* would be like Stendhal writing his *De l'amour*. Maybe it would work if I tried to do so with the same weightiness he did. However, I am a zealot and a Jew, and the Bible is in my blood, it certainly being not one of *his* favorite books.

49

The discipline of death begins quite early. Does it ever stop? (When does it stop?)

Of course I don't believe in a happy planet, the Earth full of good people who get along with one another and lead a full life as well.

What then do I believe? The thought of the *overcrowding* of the planet and the necessary castration of masses that will not be allowed to increase in number terrifies me greatly. It is as if my faith in the potential worth of every individual is taken away by a flawed focus on the sheer number of people. While earlier I conceded *to anyone and everyone* that I wanted neither myself nor others to be placed above *anybody*, now I must acknowledge how many are prevented from living extended lives. It's as if an executioner were deciding that many others are not allowed to exist, whether they are selected before birth or selected for the future. It is so disturbing I cannot stop thinking about it. My sympathies toward humankind, which once enjoyed something unlimited and indestructible, are now infected by the idea of necessary destruction.

I consider ignominy and despair the consequences of this.

The book about death I hope to write stands ominously before me. I am full of so many things I still want to write.

I think it is the presence of my child that fills me with shyness before the prospect of death. It seems to me heinous to speak of things that would also touch upon its death. I don't wish to burden its time, which is just beginning, with my thoughts.

It's clear that many terrible things come with constantly thinking about death, as if one is made responsible for it as a result of such thoughts.

Thoughts about death are themselves deadly.

He cannot find enough religions. He needs more of them. Until he has grasped *all* facets of death, he must find and invent new religions.

Can one die dreaming?

The "closed" books are those that account for death, namely as the last and only terminus. Either it is an unconquerable finality whose growing power advances, and through each of us the final stop of an unalterable debacle, or the effort is made to erect a fortress against it, one completely sealed off and without a single crack through which it can force its way in. The "open" books are those that set death aside, that ignore it, that wish to strip it of its weight and significance.

The Mourning Herd of Elephants
"Toward the end of 1964, on the slopes of Mount Elgon in Kenya, Warden Winter had to cull three animals from a herd of bulls, cows, and young elephants in order to control their numbers. Right after the deadly shots, all hell broke loose among the survivors. They whirled their massive bodies around, trumpeting and shrieking horrifically. Then they tried to lift their dead comrades from the ground."

Warden Winter writes: "The frantic animals shoved and pushed the cadavers with great force. They entwined their tusks with those of the dead and in this way tried to lift them up. That lasted more than a quarter of an hour. Suddenly a large cow galloped over to a dead bull, knelt down beside him and shoved her tusks under his belly. Then she tried to lift both herself and him up. Her body tensed under the immense effort. All of a sudden there was a loud crack and her right tusk flew in a high arc ten meters into the air."

To help the bull, which was perhaps her mate, she had sacrificed a tusk!

"Shortly after this happened the herd vacated the area with a tremendous noise and flattened every tree that stood in their path. Suddenly the giants returned, trumpeting and shrieking constantly and tried again to lift their dead comrades. Three times they repeated their efforts. At last the head of the herd struck a majestic pose and gave several loud signals, as if he wished to 'speak' to those who had been shot. When that did no good, he trumpeted loudly, and the herd finally wandered off."   *Winter, "Elephants Tried to Move their Dead"*   50

The hypnotic lake which draws all those who live next to it to swim to their death.

The end looks different since my child was born. The danger of reconciliation. Procreation's trick.

O my child, my child, how much longer shall I remain your father?

I have nothing to complain about, for I have indeed known you already. I have experienced your first steps, your first words. Yet not once have I done anything for them, as I have done nothing at all, for I have protected no one from death. My one true passion was otherwise, and the only thing I have brought to the cause is a repugnant, inflated name.

Only within his scattered and contradictory sentences is it possible for a person to keep himself whole, to hold yourself together, to entirely become something without losing the most important thing, to reiterate it, to breathe it, to learn its every gesture, to manifest its accent, to practice wearing its masks, to fear its truths, to dissolve its lies into truths, to piss death off, and once rejuvenated, to disappear.

The murderer who never utters a nasty word.
The murderer who murders the innocent before they
    become guilty.
The murderer who *rescues* his victim.
The murderer who tenderly mourns all those he has rescued.
The murderer who sets up a graveyard for all those he has
    rescued.
The murderer who honors their memory, *his* great family.
The murderer who talks about how wonderful they were;
    who jealously guards their memory: the best he encoun-
    tered, the best there ever was.
The murderer who remembers names as if he bestowed
    them himself, who transports no one until he can name
    them, who asks their name as a lover would, each of them
    more precious and beautiful than the previous, and each
    all the more deserving to be rescued.
The murderer who wove garlands for his victims and
    awarded himself medals for saving them, and who be-
    cause of their growing weight, no longer was able to walk
    or to murder.
The murderer, who full of self-denial, removes the weight of
    medals to start all over again.

1974

How many things you evaded in order not to lessen the full force of death!

Every death sunders the nexus of the spun web of the world.

It is especially important to figure out whether death fades for he who sees his child growing up, whether it matters less and less to him, whether the presence of new human beings is enough to avoid death, or whether it is not another form of self-delusion that longs for reassurance.

It is *not* sentimental to think of a dead person as long as you have not accepted his death.

1975

You are less credible than Kafka because you have already lived so long.

However, it could be that the "young" might turn to you for help against the scourge of death found in literature.

As someone who with each year despises death more and more, you could be of use.

The picture of my father, who was no longer alive, hanging above the beds in the Josef-Gall-Gasse, where we lived in Vienna. A faded picture that never meant anything to me.

Inside me was his smile, as well as his words.

I have never seen a picture of my father that I didn't find absurd, never read a written word of his that I could believe.

Inside me he was always more because he was dead. I tremble to think what would have become of him inside me had he lived.

And so you hold up death, as if it were the meaning, the glory, the marvelous, and the honorable.

But it is only that because it should not exist. It is only that because I hold it up against the man who died.

Any death that is accepted is dishonorable.

No death has yet taken away my hatred, and how I have truly hated. Perhaps that is also a way of not recognizing death.

To be extinguished for a time, but to be certain that one can reignite oneself again.

An important testimony:

"A man said to me that he believes that white people are not so worried and anxious when a white man dies as are bushmen when one of their own dies. 'There are plenty of white people,' he said, 'but so few bushmen.'"   *Lorna Marshall*   51

This indestructible feeling of lasting, not to be reduced by death, by any kind of despair, by any passion for the other better ones (Kafka, Walser): I cannot come to grips with it, I can only reluctantly record it.

However, it is true that only here at my desk, before the leaves of the trees, whose movement, twenty years on, still excites me, am I myself. Only here does my terribly wonderful sense of security remain intact, that feeling which perhaps I *must* have in order not to lay down my arms before death.

You can only escape through another approach to death. Therefore you can never escape.

Letters from the dead. The dates changed.

Herder did not choke to death. Otherwise Jean Paul could not have loved him.

It's still surprising that Goethe did not choke to death.   52

It's hard to estimate how much Wagner helped the world become accustomed to death through his bombastic feeling.

I still do not believe that I must die, but I do know it.

Death's Enemy never came to life, therefore I have done nothing. The ridicule that I engendered because of that character's views, I have indeed deserved. If he really existed, if he were there incarnate, no one would dare ridicule him.

Children rather than survival: it's possible to consider that, a great temptation.

I've always felt metaphysics is a distortion of *this* life. As if life could be reduced to physics or even fully comprehended.

The hundred-year-old woman who knows the names of all her dogs.

I have begun tearing up letters, and it brings me great pleasure to do so. I first decided to do this to make it easier to move out of the apartment, should that occur. Papers and letters have gathered here over the last twenty years, though before now I could not bring myself to rip up any paper that had anything written on it. But since I have begun to do so, it no longer has to do with my original intention: the ripping up has become *the point*. Each day I spend one or two hours doing it. Bag after bag full of paper stack up, which are then hauled away each Saturday.

The feel of ripping paper is itself a pleasure. But what excites me even more is to read through old letters before I decide which to destroy. The *decision* is a kind of damnation that I pronounce over the writer of each. Which are worthy enough to remain with me, which are only worth getting rid of. It's like a decision between life and death. I notice, however, that it is always the dead whose letters I *never* destroy. I am much more heartless to the living. Some of them I *want* to bury. A murderous occupation, which I pursue day by day. Nothing relaxes me more at the moment, neither the purchase of new books nor even writing.

I think it is possible that we really live off of the dead.
I dare not think what we would be without them.

Goethe configured his life as landscape. Now he is a part of the earth, but with birds flying above.

1976

Each must grapple with death anew.
  There are no rules that one can adopt.

This B. who pretends we can discipline death through suicide. He won't kill himself before he has convinced everyone that death is the best thing of all.

There are too many. We die from the massive weight of the dead.

He forgot to die, that's how satisfied he was with himself. However, he made sure that others didn't forget to.

To hope that you alone will be the one remaining, that's the deadly sin.

He is not old, but he still hates death, thus he will never be old, for he will always hate it.

A very old man—a kind of Jain monk who has never killed. When the only point of your life is not to kill—what kind of person remains?
  I'd like an honest answer to this question: just what does such a person know?

I've had to keep routine murder at a great distance. I've never read crime novels. If I did read them, I wouldn't be so astonished by it. Still I cannot fully grasp *any* murder. It's a puzzle I'd like to solve, and because it cannot be solved, I am still alive.

The reconciliation of two mortal enemies after the death of a mutual friend. He was what they fought over. He took their hate with him to his grave.

Disturbing and inexplicable what elephants do with the bones of their dead.

It is useless, it is senseless, it is also despicable to think of people as utterly lost.

There is only one possibility: until you draw your last breath, to hope for a way out not yet known to us.

It does not matter what one calls this hope, so long as it exists.

It is by now impossible to raise an untested view, one that has not already been put forward, against the knowledge of religions, given the mastery they have acquired in dealing with death. It is also doubtful if such views can ever be fully thought through, each one perhaps nothing more than a push toward new and other knowledge.

"Each of these stories testifies to what has appealed even to the most advanced nations as the supreme hint of immortality— the energy and power of the human soul. Death is unnatural; man was made to last forever; only the most drastic means can conquer his strong and vivacious soul. "It is no matter for astonishment, therefore, that this energetic soul, once conquered by death, should be essentially dangerous."

Verrier Elwin, Myths of Middle India   53

On the night of the 16th to the 17th he died in the middle of a dream, calling out:

"What the devil!"

Dear Thomas Bernhard,

I have criticized you harshly, and now you senselessly flail away at me.

You know very well how seriously I have taken your plight, having been deeply moved by Gargoyles, as I told you myself. Then you said to my face, "Death is the best thing we have." Coming from someone who nearly died and barely escaped it, I found that to amount to nothing less than abominable cynicism. No one knows better than you how thoroughly we are infested with death. That you wish to serve as its advocate has filled me with mistrust for your work. I am convinced that this view cannot help but weaken it, and I wanted to say that to you openly.

You always respond to critics with blind rage. But because I am not someone doing a hatchet job on you in the newspaper, I thought a harder blow coming from me might bring you to your senses rather than set you off on one of your tirades. Have you no one who can tell you the truth, and does the truth no longer matter to you?

Yours,
Elias Canetti

I wanted to mail this letter, though I was *very reluctant to do so*, lest Bernhard be too hurt by my criticism, and it wound him badly.

I then thought it over, concluding that I *just could not* do it, given that his reactions, no matter what they originally stem from, are so infamous, indeed the worst unleashed by any person who has ever succumbed to anger. He might proudly consider this an effort by me to escape one of his tirades. If so, he would be triumphant and confirmed in his stance. That would be the opposite of what I had hoped to achieve. Therefore the letter will remain just as I wrote it, a symbol of what I was afraid of.

The ethnologist who, after the war is lost, goes begging the most ancient peoples for ritual killings to vindicate the murder of his own people.

When you wish her to have eternal life, do you imagine she will have no innards?

I have never killed anyone, but I am responsible for the deaths of some people.

Absent me, would a single one of them still be alive?

A horrible question. To answer it I would hope to find the youngest judge of all to whom I could pose it.

A people that buries its dead in anthills.

1977

To experience the death of an animal, but as an animal.

To come up with some way to disappear that somehow conquers death.

"You go to sleep," he says to the child, "but you don't wake up again." "But I always wake up!" the child says joyfully.

He wants to find words that people will not forget. The words should belong to anyone who wants to hurl them at death.

When you wish to arrive at your true reckoning, you must also consider this:
The change, even if only imagined, that occurs with the approach of death, the intensity, the seriousness, the feeling that the most important thing to you is all that matters, and that it must be correct, nothing off the mark, because there will be no other chance to get it right.
Now if one could really push back death to such a degree that we no longer sense its proximity—what would become of this *seriousness*? What else could be more important, and could there be anything else that approaches its importance, that would be equal to it?

This reckoning is on me. I cannot vanish without having completed it.
It is the only thing that to *me* is not useful for anything.
This reckoning cannot add any force to my opposition to

death. As a form of apology, it can only weaken it. It is not possible for a defense, which is what it would be, to have the same effect as a merciless attack.

In this reckoning, and only in it, can I be what I have always tried to be my entire life: someone who lives with no fixed goal, no practical use, without intentions, without garbling, as free as a person can possibly be.

Whoever opens himself up too early to the experience of death can never close himself off, a wound that turns into a lung through which you breathe.

To say nothing about death.—How long can you keep that up?

Among the Mohave "there is a running conflict between the desire for the dead and the impossibility of finding them should one live a long time after their death, which leads to a frightful number of suicides."

Verrier Elwin, Maria Murder and Suicide 54

—This would be *my* rationale for choosing suicide, and the only one.

I don't want to know when it will arrive for me, but I *must* know whom I will hold on to when it does.

Heaven forbid—what a phrase!

Death and love are always set side by side, but they only share one thing: parting.

As if it were about me! Without convulsing into a whimper, I know I could collapse at any moment. The same is true for all.

"That which moves the reader of a novel is the hope of warming his chilly life with the death that he reads about."

Walter Benjamin

1978

There is nothing more horrible than singularity. Oh how these survivors delude themselves!

He died for the sake of his money's last wishes.

He is now nearly everything he used to abhor. The only thing left would be for him to beg for death.

The *last* book that he reads: unimaginable.

To be candid about death is dangerous: You should never think you are protected from it. For if you never grant it respect, no matter what the circumstances, if you consider it a sin to *ponder* it, if you also forbid others to do the same, you become so susceptible to its every threat, as if they were being made for the first and only time.

You cannot tell yourself: No matter how it comes, I'll accept it, since it's not like I have any say in how it comes, nor do I know if there is someone who will decide it for me. Whatever comes to pass is beyond me, for it's not like I'll be the one summoning it, for when it comes it will be because I can't fend it off, not because I don't have the will to do so, for my will is plenty strong, but what will happen is stronger than me, there being nothing that can stand up to it.

This kind of talk is not allowed. Your soul's flesh is naked and raw, and it will remain so as long as staying alive means something to you, and it will always mean something to you.

What weapons are available to you? Is there any kind of

shield you can use to protect your loved ones and install inside you a clever speech, a courageous sacrifice, a lofty excuse for the injustice done to all of them, a thought that rises above it, a halfway certain resurrection, a promise and full trust in it, independence from your rotting or incinerated body, a soul you might smell with nostrils opened wide, a dream that lasts, a hand taken while asleep, a creed equal to such a threat—no, there is nothing, nothing, nor does it soothe you to say *nothing*, nothing, because the hope that you could be wrong cannot be quelled.

In his new life, which began when he turned seventy-five, he forgot the death of his father.

It's happening. What? What he was always afraid to think might happen. That it's all headed toward declaring one's love of death? Is he drawing close to the cowardice he has staunchly guarded against? Will he join the psalmists of death? Will he become weaker than all the others whose weakness he despised? Will he savor the putrefaction that fills his stomach and transform it into the law governing his spirit? Will all the words he took pride in and used in order to make sense of his life be renounced as he professes the one true faith to be the church of death?

It is possible, anything is possible. There is no miserable self-betrayal that was not once tied to the truth, which is why in place of the history of the words, the words *in themselves* must remain in effect, independent of everything after or before them.

There is no such thing as a dignified death. For others there are only deaths that can be forgotten. These, too, are undignified.

To live *unjustified*. A necessary, fundamental feeling for anyone who loves life. Only the *friend* of death, who hates life, walks around as if he's *owed* it.

Not a single individual is ever exhausted. Neither when reduced to his greatest extreme, nor at death, for not even when destroyed is a person ever exhausted.

"We couldn't stand it anymore, allowing so many people to sing a requiem right before they died." 56

Let me breathe pain, better pain than nothing.
   O ancient wound, conceal yourself no longer, I'm searching for you, I need you.

He kisses the earth that is preparing to no longer bear his weight.

I'm curious about the *last* conversation. With whom will it be?

I don't wish to bury anyone else. It would be much better to just bury myself.

It's not quite true that teachers no longer matter to me after I have depicted them in a book. Quite the opposite, for I honor their legacy, seeking always to learn as much as possible from them. The process by which lives are enshrined is much more peculiar than I thought. What one depicts, what in so many words is unchanging when set down in black and white, then has its own life that harkens back to a person's story, to the degree that story can be traced, retroactively. Sometimes it seems to me that my rendering of the lives of my teachers retroactively becomes their real lives. Exactly how that happens is what I'd like to fathom.

Is this the yard that I was looking for, is it that yard? The sun, the lake, the yellow house, all the windows covered in cobwebs, inside of which victims twitch, themselves so small that I can only think of them when I come across them, though the minute I look away, they are forgotten.

And indeed I cannot really be so caught up with these victims. There are others who are not as small as these gnats.

What will become of all that has piled up within you, so much, so much, an enormous stock of memories and habits, deferred questions, frozen answers, thoughts, emotions, tender feelings, hardships, everything there, everything there, what will become of it all the moment life extinguishes within you?

The disproportionate size of this stockpile—and all of it for nothing?

The child wants to know what war is. Since I don't want to talk to her too much about death (as even in her youth she could be facing the death of her father), I limit myself to talking about war as a time when there is little to eat.

That has more effect upon her than if I told her the truth.

To carry the heart from autumn to autumn until it sinks into the leaves.

Last rites given upon the spot where one lived and sinned. Last rites as a *journey*.

Death has become for him a governing authority. So long as he is subject to it, he remains alive.

He believes in all seriousness that the greatest undertaking involves submitting oneself to death, and he celebrates the fact that he is a willing lackey who openly volunteers to give himself over to his own dying hour.

"The hunchback on Mallorca who starved to death. The hunch on his back turned out to be full of banknotes worth ten million lire."   *written in a notebook, October 1929*

Hans Mayer
The most interesting part of our conversation was always what he had to say about his time in Leipzig. He spoke of Becher, who always supported him, and praised his manner, even though he didn't appreciate his poetry. He talked of visiting Döblin on his deathbed with Huchel in Emmendingen, the two of them having been sent by Becher to find out if he could do anything for Döblin. During the visit Döblin commented sharply on an essay by Bloch in *Sinn und Form* titled, in all seriousness, "The Wise Stalin." Mayer knew nothing about it, but Döblin, who was completely with it, said that it was in *Sinn und Form*, at which Huchel lowered his head as if guilty. Supposedly they then took the opportunity to leave with the manuscript of his *Hamlet*, which was then first published in the West.

He also spoke of Fallada, who died a morphine addict in East Berlin, about the same time that Becher, who had also become a morphine addict, but who by the end had kicked the habit. Becher, who as a young man in Munich shot his beloved and then tried to kill himself, lodged a bullet in his body but then was saved. He carried the bullet inside him from then on, and indirectly it was the cause of his death. He had cancer and was examined by Russian doctors, who when they discovered a growth in his chest told him, that's the bullet that he had

always had inside him. They didn't give the matter a second
thought and his cancer remained undetected.

"How do the immortals measure time?"

written in a notebook, January 1932

"The first blessings of extended life we will most likely extend
to animals. We will gaze at ancient mice and guinea pigs like
we do petrified snails today." *written in a notebook, June 1932*

1979

To write without a compass. I have always had the needle inside me, always pointing to magnetic north: The End.

He died with these words on his lips: "Finally I know nothing."

When dead, one is not even alone any longer.

Pythagoras
"Hermes allowed him to choose what he had always wanted, except immortality. So he asked to have the ability to keep in his memory all the events of his life as well as those after he died. Everything then that he had lived through remained within his memory, and after he died the strength of his memory persisted.

"He also told of the journey of his soul and of all of the plants and animals into which he transformed himself, and of the experience of his soul in Hades as well as what the other souls there suffered through."

58

The *memory* of all of life, a gift from the gods.

How uncertain life was before the telephone. You didn't know things for a long time. And yet now your worries for others are no less. Perhaps they are even greater, because with every unanswered call they only increase. Death is now as swift as a single phone call.

The suddenness of the call always makes you think someone has died. What should set us at rest at first fills us with dread.

It is difficult to believe in the transmigration of souls. Yet wouldn't it be much harder to believe that one never returns?

"The dead themselves, it is said, wish to be multitudinous."
59 *Madagascar*

The well-known hospitality of the Massaliots: "When friends parted they loaned each other sums of money, which were paid back in the hereafter.

"Whoever intended to commit suicide had to ask the senators for approval. If he had convincing reasons to do so, he was
60 given the hemlock gratis." *Momigliano*

Of what value is the past, upon which we expend so much effort, if there is no future? Or can one finally rid oneself of the image of the *river* of time and get it out of your head?

Think of time as a room full of winds that blow hither and yon, and without a river.

"The smell of corpses … I do not find unpleasant, a trifle on the sweet side perhaps, but how infinitely preferable to what the living emit, their feet, teeth, armpits, arses, sticky foreskins
61 and the frustrated ovules." *Samuel Beckett*

"We owe our first detailed description in the West of a well-equipped concentration camp to Dante's deeply Christian,
62 perverse imagination." *Arno Schmidt*

I cannot give up the apartment in Thurlow Road. Even if I am *never* there, I need to know that I can go there.

It is somewhat squalid, not at all beautiful. Thousands of books are there, and I read them as if they will soon be lost, and surprise myself when I find them again. A library, which for weeks on end, and sometimes even months, is never used, awaiting me with its awesome power. I am astonished to escape it alive. But it is to be expected that someday I will be struck down there, either by the books themselves or someone who uses them to take their revenge upon me.

Brittany's Île de Sein
A very ancient *death cult*: No more than a generation ago people on the island greeted one another with the saying, "Joie aux morts. Amen"—"The joy of death. Amen." At any wedding a visit to the graveyard is part of the ceremony. *Bag Noz*—the Ship of Night, a ghost ship with full sails crossing the horizon, but without a crew.

Bag Sorserez, the Ship of Witches, on which the damned widows of the sea ply the waves.

"To the seafarer who approaches it, the widows impart a terrible secret, and should he betray it, he is certain to soon die."

In the last world war—after de Gaulle's call to keep on fighting—"all the men of Île de Sein came together and launched every available ship they could find in the direction of England. They consisted of 144 sailors and fisherman, 36 of which died in the war."

63

I must salvage my mornings, which earlier I dedicated to sleeping after nights spent awake. Time passes so quickly now, I must write just as quickly. It's now easier for me to write than to read. When reading I feel dazed, nothing remaining of my former sharpness. When writing I feel free and at ease inside my head. Should I no longer read? Reading has become for me a kind of annoying habit that I can no longer get rid of. Most likely I will still be reading even on my deathbed.

There is something immensely primitive in your desire to extend every life at any price.

Would you have the same wish for others if you were no longer alive?

The slaughterhouses of the cities butcher me.

The feeling that I am becoming ever more boring because I continue to only mine my own past.

Can one exist without it coming *to* something?

Or is it actually the opposite: that one persists without it coming to something?

A still point, all movement ceasing, by which you demonstrate how deeply you are able to breathe without it coming to nothing.

Corpse Carrying Month

"This was the month in which reverence was paid to the dead. It was the custom to take the corpses out of their tombs and put them on show in the open air. Food and drink were placed beside them, they were dressed in their best clothes and feathers were stuck on their heads. The people danced and sang in their company.

"Afterwards the dead bodies were put in litters and carried from house to house by way of the streets and squares. Then, when the procession was over, they were put back in their tombs. Quantities of food were provided in gold and silver dishes for the noble corpses, and in earthenware dishes for the remains of the poor. Also, domestic animals and a variety of clothing had to be provided for the use of the dead, so that this ceremony was liable to be extremely costly."

Aya Marcay Quilla, Huamán Poma de Ayala

64

Bull Sires 200,000 Cows

The Friesian bull "Alsopdale Sunbeam II" has reached the grand old age of fourteen. As reported by the British Milking Association, Alsopdale has sired more than two hundred thousand young. As a result of artificial insemination, his off-spring are spread across the entire world: Australia, New Zealand, Zambia, Greece, and numerous other countries. Two of his sons are already following in their father's footsteps on the Association's farm for research on breeding.

65

I need to find out what death masks are. I still don't know, but for more than fifty years they have continually meant a great deal to me.

The Yamana claim not to know the nature of the hereafter, and that is also one of the reasons why they are so sad at the death of their loved ones.

1980

For me it is not about abolishing it, which is not possible. It's about *condemning* it.

It is not possible to even *imagine* one's own death. It seems unreal. It is the most unreal thing of all. Why have you always called what you do defiance? It only shows a lack of experience.

After a life spent fearing it, he succeeded in being murdered.

To record the precise point at which one gives in to death.

To threaten someone with your own death, one of the most important means by which to live among human beings.
    A person who thinks a great deal about death cannot remain forever silent about it. But how can he speak of it without turning it into a threat? Should he *feign* belief in his own immortality without really believing it? Should he pretend health and vigor amid the frailty of old age? How does one pretend health? How can one evince strength?

People who write about death as if it were long gone.

To be one of the powerful is a bitter fate, even if you belong to them only in the future, after your death.

By tapping his earliest life he managed to secure an audience for his later life.

Not without good reason, for with great force everything back then was set in motion.

Death was present in its every form: as threat, salvation, event, and as lament, as an ever-changing guilt stretched out over years. Thus he gained the strength necessary to fend it off. And so he keeps putting it off to this very day.

How many dead can you endure once you have denied the baseness of survival once and for all?

"And out of the community of creatures death disappears."

Hyperion 66

You shy away from taking too much along. You'd like to un-pack some things. Since you know that most of it will remain still packed, you want to destroy it.

Unbearable to imagine carrying heavy baggage from one world into another, or to journey from this one into nothing-ness.

The cloud in which you think you're suspended while others die below.

As long as I have not formulated clearly and wholeheartedly what death means, I will not have lived.

Everything else that I have done, whether it was finished or remained only an attempt, means nothing in comparison. Do I really want to content myself with such babbling? Have I not sensed something much more *certain*, and have I not the determination to grasp it comprehensibly?

The incredible shouts of rage by those who act as defenders of death have bewildered me. Too often I think that they exist as, God knows, something entirely new. But of course they exist, of course they always have. For that very reason I must disregard them and tend to my concerns as if they didn't exist.

The weight of all who have died is immense. What strength is needed to forge a counterweight, which if it cannot be forged now, it perhaps will never be possible to forge, especially when you consider the weight of the dead that increases by the hour.

Visiting the dead, locating them, is necessary, otherwise they can be lost unbelievably soon.

As soon as you find the place, the place where they *could* be if they were still alive, they win back their life in a powerful hurry. Suddenly, in a flash you know again all there is to know about them, what you thought you had forgotten, as you hear them speak, touch their hair, and blossom within their shining eyes. Perhaps back then you were never quite sure of the color of their eyes, but now you know it without even needing to pose a question. It may be possible that above them everything is now more intense than it was; it's possible that only in this sudden flash they become entirely themselves. It is possible that each of the dead awaits his full perfection through his resurrection, which is offered by someone left behind. Nothing certain can be said about any of it, only wishes made. But those are the most sacred thing a person has, and is there even one single wretched person who does not cherish and nurse them in his own way?

Why after all are you so proud that you cannot stop thinking about death?

Does it make you feel more truthful or brave? Is that your way of becoming a soldier: receiving no orders, and yet dressed in a type of uniform that is the same for all and which no one has ever cast off?

Would you always still have to think about death if there were just one person who had escaped it?

The twin charges by the idiots: that for a long time before getting old, you remained unknown; that now, when you are old, you are known.

The charge against me should be simpler: that *The Book Against Death* does not yet exist. That would seem a much stronger, perhaps a more damning indictment.

By playing possum he will manage to be forgotten by fame.

The way that he is thought of when he dies will cause his fame to be forgotten.

Whether perhaps more *restrained* and more *chaste* mourning can rescue more from the dead?

Imagining the horrors that await you makes the pain of leaving behind your people easier to bear. Yet worse than anything that awaits you is what would happen to them.

The attempt to set up a life in which one dies more than once. Followed by a *modest*, not grand return.

It is already almost impossible to write *The Book Against Death*, for you simply do not know where to begin. It's as if you were given the task to write everything, meaning everything about everything.

Things progressed nicely. He was immortal. Now he can become mortal again.

The Numbered was born of a feeling that lasted a year and a half. How could you have ever written something more solemn?

Why does my attack on death fill people with such hatred?

Have they been hired to defend it? Do they know so very much about their own murderous nature that they feel *themselves* attacked when I attack death?

Soon it will be four years since, under the threat posed by Hera's first operation, without knowing there would be a second, I decided to write a book about death.

Instead all that exists is the second volume of my memoirs, *The Torch in the Ear.*

Perhaps in setting it aside I have lost the chance to write the book about death. But it could also mean that it will be *better* if I write it now. Whether or not I still have enough time to do so, I do not know. It would be appropriate and in accordance with the meaning of this book to wrest away the time needed for it.

That which I seek above all is justice for death as well. I want to try to truly understand everything that is said on its behalf. I want to also express it myself, for only then can I counter it. I want the confrontation with it to be *complete,* and not just involve my earlier partisan yapping. Dogs have also howled at the moon, and yet has it not been reached by others?

The man, handsomely dressed, took him by the hand and said, "Come!"

He, however, inquired about the carcass and did not budge.

The greatest secret of any person is the date he will die. It is no less so just because I've written something about it.

Archaeology fascinates him because of the skeletons that are found and images of the living derived. Everything else, objects that provide no image of the living and any remains can, according to him, be stolen.

lasted a full year. During this time the mind of man was extremely self-conscious and sometimes also abnormally excitable.

"Many saw strange figures on the street, strange and malformed people they encountered and who walked along with them, such that they could strike up an actual conversation. In these conversations that sometimes occurred after their return home, they learned of things, namely the death of others which future events soon confirmed. Others saw such figures entering the houses of people they knew and there apparently strangling or stabbing to death those already fated to die."

after Nikephoros

In the *Chronicle of Theophanes* one finds the following account of this time of plague:

"In one year many died from the plague that started in Sicily and Calabria before spreading like wildfire throughout the entire 14th Indiction across Monemvasia, Greece, and the neighboring islands. That was a warning sign for the godless Constantine and caused for a time his rage against the Church and venerable pilgrims, even if like the Pharaohs of old he remained unregenerate. Then in the 15th Indiction the bubonic plague raced through the imperial city.

"Upon people's coats and on the holy vestments and curtains there began to suddenly appear, without anyone knowing just how, little garlands painted in oils. These symbols caused people great sorrow and confusion. A madness imposed by God not only took root among people in the city, but also in the surrounding area and wreaked havoc everywhere. Many people had visions and in their ecstasy believed they were walking around with strange and giant creatures who appeared to talk to them like old acquaintances, and with whom they conversed as well. They wrote down their words and later shared them with each other. They saw them enter their houses, whereby they killed a portion of the inhabitants, then wounded others with swords. Most of what they relayed had to do with what they had seen. In the spring of the 1st Indiction the plague got worse and held such sway that summer, entire households dying and no gravediggers to be found.

"Amid great panic it occurred to them to do the following: they fixed four baskets on the saddles of pack animals, laid boards across them, and carried off the dead, also piling them up in wagons one atop another. Since all the cemeteries in and around the city and even the dried-up cisterns and pits were filled with the dead, not only were most of the vineyards dug up, but also the gardens within the ancient walls that were used to feed the people. But even that was not enough. Each house having been visited by misfortune because the emperor had ordered holy images removed from their walls in godless fashion, finally the Arabian fleet unexpectedly sailed from Alexandria to Cypress, where the Byzantine fleet lay ..."

Iconoclasm and the Arab Invasion of
Byzantium in the 8th Century (717–813)
from Theophanes's World Chronicle

67

The promise of a life *beyond*, somewhere, where it will always exist, creates a sharp separation from life here. It is a disguised expulsion: stay over there and away from me!

But should we stay away from death? Shouldn't we expose ourselves to death? To the degree that death is constantly allowed to carry out its charade, the living *deserve* the same.

But what happens when exposure to the dead creates so much fear that it weakens our resistance to our own dying? When in fact death entirely succeeds in our being co-opted by the dead? Shouldn't we then relent and not seal ourselves off from it?

There is still much to be said about carrying around his dead.

 After years of pain, he can feel something like lightness and grace.

Try to think about death as if were *past*.

He clapped his hands and death was there. It was the only thing on which he could rely.

A radiant figure which would never arrive unwanted—could that still be death?

"If I must die,
I will encounter darkness like a bride,
And hug it in mine arms ..."

Measure for Measure, Act III, Scene 1   68

The Earth, itself saturated with graves. What would the Earth be without its graves?

There is nothing more *specific* than death. Yet everything that is said about it is so general.

The earthquake is the *cleanest* form of death: the Earth as murderer.

It is as if I must always *paint* the same thing, my Mount St. Victoire.

That animals eat each other is not horrendous, for what do they *know* of death! Rather it's that humans, who *know* what death is, continue to kill, that is what is horrendous.

"We cannot see death, and even if we could see it, we would not recognize it. I mean, it now may be moving about somewhere nearby, but where else might it be ... Yet one can hear it very well. One time I was asleep and felt someone's cold breath upon me. I jumped up, but there was no one there to see, yet I could hear someone walking away, moaning with every step.

"I have, however, seen death. In the middle of a field there stands a tall, thin woman. She has shrouded her face with a black scarf. Then she begins to lift her head while not moving. I cannot look at her, so seized am I with dread." *Ivan Speaks*

69

Reading Montaigne, I find it all again, all the ancient banalities about death, and his own as well.

He, whom I cherish so much and love, has only a single redeemable aspect when it comes to death, namely that he cannot get it out of his head.

Otherwise, he also belongs to the *appeasers*. Yet he does not allow himself to be terrorized by death, for until the end he thinks life is precious and knows that we cannot relinquish it.

The *sacrificial death* that I respect, the one for which I feel the deepest veneration, is that of Sophie Scholl.

The one single death is acceptable.

But what about those who celebrate it? Does it seem to you as if such celebrations are allowed in order that the living can rid themselves of their bad conscience?

Can the death of another free *us* from our sins?

70 The central question of Christianity.

Murder occurs everywhere. But there are some civilized nations in which murder is not decreed. That doesn't sound like much, yet it is infinitely important.

That which is boring, and which is tied to the idea of human kindness: we detest so many and really should love everyone.

But we would not detest anyone if we knew they would soon die.

The commandment to love others feeds on their mortality.

There, at the moment of death each sank into complete oblivion.

What a conversation with Georg!—According to him, I shouldn't have thought about him at all these last nine years. It is best if the deceased is *always* kept at a distance, absolutely, completely, as if he never existed. Where he lived, his name, his eyes—nothing! A brother is not a brother, for he is nobody. A father? A mother? Nobody. You come into the world an orphan. Your best friend, what's his name, it doesn't matter. A lover? Just like any other! A wife? Who was she? A child? Was it a girl or a boy?—if you really have to know, check the public records.

What deep, what total concern for the survivor! Only he counts. Only he matters. The survivor is king. Not a hair on his head should be disturbed. No burden, not an ounce, nor any pointless commemoration of the dead. Not a tear should be shed. His days are numbered, what a waste, not a single one should be weighed down with the dead!

The soul circles a person like a fly that will not allow itself to be shooed away. Might there be more flies?

Can you actually admit that you don't at all care what happens with your works?

It doesn't matter, so long as I still write.

We think you can finally stop writing once this book is finished.

I can't do that. I wouldn't be able to do that.

Then you will never make your peace with death. Never.

"For Eastern-European Jews there existed the custom of gifting a sick loved one time from your own life. That was actually meant in real terms, which is why in general you gave at most a couple of minutes or at most an hour. Once the daughter of the synagogue's sexton gave the sick rabbi her entire life. The moment she did she collapsed and was dead. The rabbi recovered and lived to a ripe old age. (In ghostly fashion the unlived life of the girl mapped itself onto his. During night visions he would hear wedding music, or he heard the excitement at the birth of her children. His heart banging, he listened to see if finally something bad erupted in her life which her early death would have spared her. For then the sacrifice he had not wanted would weigh on him less. But in the life of she who had gifted hers there was not a single shadow.)"

after a ballad by the Russian-Yiddish writer Frug,
as told by Michael Landmann to Ernst Bloch, summer 1968,
on Korčula (the birthplace of Marco Polo)

71

Bruno and Elettra Schärer visited us yesterday afternoon. They said that Frau Brock-Sulzer has been in the hospital for half a year, in a nursing facility where Hera was twice operated on.

Frau Brock-Sulzer was by far the best theater critic in Zurich, and you could even say the only one. She is now nearly seventy-eight years old. Phoebe, the Schärers' daughter, who visited her a couple of months ago, was taken aback when, the moment she arrived, she asked her:

72   "How did you know I died?"

Hundreds of Applicants for Executioner Position
Springfield, June 10 — Some might do it out of a feeling of

duty, some out of a desire for revenge, while others are just looking for a job. The Department of Justice in Springfield, Illinois, has received hundreds of applications from all over the world for the position of "volunteer executioner."

The flood of letters started after officials let it be known— following the death sentence handed down for John Gacy— that they want a volunteer to carry out the sentence, since they are uncomfortable with asking one of their employees to consciously flip the switch.

Some letter writers have sent detailed resumés and point out their relevant professional experience: "I am thirty years old, male, single, and am described by others as a cool, quiet, reliable, grounded, and discreet young man. I firmly believe in the death penalty," wrote a bank cashier from London. A police official from Wisconsin highlights that it used to be his job at an animal shelter to "exterminate the animals." For another man from Vienna, it is just a job. "I take no pleasure in killing, but I'd do it for the money." Another volunteer, a forty-two-year-old Marine veteran writes from a New York prison, "I'll soon be out on parole, and I need a job."

73

His rubber band, from which he hangs himself each day.

My only hope now is the book about death. In the past weeks and from a great distance, I have nearly finished a tiny piece of it. If nothing else, I am aware of the surprising abundance of things that I would have to say if only I could just figure out how to begin.

This does not mean things that I have felt I had the responsibility to say throughout the course of my life are linear, somewhat limited, or all that certain. I want every possible doubt to be put into words, even those of every *friend* of death. They should be spoken in the strongest and most convincing of voices. I want to allow such things to be spoken as if there were no possible way to refute them, for once everything has been said, when it is said so powerfully and forcefully that it appears I have annihilated myself, that is when I will want to find new strength to refute and vanquish them all.

Up until now I have made it too easy for myself. My clamorous assertions affirming life were ridiculous and childish.

Any of the most base and envious of my enemies could complain and declare my crowning thoughts, my lifelong undertaking, to be ignoble.

That's not how it goes with assertions and counterassertions, with the constant repetition of the same sentences. I might as well crouch down with legs folded underneath me in a corner of my room and say Allah! Allah! Allah! five thousand times a day.

Has it never occurred to you that perhaps the fundamental undertaking could have been *wrong* from the start? Have you never *really* had any doubts about it at all? No, I have never really doubted any of it. I must first manifest real doubt and hold it up to myself and others in order to earn the right to not doubt myself at all.

There is something *rigid* in all I have done, which doesn't have to do with the language, but rather with the substance itself. It is as if for sixty-eight years, since the sudden death of my father, I have remained the same. Death lodged itself inside me, formed me, and I cannot get away from it.

I must *change*. It might be ridiculous to say that at seventy-five. But now for the first time I know I *must* change, and to a great degree.

It is highly unlikely that I will succeed. But the attempt to do so would be interesting, especially since it is so unusual.

Try to imagine *how* you could change.

"Sky Burial" in Tibet

"I climbed high up the mountain to the cliffs of the vultures. Below, in the next deep valley through which a silver river ran, I could see the ritual which the Tibetans have performed for centuries.

"Because in a country where the earth is too hard to dig graves, and there is hardly any wood with which to cremate the dead, nature forces one to hold a 'sky burial.'

"This was happening now below: Family members brought their dead to a huge flat stone. They stripped the lifeless body and laid it face down on the cliffs. Then the skull was split open so that the soul could find its way to a new life.

"Finally the undertaker opened the chest of the deceased and gave the heart and liver to the largest vulture.

"After that they cut various other parts from the body and gave them to the ravens. Finally a man took the leftover bones and pummeled them into meal for the birds to eat.

"At the end three exhausted men remained behind, resting on the stone after their efforts. An old woman brought them something to drink.

"The river shimmered in the valley. In the distance the ceremonial temple of Potala with its hundred windows floated in the mist. In the sky there was only the cawing of ravens and the sound of vultures' wings.

"'What's the difference?' asked a Tibetan that evening. 'You let your dead be eaten by worms, we by birds.'" 74

"At his birth he wasn't breathing, and it was thought that he had been born dead. An uncle nevertheless blew cigar smoke up his nostrils—Picasso later saying, 'I twisted up my face and began to cry aloud.'" 75

His strength: that in the era of Freud and Henry Miller he turned away from thinking about sexual matters. The others do that already, so they don't need him to. He has something much more ominous to focus on which *nobody* knows about: Death.

A very beautiful death: to fall asleep in the snow before the Earth explodes in the next war.

A Diary Entry by Sophie Scholl
"Many people believe our time shall be the last. All the terrible signs can make it seem palpable. But is this belief not founded on circumstantial evidence? For must not each person, regardless of what time he lives in, continually reckon with the fact that at any moment he could be called to give his account by God? Do I even know if I will still be alive tomorrow morning? A bomb could kill us all tonight. Nor would my guilt be any less if I died along with the Earth and the stars."

A Memory of Sophie Scholl's Last Night by Else Gebel, Her Fellow Prisoner
"For me the night stretches out endlessly, while you, like always, sleep soundly and deeply.

"Just before seven I wake you to this awful day. You wake up right away and tell me your dream while sitting in bed: On a sunny day you carried a child in a long white dress to its baptism. The road to the church traveled up a steep mountain. But you held the child safe and secure. Out of nowhere a fissure in a glacier opened up. You had just enough time to lay the child down on the secure side before you plunged into the deep. You interpreted the dream so: The child in the white dress is our cause, and it will succeed despite all setbacks. We are trailblazers, but first we must die for her."

How long must one live to survive that which poisoned him in his early years?

The horrible consequence of producing leather: flayed skin.

1981

There is nothing that I have inured myself to, nothing at all, and least of all death.

How many lives must one live to figure out death?

And if death were not to exist, where would the pain of loss be? Is it the only thing that speaks for death: that we need this immense pain, and that without it we would not be worthy of being called human beings?

Such pettiness: instead of facing death, he carps about his age.

He succeeded at turning the dead into the enemy.

Lying letters. Sport of the dead.

A year before dying everyone there can completely forget who they are and lead an entirely new and unexpected life.

"Oxen die young if forced to bear a twisted yoke. Under pack saddles that are too big, the backs of donkeys erupt in bloody sores."

What is more awful than to just go with one's times? What is deadlier?

"Research," he said, and meant graves.

G. decided to not recognize anyone who has died.

Of all things what has upset him the most of all is *The Resuscitation of a Child.*

What fascinates me about religions is their conception of death, and so long as I have not yet understood every such belief that has ever existed, I know nothing.

"According to the Tukuná, many of the immortals are still alive ... at the headwaters of a stream and there celebrate beneath the full moon. Anyone who tries to draw near is driven mad."
Nimuendajú, The Tukuna   77

"No, rest assured, the good sense of a twenty-year-old to not forsake his life without a care means little, and probably even less so, in the eyes of a hundred-year-old."
Marcus Herz to Moritz, during his illness, as set down by Herz in Hufeland's Journal of Practical and Magical Medicine, Vol. 5, Jena 1798, quoted in the Insel Almanach, 1981.   78

"Today in Japan it can still happen that a woman takes her life so her corneas can be transplanted after her death into the eyes of a blind loved one in order for that person to see again."   79

"Death cannot be evil, for it is something common."
Schiller, ill, speaking on the last day of his life to his sister-in-law Karoline von Wolzogen

"I choose not to lay down before death."   *Goethe to Forster*   80

"It is in a sense an impossibility that suddenly becomes a reality."   *Goethe to Eckermann*   81

"I cannot conceive of any thought that would not have death carved into it."   *Michelangelo in his old age*

Have you made death any easier for yourself with phrases posed against it?

He cannot get enough of the sound of the gamba, his only comfort.
    He begs her to play for him after he is gone.

The worst is nothingness. Ideas about the afterlife were wonderful. How could it have disappeared? How easily it happened! How suddenly! I always think of it in tandem with the detonations of atomic bombs. They are what, it seems to me, killed off the afterlife.
    Before the detonations, death was different: something clear. Despicable perhaps, but one could imagine it.
    There is nothing left, however, when everything splinters into uncountable, unfindable pieces that can never come together again—how can we then think of the afterlife?
    The atomization of death amounts to our deepest despair.

A frequent notion: that I need to go to *Hampstead* in order to die there.

"And God firmly bound the soul to man's body. The soul of man is attached to the body so that, when sorrow overwhelms him, he does not remove his soul and toss it away."

On the great square they all gathered together again and formed a circle. They all bowed to one another. They then turned about and walked, each of them alone, away from each other for the last time.

What do you see ahead of you when you die? No paradise for the good, no hell for them, the bad ones, but instead a hell for all, the good and the bad, and soon, here.

It's strange that you should say that *every* faith, even the most awful, was too optimistic in containing no penalty, no threat that touches upon the kind of fate we have prepared for the Earth.

But that also means no reconciliation with death. For we can presume that we have come so far because of it, because of our knowledge of it, because of the possibility of employing it for any kind of ends.

The child who refuses to eat anything that once lived. But that's not good enough for him: now he also refuses to eat anything that is *shaped* like a living thing, be it a beetle, a rabbit, or a lamb made of chocolate.

Reincarnation had to be enough for the animals. They never got as far as resurrection.

And although it will soon stand before me, for the most part I am offended that *others* suffer death's arrival.

He was old enough to experience the self-destruction of the Earth.

The Prolongation of Life
"There was once a man named Fu-hsing (Fortune Rising). He was around fifteen years old and his family was very poor. He made a living by chopping wood. His father was long since dead, and there was only the mother, who could no longer work and was supported by Fu-hsing's labor.

"One day when he went searching for wood in the mountains he came upon two men playing chess atop a mountain. That was the Little Dipper and the Big Dipper, both of which watch over the fortunes of humankind. They played chess and talked at the same time, saying that a certain man would live to be very old, 287 years old, and that a certain Fu-hsing had to die very young at nineteen years of age.

"When Fu-hsing secretly heard this, he became deeply afraid and quickly headed for home, where he told his mother everything. She replied, 'That is without a doubt the Big Dipper and the Little Dipper. Borrow some money from your friends and buy a large bushel of fruit, for that's what they love to eat. Then kneel down next to them right when they are about to eat, which is when you can appeal to them.' Fu-hsing then purchased the fruit and climbed the mountain again in order to kneel before them.

"The two of them were about to eat the fruit, and as they were about to, the Big Dipper looked at Fu-hsing and asked, 'Why did you come here?' Fu-hsing responded, 'I heard the two of you say that I can only live to be nineteen. I'm here now to ask that you grant me more years than that,' at which he kneeled again. The Little Dipper then said, 'So you are Fu-hsing?' And after the boy confirmed this, he added, 'Well then, I will grant you ninety-nine years.' Then he spoke nine magic sentences. Fu-hsing thought about it and was overjoyed. Then he was about to ask if he might be granted yet one more year, but before he could speak, they both disappeared.

"*Comment*: The Little Dipper is usually linked with Shou-hsing, the god of long life. He has a very big head, a stag as his companion, and as a symbol, the *life-extending peach*. That is why the sacrificial gift made to him is fruit. He is in charge of the register of lives, which in other legends is controlled by one of the gods of the underworld."

83   *Eberhard, Folk Tales of Southeast China*

"Thus death is never what we think it might be while alive. It is the opposite of basically everything said of it. Because we must die, our lives have no meaning, because our problems remain unsolved, and because even the meaning of the problems remains unclear."   *Sartre*   84

After *Sartre* it is useless to complain or to rebel and to naively ask why death exists.

"To love a person is to say, you will not die."
   ...
"Because I cannot love someone without wishing for the one I love to be immortal ... I cannot accept death."
                                        Gabriel Marcel   85

Dog as Funeral Mourner
"For over a year in the Sicilian village of Ribera, a medium-sized dog no one knows and belonging to no one has attended every funeral. Whenever preparations are made for a funeral in the village, the dog, a light-brown mongrel, lurks for hours near the threshold of the house, waiting until the coffin is carried out. The dog follows the hearse to the church, listens for when the chapel bells signal the start of the funeral march, and then accompanies the funeral party to the grave. At the end of the funeral, he disappears without a trace, only to show up at the next funeral in Ribera."   86

Generations of "prairie birds, who learn very quickly to pounce upon freshly burned plains in order to eat grasshoppers roasted in the fire."   87

"Death. I take death, when it does not occur too early, to be a natural and fitting event. Over the course of decades we have plenty of time to become familiar with the defects and limits of our person.

"Gradually you know yourself through and through, and only wish to move on."   *Late Döblin (a "fitting event"!)*

"On May 1, 1968, a contingent of government officials went to the Shanghai home of the mother of a young woman named Liu Zhao, who had been jailed for keeping a diary critical of the party.

"As three Chinese reporters recently recounted the incident, the officials told the mother that her daughter had been executed three days earlier as a counterrevolutionary.

"They told the mother that the money spent on her daughter's execution had been a waste, and they demanded that the mother pay five fen—a little more than three cents—to cover the cost of the bullet they had put through the back of her 88   daughter's head."

"As the Chancellor of the Order, I must share with you that the Order mourns the death of Herr Professor Dr. Carl Ludwig Siegel on April 4, 1981, at the age of 84.

"The funeral service will be held on April 9, 1981 in the chapel of the metropolitan cemetery in Göttingen. *Herr Professor* 89   *Siegel leaves behind no relatives."*

You have lived longer than Kafka, than Proust, than Musil, as well as Broch. What does this *monstrous* injustice compel you 90   to undertake now?

Certainly I will eventually submit to death without a hue and cry, but only because there is no choice, rather than giving my blessing.

I also swear that at the end I will not close down any of the temples of death.

In the time that Goethe lived, Jean Paul, Hölderlin, E.T.A. Hoffmann, Kleist, Novalis, and Hegel lived too.
There is a lot of room in this life.

The *Sibyl of Cumae* was awarded a thousand years of life by Phoebus. It was determined that she would be granted as many years of life as a handful of sand contained grains. However, she forgot to ask for years of youth. Thus, she was condemned to old age and was already seven hundred years old by the time she spoke with Aeneas, and still had another three hundred to live. She became so shrunken and lost so much weight that she could be recognized only by her voice.

Ovid, Metamorphoses, XIV

Butterflies hatched in the classroom. Each child takes one home, promising *not* to mount it on pins.

The Bible slept and awakened as if it was no longer day.

I could have accomplished a great deal after Veza's death if I had not *shed* the obsession I brought to *Crowds and Power*. Because, really, I was only obsessed with death.

The murderer as critic: he whose victim doesn't *suit* him.

Protozoa (like bacteria) procreate themselves through division: out of one individual two of the same are born, and so on. Each generation is the same as the last, and the following as well.

After dividing themselves there is nothing left over that is wasted. *There are no—not even the smallest—corpses.*

1982

It [the Nobel Prize] might have pleased some who are no longer alive, but not so much so that, out of joy, they could return to life.

You cannot make much of a fuss about your coming to an end. You've been making a fuss about the end in general for a long time, and that it can't help but come for that one, this one, for all.

The careless proliferation, indeed, the blindness of nature, its senselessness, lunacy, brazenness, and vainness became a law only through the declaration of hatred against death. As soon as proliferation is no longer blind, the moment it has to do with each single thing, then it begins to make sense. Out of the horrible notion of "More! More! More! Destroy them all!" arises "In order that everything becomes sacrosanct: more!"

Before it leads to decay, death involves confrontation. Grant him the courage to face it, to defy all futility. The courage to spit in death's face.

For a long time his experience has been: whenever his jibes at death increase, it takes another dear one from him.
    It either anticipates or punishes. But who metes out the punishment?

He's become more defenseless in the face of death. The faith that he adhered to is no protection. He is not even allowed to defend himself.

Yet there were others there by his side. Did he not defend them, either? How did it occur that all the others around him were killed and he is still here? What kind of secret, disgraceful, incomprehensible relationship does that imply?

There is something *impure* in the laments about the dangers of our time, as if they serve to excuse our own personal failures.
Something of this impurity has existed in every lament for the dead from the very beginning.

Each time, before every rebirth, he put up a fight.

He tries to imagine how old he would be if no one had died.

Those who grasp the horror of power do not see to what degree it serves death! Without death, power would have remained harmless. Those who talk about power think they fight against it, but leave death by the wayside. They think it's natural and of no concern. This nature of theirs leaves much to be denied. I always felt terrible when nature presented itself as immutable and I believed it to be so. It's clear now, everywhere, on all sides and in every direction, that nature is changing. I feel even worse, for those changing it do not appreciate that there are some things that must never change under any circumstances.

Juan Rulfo: "A dead person cannot die. On All Soul's Day one speaks to the dead and gives him something to eat. The betrayed widow visits the grave of her dead husband, reprimands him for his affairs, scolds him, threatens to take revenge. In Mexico death is neither sacred nor alien. Death is the most everyday thing there is."
...

"And what, Herr Rulfo, do you feel when you write?"
"Remorse."

If all is to collapse, it should be *said* that it will. When nothing more remains—we should not just obediently exit.

I do not feel at all weak so long as I think about what I am here for. The moment I stop thinking about that, I feel weak.

Should you from time to time commit treason against yourself, i.e., accept the impossibility of ever beginning and lay out the consequences? Why do you like the people who can't do that so much more, those who, as it were, believe themselves to death?

He smashed his coffin to pieces and chased off the mourners, gnashing his teeth at them.

He shed tears for a friend whose name he had forgotten.

You are accused of not having scolded your mother and father, or at the very least of not having stripped them naked. You are accused of respect, veneration for the dead, gratitude.

Why is it that those left with nothing are also grateful? Why do they respect someone who left them with nothing? Why do they memorialize the dead who disowned them in disgust?

The accomplices who *beckon* the final end:

That someone can say, "It doesn't matter, since I won't be around to see it!"

The employees of death, who write one book after another justifying it.

One needs a bit of hope to mount the attack. The hope is that others will also fight it.

"If I am not around, then no one else should be, either."

Self-love and love of death. The relationship between the two needs to be pursued.

The main argument for death: the rapid increase in the number of humans. It looks as if Malthus was right about this, as well as in his influence on Darwin. But the fact that today *everything* is threatened with obliteration, Malthus could not have completely understood.

That is what has changed since Malthus's day. A universal catastrophe was not conceivable then.

You are no longer obsessed with crowds. You no longer are interested in formulating recipes for their good conduct and welfare.

You are more obsessed with death than ever. Mass death has replaced your concerns with the masses. Your own death can only be seen as irrelevant. It is undoubtedly clear that it is death itself that matters most.

Your aversion to the element of *sacrifice* in religions, which begins with Abraham's sacrifice of Isaac, involves *mistrust*. It turns death into a transaction and sanctions it. It allows it to be repeated and wished for.

The sacrifice of insects. The burning of anthills.

It is easy to antagonize you. As soon as matters look hopeless for someone mortally ill, everything beyond what is happening to him seems a senseless waste that only matters to the living. Many think this is the battlefield on which death is fought. But that is not what I am talking about at all. I am talking about a false *attitude* which is found particularly among the healthy, a division, namely between life and death, as if both were two equal entities. It is this attitude which grants death the same standing as life. To equate them is a distortion, one nourished by every kind of faith that ascribes more and more life to death. We don't end up just fearing their rancor, we try to preempt it, contemplating and endowing the dead with life. "There you are! We are here for you!" In order to convince them how serious we are about being there for them, we end up doing something exceptional, something life-affirming. We endow them with life through reverence.

Whom we believe: the central question of every life. The changing course of life. Changes in the types of people we believe in. The shedding of those we believed in earlier.

How swift the change, and why the shedding of earlier influences? In part it has to do with how many still believe in them. But there are also transformations in the content of our beliefs that have nothing to do with how many others feel the same.

Beliefs somehow deflated (one could also say their language, as well). The drying up or suffocation of belief. Beliefs which eventually and gradually are insinuated. We hear something for such a long time, but without listening. Then suddenly we hear the same thing again and it makes sense. How does such meaning come about? Through repetition or the weakening that occurs over the course of a life? Teachings, experiences, determinations become reasonable commonplaces that are not too upsetting, and we gain the ability to confront without hate the greatest monstrosity of all, namely death.

The souls of the dead engender wind as they leave their bodies. This wind is especially strong among suicides. Someone must have hanged himself in the woods, we say when a sudden wind rises.

The brevity of life indeed plays a role in Schopenhauer's thinking, as does death.

But does it not grant life a great deal of value if we denounce its brevity, and death as well?

"I'd love to rise from the grave every ten years or so and go buy a few newspapers. Ghostly pale, sliding silently along the walls, my paper under my arm, I'd return to the cemetery and read about all the disasters in the world before falling back to
92   sleep, safe and secure in my tomb."   *Luis Buñuel at 82*

All Souls commemoration of all the faithful departed. Its earliest object was to commemorate all the dead of the Monastic Order. Under Odilio of Cluny (962–1049) it was decided to extend it to include "all the dead who have existed from the
93   beginning of the world ... until the end of time."

A great deal of time has been lost, and there cannot be much more remaining, but I cannot manage to reckon with it soon enough. How little I have done with my life. What has it all amounted to? December's spectacle only belies this fact. For the very few works that I have produced I have been honored ... Kafka looms high above all prizes, or better yet: he would have escaped them all had his work been destroyed. Now today he deserves the highest prize that can be awarded, and for such special, very rare cases there should be a prize that could be awarded fifty years after death ...

As for what I've been awarded—what am I to say? I always thought that I would earn this prize for *Crowds and Power*, for the years and years that I devoted to it. I was of this opinion because of Veza, who bore the brunt of that endeavor. But then, three years after the book appeared, she died. What was there to be gained after her death? *Nothing*, because I found Hera and for eight years, between 1963 and 1971, lived a life that for someone my age can only be called wild. You could say that for the first time I *began* to live. During this time, I wrote some essays. Good, so it was, but so few of them that perhaps they don't really count at all. Georg's final illness and death was the next terrible blow. Then followed the period of the memoirs and the birth of the child ...

But it's certain that this honor would not have come if I had not written the memoirs, and that's why I do not know if Veza's and my great efforts, even on *Crowds and Power*, would indeed have been enough to carry the day. It all feels neglected, in the past, played down. It is as if in the midst of a *new* life I have been honored for something much earlier and long gone by, and indeed only because I have written down memories of this earlier life.

"When the flames reached the upper floors of the building, the Jews appeared at windows of the attic. These were their last minutes. They ran from window to window, waving their arms desperately, jumping onto the windowsills. Their black silhouettes stood out sharp against the red glowing wall of flames. To avoid a painful death by burning, they leapt from the heights, landing not on any kind of cushion but rather directly on the asphalt street. Like black dolls with red colored heads, the suicides lay there. Burst skulls, splattered brains. The buildings continued to burn, even though one roof after another collapsed with a crash. The ruins burned for days on end, the May rains finally extinguishing what here and there still smoldered."

Stroop on the events of May 4, 1943   94

Saturday, May 1, 1982

Veza died nineteen years ago today.

What a life I could have given her in her fifty-eighth year!

Many wrote to me in the autumn about it all being well deserved. But that's not true, for Veza was not there to see her triumph. It *would* have been a triumph for her, because she was like Deborah, a warrior and judge of the Old Testament.

A few weeks ago, I visited her in the Hampstead apartment, which has become her tomb. She is not pleased to be there so much anymore, but I found her there. Maybe she loves the child that she always wanted me to have, and who is often with us. Hera is well-disposed toward her, and I know how much she likes Hera. I feel her blessings upon our life. In many languages her name is now known, and soon they will know the very best of her *everywhere*.

Today I was on the *Titanic* and have learned what the orchestra really played as it sank.

In autumn a person wrote to me saying he wanted to do a piece about suicide. Enzensberger told him about my "close" friendship with Jean Améry. Now he wants to contact me to learn more about Améry's suicide.

I have not answered him, although I would have happily murdered him. That's why I should have let him come visit.

More and more I am convinced that the responsibility for Benjamin's death lies with his friends, above all Horkheimer and Adorno, though also Scholem.

However, I am always inclined to find someone *guilty* for any suicide.

95

From fireworks to the final rockets. China's contribution to the apocalypse.

"Grillparzer recently said, 'There is nothing more grave than to recall that people are born in the morning and die in the evening.'" *from Bauernfeld's diary, October 24, 1836*

96

Any opposition to death can appear to be only about your own death. That would be too little. That would be nothing at all. How can I make it obvious enough and beyond any doubt that what I am *really* opposed to is death, and less so the brevity of life, as opposed to the *consequence* of death—which poisons every thought.

Death is our cancer, it infects everything, it *cuts into* every life, it is everywhere and always possible. You *reckon* with it, even when you least expect to.

What's astonishing is that we live as if we had nothing to do with death. This duality: that we encounter it everywhere and nevertheless behave as if we can avoid it, that everyone recognizes its worthiness and yet some deny it (since we build houses, make plans, give assurances)—this duality is a kind of fundamental falseness at the heart of existence.

You have touched both central nerves: crowds and death. However, you have not said anything *decisive* about them. You have made great pronouncements. Could you or anyone else have succeeded at doing more?

They suspect that you are *afraid* of death and don't want to believe that you *hate* death. What terrible readers!

When my mother died, I swore to myself to write the book against death. I read the letters to Veza again the day before yesterday. I spent half the night reading them (just like in the old days). I also wrote back then that my mother had to remain immortal. Since then, she has become that, as has the one to whom I wrote. So long as humankind exists, no one can take that away from my mother or Veza.

But what I did not write is *The Book Against Death*. Since June 15, 1937, forty-five years altogether, I have failed to do so.

I must find a way to steal away the time needed for this book.

I am not capacious enough to think of someone who has died. How could I contain him?

It's high time that you investigate the *danger* of your sentences against death. There is something in them that could inspire others to murder. What is it?

Certainly your expression "Death's Enemy," which you understand in your own way, namely as the enemy of death, has something *infectious* about it. Whoever is struck by it strongly enough suddenly feels themself to be an enemy of death, not of the mythic or abstract figure of death, but instead a *person* whom one takes to be one's enemy and might want to strike. That leads to the *need* to strike that person. The *implacability* of my rejection of death, which I wholeheartedly let others feel, has something *murderous* about it. That is indeed what is infectious, whereby others who have not yet settled the matter for themselves turn this murderous desire toward someone else. They adopt it *for themselves*, and appropriate it for their own needs, which they then set in motion.

Mass "Die-In" in Osaka
"Osaka, October 15. Around 450,000 opponents of nuclear weapons have taken part in a so-called Die-In, a *simulated mass death*, in a park in the Japanese city of Osaka. Across ten different sections of the park, they arranged to fall to the ground simultaneously as if they had died in a nuclear explosion in an effort to call for a worldwide end to the deployment of nuclear weapons. Their protest was also directed at Japanese nuclear plants. The fact that the "Die-In" involved so many participants in a city park of Osaka will likely lead to more such demonstrations occurring sporadically."

97

1983

There, people are most alive when dying.

How wonderful Buddhism appears in contrast to our deniers of life!
It manifests disgust with life, but also a thousand stories of reincarnation.

You shall grow so old that you no longer notice it.

To them it looked as if the dead lined the road like flowers.

Since he knows that he must die, he no longer looks anyone in the face.

He knocked on her door, walked in, saw her smiling, and his fear of her dying disappeared.

The chronological order of the dead disgusts him. Who determines it?

In 1804, *Frau von Krüdener* went back to Riga for a visit. "One day from the window she saw an acquaintance who lifted his hat to her in greeting and then dropped dead."
This grotesque episode happened during Julie's journey to Damascus, having joined up with a group of Moravian monks.
In Baden she came under the influence of *Jung-Schilling*, who, on the basis of a simple calculation, could pinpoint *1819 as the date for the world to end.* 98

211

It would only seem fair that you should cite a good deed on the part of death, but which?

Perhaps the cost of the new bombs will save us from them.

In each issue, on the same page, one and the same squashed insect.

Burial of a Tribal Chief
"One of the women after a while begins to cut the hair of the deceased. Another one, and indeed his most prominent wife, lays herself out mouth to mouth, hand to hand, and feet to feet upon the dead man. The first woman continues to cut his hair, and the second begins finally to both weep and sing. This lasts for many hours."

99

"'There was Dresden,' said Vonnegut, 'a beautiful city full of museums and zoos—man at his greatest. And when we came up, the city was gone ... The raid didn't shorten the war by half a second, didn't weaken a German defense or attack anywhere, didn't free a single person from a death camp. Only one person benefited.'
    "'And who was that?'
    "'Me. I got several dollars for each person killed. Imagine.'"
Conversation with Kurt Vonnegut

100

"It is well to remember that in the war that ended with the Peace of Westphalia, Germany lost 35 percent of its population. Bohemia's population fell from 3 million to 780,000. This was at a time when people had to be killed one at a time, often with muscle power."

101

Buñuel: "When people ask me why I don't travel more, I tell them, Because I'm afraid of death. Of course, they all hasten to assure me that there's no more chance of my dying abroad than at home, so I explain that it's not a fear of death in general. Dying itself doesn't matter to me, but not while I'm on the road. I don't want to die in a hotel room with my bags open and papers lying all over the place.

"As I drift toward my last sigh I often imagine a final joke. I convoke around my deathbed my friends who are confirmed atheists, as I am. Then a priest, whom I have summoned, arrives; and to the horror of my friends I make my confession, ask for absolution for my sins, and receive extreme unction. After which I turn over on my side and expire.

"But will I have the strength to joke at that moment?"

102

Saturday, March 12, 1983

Today Hera is fifty years old.

To have experienced this day reconciles me with a great deal.

The three of us sat in the sun at that table with its yellow roses in full blossom, it having become a favorite place of ours since we moved it there.

The day was completely still, except for Johanna's happy laughter, Hera's brilliant smile, my relentless joking.

No one can know what will come, when news brings pain on every front. Up until now it was behind us. Perhaps it will return again, perhaps everything will be finished for good, but no matter what, this day occurred. I sat with my loved ones, with that goddess and the child, and should I have to depart, it will be this image I will hold in my eyes.

The chief of the Bajau Laut, an old man, left his sons very little: upon his death his boat was taken apart and reconstructed as a coffin.

103

It is possible that a home means more to one when it is not the only one you have, but instead one among several. And yet there is much more to this. I always feel good in places I have *known* well—such as Vienna, such as Paris—but the places that mean the most to me are those where my dead once lived. It's not their graves that draw me to them, but rather the places where they lived. I am ashamed to visit the *graves* of my own relatives, for when I am confronted with graves, I feel guilty for having survived. I have never visited the grave of my mother in the Père Lachaise since the day of her funeral in June 1937, nor have I ever visited the grave of my father, who died in Manchester in October 1912. I was at Friedl's grave in 1953, in Grinzing, but her name has yet to be carved into the stone. Meanwhile, Veza's ashes are with me in the Hampstead apartment. I have not been able to bring myself to find a grave or even an urn for them. It is obvious that I shun my most private graves. Far more do I frequent the places where my dead lived.

This talk of doomsday! This talk of doomsday! Enough with such a threat, for it will be happy to take its own sweet time.

"As happens to many others, I would dream of my father. He sits at the family table, his face serious. He eats very slowly, very little, and he hardly speaks. I know that he is dead, and I quietly say to my mother or to one of my sisters sitting next to me, 'We simply shouldn't tell him.'"   *Buñuel*

He survived his fame and happily died later on.

For *Theseus and the Centaur*, Canova had a horse killed in order to study all the stages of its death throes and utilize them.

A race between medicine and nuclear physics. Neither has reached the finish line.

You would always ask yourself whether you have known a

single person who was *good*. Is that what matters? Only that. Even if it is the last question, only that.

The breathing of these children, that of all children. And shall that not be our salvation?

They discuss, they discuss. The final clocks tick.

He says realism and means machines. I say breath and mean not dying.

4.7 billion people. The justification for nuclear warfare. The reduction of the Earth's populace to a single family. The new ark.

I am now starting the book that I resolved to write years, decades ago.

It is not enough to continually assert that I oppose death. It has been talked about, but *nothing* has really been said. The time is pressing: even if I am still allotted more years, my powers could fade, and it would no longer be possible for me to find the words for all that would need to be said. I will begin today and never again stop.

The dimensions of resistance: it is important to know *how long* one has put up a fight against death, and with what kind of conscious effort and decisiveness.

On *every* day of a long life, one should write something down about it which is *new* and has never been thought before.

He raises animals only for them to die, and when the time comes, he shoves another one forward.

He has no name for it. He has never spoken it aloud. But he knows it.

Can one resent what someone has died for? And for what have human beings not died?

One can resent someone for what they have killed.

People came to realize that even animals were not as clueless about death as had been thought.

People who live like flies, for a single day—would that at last be infuriating enough?

The butterfly—a ghost of the caterpillar.

Something to consider: does the resistance against death in the end only increase its allure?

Tännerlin's Death
"Thus he died and was buried in his kingdom with great fanfare. I will share with you *that even after an entire year he still complained from within his grave.* The priests who tended his grave could hear it clearly. Friends of the king made great sacrifices to get him to stop, but it did no good. The priests conferred amongst themselves and went to his son and asked if he would free all of those his father had captured in other lands, especially those imprisoned in the capitol. For all the craftsmen among the prisoners had been brought by Tännerlin to the capitol, where they were forced to work for him. His son and his followers set them all free. As soon as that happened, 105   the deceased complained no more."   *Schiltberger*

All of his questions contain an idea that he does not express: how is it that you are still alive?

He returned as an ant queen and founded a new country.

No, you will not get any better, just shrewder. What then do you hope to do with further years?

He trampled the untouchable and protected the cow, and in the next life found himself again chewing his cud.

The last time I saw Veza, she had already been eviscerated. But you wouldn't know it looking at her face.

Georg was with me. Eight years later he died.

How many years later will I die?

1984

The survivor's *guilt* you have always felt.

Death as an insult. — But how does one describe that?

Death, which he cannot stand, carries him in its arms.

No slowing down before death: faster, faster.

A full supply of dead, something to *rue*.

I think of my miserable dealings and my inner life, as well as the fact that the older I get the more powerfully and strongly I love, constantly preoccupied as I am not with my own death, but with that of my loved ones. I realize that I am less and less objective and *never* indifferent to my next of kin, and that I despise everything that does not have to do with breathing, thinking, and learning.

I also realize that I do not want to see *others*, that every new person I encounter upsets me in my deepest depths, that I cannot protect myself from feeling upset either through disgust or scorn, that I am completely at the mercy of another (even if he doesn't know it), that for his sake I can find no peace, nor sleep, nor dream, nor breathe, that each new person is for me the epitome of all that is vital, the most vital, which I compare with Goethe's more practical (more courteous) and more comfortable serenity, which in the end he *deserved* more than any other, and I don't know which I prefer. I am as much ashamed of his serenity as I am of my naked soul, and would like to be like him and not like him, though one thing I know for certain: the death that he escaped I have handled better than he.

He felt terror, but he concealed it. Both of us grew old. His work stands, I have sacrificed mine to the horrors, and by now there is hardly anything of me left within it—do I even know if I'd like to trade places with him?

It is astounding to find myself right now recalling Michelangelo's *terribilità*, as well as how Wotruba was as inspired by it as I was, though each independently of the other.

I travel back in memory and through milder places, feeling protected in having a child.

Have I become a Christian right before they threatened the end of the world? Will I suddenly pray to whoever it is that will destroy us?

The death of the forty-year-old strikes close to home, a death that Wotruba and I feel like no other. It's been eleven months since I thought of this death. D.S. died in Ludwigsburg on the day that *The Numbered* opened in Stuttgart, as if more than anything he wanted to be a part of this play about those who had to die. Three times he had spoken to me, but in between the paintings I forgot his face. I refused to talk about Wotruba with him. He found words for it on his own. I deeply hope that they will be taken seriously.   106

D.S., half as young as me, died last year. He who very early on understood what Wotruba and I meant to each other, our shared sensibility, that which we held *together*, this he had grasped and wished to express.

I mourn for him as if Wotruba and I had died with him, nor am I ashamed of this grief, which might appear self-involved. For it is for the most intense friendship of my life that I grieve, not for myself, since for he who died last year in an accident, this friendship was completely and secretly understood.

Why do you deny the thought of another life, be it an earlier one or a later one, and why do you loathe the idea of transmigration?

Are you only addicted to this sturdy desk at which you now write? What of this child, this woman? Can you grant no one at all any truck with another life? Is there no room for unexpected realizations and encounters? Are your dead completely dead to you and you alone?

No, it's only because of the idea of seeing again someone who has died that I loathe all notions of transmigration.

The cause of the earthquake ... the dead congregating.

Pythagoras

Sunday, January 1, 1984
I begin this year with the feeling that it will be my last.

I am determined to counter this feeling by writing.

Because if I have something to say that surprises me, then it will not be the last.

Since the visit yesterday with W., he has thought of the most horrible thing of all, violating a divine command which he never before—not even in his private thoughts—would have dared to do.

He doesn't want to decline into complete helplessness. He wants to decline to a certain point, but no further. As long as he says it, i.e., writes it, things can get worse and worse for him. Writing down his *testimony*, that is the only thing that justifies his condition. But if it were about nothing more, when the decline prevents the need to bear witness, and every possibility of doing so disappears—what then?

Is it then enough to hope for the miracle that can reverse his ultimate decline?

An enemy has died. Where is your magnanimity? You have accepted it, feeling no shame, a trace of satisfaction rising within you. What have you turned into?

Yet you have always said: Perhaps only weeks will separate our passing.

He is too old to die, for now, ghastly creature that he is, he has survived them all.

How long have you been old? Since this morning.

The TV President: his smile, his star quality, his stupidity.

He, and only he, do I hope will die smiling.

When all you can do is feel demoralized, it's better that you go.

Ro-lang, the floating corpse
"The sorcerer is locked in a dark room with a corpse. To bring the dead to life again, he has to lay his mouth upon that of the deceased and then continually repeat the same spell without his thoughts ever straying. After a few minutes the corpse begins to stir, rises, and wants to flee. The sorcerer must then hold him fast by the arms. The deceased moves ever more vigorously, his body thrusting upward, while the sorcerer has to make sure to never take his mouth off of the corpse. Finally the deceased sticks out his tongue, and that is the decisive moment: the sorcerer has to grab hold of it and rip it out, at which the corpse once again lies there lifeless. However, once the sorcerer has dried and preserved the tongue, it turns into a powerful magic weapon.

"Ngays-pa knew especially well how to mimic the gradual

return of life to the corpse, how the glassy eyes first began to look around, and the shaking of his body more and more turned into vigorous movements, such that the sorcerer could hardly hold the body down any longer and had to focus all of his powers on the deceased. He described what it felt like when the tongue first appeared and touched his own mouth, for then the terrible moment had come when he either would be victorious or the deceased would be sacrificed.

"I asked, since I was doubtful, to see 'the tongue,' at which the magician presented me with a hardened black thing that perhaps once was a tongue.

"The Ro-lang's touch is deadly, and the malicious ghost lays his hand upon all who are within its grasp."

David-Néel, Heilige und Hexler

I should write the book that more than fifty years ago I set out to write: *The Squanderer*.

Now I really know what it means to be a squanderer. For I have squandered away life and yet am still here and see how the Earth is squandered, and what becomes of it, knowing what the great, the real squanderer is: Death. I can only approach it as a squanderer. The only book that I was born to write, *The Book Against Death*, and the book about the squanderer that I am, these must become *one* book.

Death is the squanderer. That's what I need to show.

Let everything else that came before fall to the wayside. Bring them together, the Squanderer and Death, reveal their secret.

Forty-seven free years, which still belong to me: 1937–1984, the unceasing horror, and I must speak of it.

August 18, 1984

A Moment's Breath—that is what I called the book, and thus was I granted such a moment. I want to make use of it. Now

I will set forth the notes about death that I began in the last months of last year.

"There is a time for everything." Not death, it has none whatsoever.

The young man who adamantly disagreed with your sentences about survival. His father was dead, so he knew what he was talking about and turned with anger and disgust against my "theory." He experienced *no* sense of satisfaction at the death of his father, none whatsoever, not even the slightest trace of satisfaction. He stood among several others who surrounded me after the lecture, wanting an answer from me, for he *knew* otherwise. He was so angry at my claims that I felt it would have been best to hug him. But I cut off his talk and simply said that *I won't discuss it here.*

You have spoken directly with thousands. You more than likely ought to have been murdered.

In imagining that you will be murdered as a result of "demands" made of you, in this you approach Christianity. The thought of becoming a martyr for your beliefs attracts you.

The good days, which he does not allow himself to believe in—no death, no resurrection, no biological aging.

"It was believed by practitioners of yin-yang divination that *a person's hour of death was determined at his birth* and could be foretold by an examination of the celestial stars governing his birth." 108

"There are certain things that can only come from the dead."
Gottfried Benn 109

"Thus he refused to acknowledge the end that awaited him:

"The thought of death was so terrifying to him (the doctor later wrote to Marie Taxis), that he denied even knowing, nor did he ever once ask about the illness he suffered from. Not once did he mention the possibility of his dying, although every day when, following his wishes, I sat with him alone, we spoke openly about his condition and his friends."   *on Rilke*

110

"In the end we no longer need them, the early departed, weaned of earthly things like from a mother's breast. But we, in need of such great secrets, for whom grief so often spells a bless'd advance—*could* we exist without them?"

from Rilke's Duino Elegies

"... I love thinking, for I know I will die. I do not need to be ashamed of my hatred of death. It's not personal. I would be very much satisfied with just one person who did not die (that is, if it did not come at the expense of others—though it would be all right if it were at my expense)."

note from June 1932

"Palmer the tragedian died when he should have counterfeited a scenic death in Drury Lane; the audience hissed because the hero did not die well but the poor actor was found lifeless."

Emerson, Journals and Notebooks, VI

111

Hodler: The Permanence of Death 1853–1918
"When H. was five years old, his father died of consumption. In 1867 (when *he* was fourteen years old), his mother died. While working a poor piece of the Thun commons, and surrounded by her children, she suddenly collapsed on a spring day and was dead. The children themselves had to load the corpse onto a cart, and, weeping, brought it back home. In the

course of the following years H. experienced the death of all his siblings (there were *nine*). 'In the family, death was general. It ended up feeling like there would always be someone dead in the house and that was just the way it had to be.'"

112

"When you are all dead, will I be all grown up then?" A girl, three years old.

The dignity of those who remain behind depends upon *how* the deceased died.

Not every comforting maneuver ends up successful. There are the dead who are truculent, just as there are survivors who are truculent.

1985

There is much to envy Stendhal. Above all for being totally exposed after his death.

You do everything you can to increase the consciousness of death. The danger, which is doubtless great, you magnify in order not to lose awareness of it. You are the opposite of a person who takes drugs, for your knowledge of the horror never eases.

However, what do you gain through the constant wakefulness of this consciousness of death?

Are you at all stronger? Can you protect those endangered any better? Can you instill a *single* person with courage simply because you always think about it?

This entire enormous apparatus that you have constructed serves nothing. It saves no one. It gives the false appearance of strength and amounts to nothing more than false boasting and from beginning to end is as useless as anything.

But I curse death. I can't help but do so. And should it make me blind, there's nothing I can do but repel death. If I were to accept it, I would be a murderer.

He will not compose his last will and testament. He does not wish to grant death the honor.

How far are you—after all the announcements—with the preparations for the book against death?

Try the opposite: its glorification, and you will quickly get hold of yourself and arrive at your true objective.

He escaped from the world, the only one to do so.

The most difficult thing for you? A last will and testament. To write one would spell capitulation.

And what if someone said: one hour more?

He shed his final fear and died.

Here he stands staring at death. It comes at him, he repels it. He does grant it the honor of coming to terms with it. When nevertheless the final bewilderment descends upon him, he will not have bowed to it. He called it out, he hated it, he repudiated it. Though he succeeded at very little, it is more than nothing.

The dummy adopted the final downfall as his own.

Sentences as simple and dreadful as the man himself.

The Death of Al-Hamadhāni. Writer of the Makamen
(1000 BCE)
"I learned from a reliable resource that al-Hamadhāni had fallen into a coma and after succumbing to it was buried. He awakened in the grave, and during the night could be heard calling out. That was why the grave was opened and they found him with has hand knotted in his beard. The horror of it all had caused him to die."   *Fähndrich, after Abu-Said*   113

Autographs Rise in Price at Sotheby's
"Among the curiosities in the auction is a letter from Sigmund Freud from May 1911, in which he wrote to Gustav Mahler's executor five days after the composer's death to demand payment for several hours of treatment he had given him, while in October he wrote to acknowledge receipt of the funds. In the

auction the demand for payment sold for 6,820 pounds, and
114   the receipt for 3,850 pounds."

"He bound my breasts, which then prevented me from nursing
my child. He wanted to see how long it would live without any
nourishment."
115   *from the Mengele forum, in the auditorium of Yad Vashem*

At the close of the Mengele forum, Telford Taylor, who had sat
for three days on the podium without saying a word, offered
a brief comment. Having witnessed it himself, he recalled the
entrance of an accused general practitioner brought before the
military court at Nürnberg who remained obstinate. Question: "How long does it take before an injection of phenol
116   causes death?" Answer: "Bring me a man. I'll show you."

The death of Heinrich Böll. My respect for this face engraved
with integrity. I hardly know his work, so I cannot say much
about it. Why did it not attract my interest more? I never saw
him in person, but his voice I know well, for once we spoke on
the telephone about the situation in Poland. It was the voice of
a deeply sad man, who did not just suffer from his own illness.
    He was worried about the fate of his friends, for someone
had told him that they supposedly had been *beaten* (something
which later proved untrue), and he wanted some prominent
names—other than his own—to file a protest against it. He
managed to inspire me to support something of which I was
not entirely certain, which is unlike me. He had taken part in
open protests and did not at all worry that his name could be
cheapened as a result. He was not stingy with his name, which
made him a lot of enemies, and even though I am shy about
signing my name too often in support of such things, I would
always find myself, or at least I believe, so far as I can tell, on

his side. I am completely certain that he *never* did anything out of his own self-aggrandizement (in contrast to G.G. who with his dictatorial airs is a complete idiot).

There are great ways of responding to injustice that stand or fall on their own persistence. If even, just once, Böll had refused to take part, he would no longer have earned the right to be called the conscience of his nation. There can be no such thing as an intermittent conscience.

117

Yesterday they buried him. Today he gets up and crows on the dung heap.

There, murderers also bring flowers to a grave.

There, portraits weep, and people freeze.

There, each is haunted by the ghosts of animals they have eaten, until he breaks down and confesses.

In any case he can now sit down somewhere and quietly die.

The same astonishment you feel about anyone's death, this inability to fathom it, which you will never understand, nor do you wish to understand it, for it is your single unchanging primal experience.

1986

Greek tragedy allows no distractions. Death—of the individual—still carries its full weight. Murder, suicide, burial and grave sites, there it is all exemplary, naked and unadorned, as is mourning (which among us has been castrated) and the pain of the guilty.

In our time the social world surrounding death has radically changed. Mass death is no longer the exception, for everything flows into it. In the rush toward it the individual death loses its weight. Given how many more people there are—can they each die an individual death? When that is no longer possible, we will have reached the point of no return.

Yet he is still capable of writing down the word "immortality." He trembles with disgust, yet he writes it down.

"One imagines life without death. Out of despair, day after day people would try to kill themselves."   *Jules Renard, Journal*

He died in his sleep. In which dream?

The focal point—you could almost say the hero—of *Electra* is the grave of Agamemnon.

There is nothing that I better understand, for the secret focal point of my life is Veza's ashes in Thurlow Road.

"Has it been emphasized enough that the type of music and the amount of music that one has listened to in life are crucial for the soul's condition and the judgment after death?"
Stockhausen

There, people are roasted before they are buried.

My mistrust of Nietzsche, my aversion, my resistance, become more hardened with each new year. But I don't wish to attack him and thereby quote him even more. As if they were contagious, I am repelled by his words when I write them. I find him to be both an open and secret lover of death.

"Jesus and his disciple passed a dead dog. The disciple said: 'It smells so repulsive!' But Jesus replied: 'His teeth are so white!' In this way he reminded them not to say anything terrible about others."

120

He died before he could unseat his successors.

What I would still like to take up:

The Trickster: an exploration of this figure, which would contain some important aspects of metamorphosis.

The Metamorphoses of Ovid: an extremely detailed study, a literary textbook of metamorphosis.

Greek Tragedy: A study of all thirty-one extant dramas. Also, in connection with these, a discussion of the comedies of Aristophanes.

On Hierarchies: stemming from India's caste system, an immense topic, the exploration of which I am beholden to undertake.

Some comments on the *Books of the Bible*.

The Book about Death. It remains my most central book. Will I finally write it *in one fell swoop*?

He would like to die while writing; before he's entirely finished, he'd like to complete a sentence, exhale before the next sentence, and die exactly between the two.

Konjaku Monogatarishu

The first story is called: "How a Man Who Bought a Turtle and Let It Free Gains New Life with the Help of Jizo."

"The fisher joyfully grabbed the line and handed over the turtle to the man. The man, who had purchased the turtle, said: 'A turtle certainly has a long life. Who possesses a life knows what a treasure it is. Although I hardly own a thing, I have let go of this line and saved your life.' As the turtle heard these words, the man let it go in the lake. The man then returned home empty-handed ...

"The man did not live much longer after this, for he fell ill and died. He was buried on the steep slopes of the Kaneberg. After three days had passed, he came to life again. About this same time the governor of Iga was traveling down the mountain on the way to his own province and found the man who had just awoken from death. Deeply concerned, he ladled out some water and poured it into his mouth. Once the man's throat was moist, he traveled on. When the man's wife heard all this at his home, she climbed up the mountain, threw him on her back, and turned toward home.

"After a while the man told his wife: 'When I was dead, an official grabbed hold of me from behind and led me away. We crossed through a huge wasteland and arrived at the gate of an official building. When I looked through the gate and into the courtyard, I could see many people lying about in chains. The fearful thoughts that came into my heart were horrendous.'

"Then a pure and devout little monk arrived and said: 'I am the Bodhisattva Jizo. This man is someone who showed me mercy. In order to bear witness to the grace of life, I lingered on the beach of the lake at Omi in the body of large turtle. When I was captured by the fisherman and should have been killed, this man bought the turtle out of sheer heartfelt concern, saved its life and let it go free in the lake. Therefore this man should be freed immediately.' The official took this all in, then let me go.

"... When he showed me the way and told me to head for home, there arrived as I looked around a lovely young woman, roughly twenty years old, who had been chased and attacked by two demons. When I saw this I asked: 'Hey there, where are you from?' Weeping heavily, the girl replied: 'I am from the Chikuzen Province, the daughter of the magistrate of Little Munakata. Suddenly separated from my mother and father, I walked the dark way alone, pursued by demons beating me, and finally arrived here.' I listened to this and, *overcome with pity*, turned to that little monk and said:

"'I have already lived passed the middle of my life, and there is not much more of it left me. This girl is still so young, and her life's end is still distant. Therefore take me instead of her and let her go free.'

"The little monk listened and replied: 'You have a heart full of great goodness. To forsake your own body to save another, that is a merciful act. Therefore I wish to appeal on behalf of both of you and free you. Thus he spoke, then appealed to the spirits, and she was freed along with me. The girl wept with joy, turned to me, swore an eternal bond with me, and then we went our separate ways.'

"Then after some time had passed, he thought of visiting the girl that he had met in the realm of the dead, and therefore headed off to Tsukushi. And just as the girl had said in the underworld, when he arrived at the house of the district head of Munakata in Chikuzen Province, there really was a daughter of the magistrate who was young in years. 'She took ill and died, and after two or three days, she came to life again,' or so said the people. When the man heard this, he told the girl about what he had experienced in the underworld. The girl listened and appeared from inside and stood there confused.

When the man saw her, he could not see any difference between her and the one he had seen in the realm of the dead. And as the girl looked at the man, she could not see any difference between him and the one she had seen in realm of the dead. Together they broke into tears, crying and weeping and talking about what had occurred in the realm of the dead.

"Then they swore anew eternal loyalty to one another, and the man returned to his home province."

"The pageantry of death is more horrible than death itself."

Seneca, quoted in Bacon's "Of Death"

What will I have to say to her someday, if indeed I'm still here. How can I say that death is not death, how can I lie to my own child.

Will I ever be forgiven for it?

The Book of Death: I will have to dictate it heedlessly, otherwise it will be worthless.

I will leave to others the meager act of making corrections.

I should also not shy away from making claims that sound a bit insane, not when they are *my own*.

Yesterday he died. Today he recalls nothing more about it.

To take apart death, its inner workings.

1987

What I have to say against death is no less unreal than the immortality of the soul posed by religion. But it is even more unreal, for I wish to preserve *everything*, not just a single soul.

An insatiability that is nearly incomprehensible.

This morning something awful began. I awoke with the feeling that I no longer wanted to live. Disgusted with everything. I don't want to go on.

"The soul journeys forth into the land of the dead, where it comes to a *giant strawberry*. Once it eats of it, there is no going back to the realm of the living. Should it not do so, then it is possible for it to return." *Ojibwa Indians* 122

"The king who never laughed because he feared death so. It threatened him no matter where he was, and when he was asked the reason why, he answered with a horrendous image: He never laughed because there were four lances aimed at his body, ready to pierce him straight through should he give any sign of joy. The first lance represented the bitter suffering of Christ, the second was the thought of death, which separates the soul from the body, the third being the inability to know when one will die, as well as the fear of suddenly dying full of one's sins, thus also denying him of any earthly pleasures, and the fourth and last was the fear of the Last Judgment."

W. Rehm, The Idea of Death in German Poetry
from the Middle Ages to the Romantics 123

"Philosophy is therefore not a comfort; it represents much more, as it reconciles and explains reality, which appears unjust. To the reasonable, it appears that it exists as an idea in and of itself, which therefore satisfies reason."

Hegel, Lectures on the Philosophy of World History
How appalling!

An incredible sentence by Schelling in a letter to Georgii, Easter, 1811: "We cannot settle for just a general continuance that postpones our eventual departure; we must comprehend its entire character." *Schelling's Life in Letters, Vol. II*

"Why is there anything, why is there not nothing at all?"
Schelling

"To philosophize means to ask the question: why is there above all that which exists and not much more that is nothing?"
Heidegger

"The way the world is, that is not mystical, but rather that it exists." *Wittgenstein, Tractatus 6, 44*

W. has "sometimes expressed a feeling of surprise that really anything exists."

Within this question lies buried the *acceptance* of death. All thought that begins with this is infected by death. When immortality was destroyed, it left behind nothing. Whoever manages to introduce immortality into his physical existence is turned into nothing, and is not even capable of asking a question about it.

"Because the most painful thing is parting ... he will give his

beloved a single piece of his fortune, his renown, his estate—
yes, even if only a shirt that he could ask him to wear and
which would make him happy."   *Al-Ghazali, via Gräf*   125

Death is depicted as a ram of cosmic dimensions, which is
slaughtered by Gabriel or John on the first day between Paradise and Hell after the Last Judgment. Life itself is symbolized
by a mare.

The Sacrifice of Isaac
"Some commentators say: Each time Abraham cut through a
piece of Isaac's throat, God healed him so Isaac could live on.
Jewish commentators of the Middle Ages thought that Isaac
spent even more years in Paradise waiting for the wounds to
his throat to heal."   *Gräf*

"Can God enable his creation to grant life and death. Prevailing doctrine says: No."
          Abu Hasan al-Ash'ari, Maqālāt al-Islāmīyīn   126

Greek Fire
"When the enemy set fire to a Muslim ship and the crew had
no chance of being saved, those who could not stand the pain
of being burned plunged into the water. It is admittedly more
proper to die by an outside force rather than by one's own
choice."   *Gräf, Conceptions of Death in Islamic Anthropology*

"A simple woman with chronic schizophrenia, who as long as
she was physically healthy, spoke hardly a sentence that did
not contain neologisms and absentmindedness, such that it
was often impossible to understand her. However with the onset of metastatic breast cancer, at the end of her decades-long

stay in a mental hospital, in simple, well-ordered sentences she
127   thanked people for their final visit to her."   *Heimann*

Zen
"Young people, if you don't wish to die, then die now! If you were to die now, you will not die when you die," said Master Hakuin (1686–1769).

    An instruction that the Zen master gives to his followers
128   says: "Die your death through and through, then come to me!"

"To breathe out, that means exhausting yourself, and completely expelling all your breath into the open air—that is indeed death. To breathe in, that means bringing the far and
129   wide into yourself again—that is indeed a resurrection."

"Among those who practice Zen is the custom of composing a very short poem upon one's deathbed that is called a 'bequeathed poem.' It is a final goodbye composed as a self-
130   reflection about the people in one's life."

In actuality, the last words of the one dying make up the bequeathed poem, no matter whether they are written out in the form of a poem or not.

Quanhuo, a Chinese Zen master of the Tang Dynasty, was murdered while traveling. His last cry of pain functioned as a bequeathed poem, and Zen Buddhism asks: "Do you hear his
131   cries? What do you make of them?"

Jesus Sirach on Death
"O death, how bitter you are, when anyone thinks of you who has had good days and enough of them and lives without worries, and who prospers in all things, and who still eats well!

"O death, how well you serve the poor man who is weak and old, who is immersed in all his cares and has nothing better to hope for or expect!

"Do not fear death! Remember it is also rendered by the Lord onto all flesh, all who have come before you and all who shall come after.

"And how can you deny God's will, whether you live ten, a hundred or a thousand years?

"For no one who is dead asks anyone how long he has lived." (*The Book of Sirach*, 41:1–7)

Curious is the last sentence: when does anyone actually inquire how long one has lived.

Does Jesus Sirach believe in a similar number of years granted one after death? Would that be a comfort? If everyone were to attain the same age in death as in life — would that be a comfort?

132

Rolling Head
"The skull of a *suicide* must roll in the dust until it has *saved a life.*"

133

Only religions have something to say about death. Philosophies say nothing at all about it.

For the umpteenth time I write out
the outrageous obituary published for Lenz
"He died knowing few people and was not missed by anyone. This unlucky man of letters wasted the best part of his life in useless activities that came to nothing. Misunderstood by all, battling against deprivation and poverty, disowned by his loved ones, he nevertheless never lost the feeling of his own worth, his pride roused even more by countless indignities and becoming finally the defiance often found among the

noble poor. He lived off of handouts, but he did not accept just any act of charity, and was insulted if someone offered money or support unasked, even though his entire nature and outer appearance really called for the most pressing need for charity." *Allgemeine Literatur-Zeitung, May 1792*

134

Given your life history, you are guilty of a kind of furious *attack* against yourself: *The enemy of death, all of whose people have died.* Does that not sum you up as an enemy of death?

Upon his dead horse, he rides onward.

The *continuousness* of an illness puts one to sleep. One gets used to it, and the continuousness makes the danger seem less.
All *duration* has calming effects, even when it causes intense discomfort. The peace in Europe since 1945 has had the same effect. There *cannot*, so they tell themselves, after such a long period, ever be another war. So then let's quietly go on arming ourselves!

Is it time to give in to death? It is gradually becoming known how much you *hate* it. Repeating it does not make your hate stronger, just more boring.

He forgot the dead, and they were alive once again.

I was in London during the election. For the third time, Thatcher won, which is enough to make one vomit. Dickens, who died 117 years ago, would again feel right at home. The same attitudes as then, minus an empire. The people who feel good about themselves only because *under* them there is a class of outcasts and the unemployed ...

Being-toward-Death

"Throughout the extended course of life, cells die off and new ones are produced. Is there a difference between this dying off of cells and the death of *all* cells? And yet once total death occurs, cells continue to live. The hair and the nails of those who have passed on continue to grow. *Even the production of sperm continues beyond death.* It is theoretically conceivable to generate a new life from the sperm of a dead person. Biology alone is only able to provide us with a hazy conception of death ...

"Where then in this process is the border between life and death? We do not know. Biology can define death no better than it can define life and human existence."

Hans Saner, *Being-toward-Death*
from a Philosophical Perspective   135

A new God has been concocted. Out of the remains of the old one.

It has become ever more clear to me that I can only write the book about death when I am entirely certain that it will not be published within my lifetime. It should be complete, or at least close enough to complete, so that it *can* be published later. Only then can I be certain that I can express everything *truthfully*, without regard for the living, especially without regard for Hera's illness. I also don't want to be alive when it appears, so that I don't have to defend it. I want to say what I think, I want to say it unreservedly, but I don't want any kind of battle.

Perhaps it would be enough to put together all of my unpublished notes on death in chronological order. But this idea does not please me, because up to this point I have always worked with the idea of gathering thoughts on this theme into a book that I would write and publish myself. However,

I believe that I can only express the last and most important things when I know that I will not see their public reception. There is something ignoble about such public scrutiny, and I can't stand the thought of it. It has nothing to do with me, it has to do with death. So long as the one who says things about death is still around, all such thoughts will seem to be about him. That's exactly what it should not be about.

What I would like most would be to write this book *as a different person*. But that will not be possible, because my interest in the subject has long been known, as has my writing style, and so it would not in any way be possible to keep secret the source of such a book.

It also needs to be considered that such a book against death, if it is read *after* you have died, could serve as evidence of the failure of its own ideas. The book could as a result lose its own power and seem more the account of a *chimera*.

He had no one left. He lined up little stones on the table and talked to them until they began to dance.

Hardly does he bend over before he feels death inside his neck and quickly stands up straight again to shake it off.

A *nobleman* cannot be thrown into the tower nor hung from the gallows. A nobleman must be decapitated (as is done throughout Europe), and in Spain it must be done *from the front*. Only traitors are decapitated from behind.

In the death doctrine laid out in his *Being and Time*, Heidegger presents death as the single, intractable, unconquerable, certain, and therefore indeterminate possibility. Heidegger's

Being-toward-Death, if one were to express it as an actuality, is really Being-toward-Being-Struck-Dead.

"The ability of the human being to kill its own kind perhaps underlies more of human history than the fundamental fact of our having to die."   *Koselleck*   136

"The last company of an artillery regiment was killed by hand grenades." Muo asked what the soldiers could have done, given that they had no ammunition. Schmidt replied: "They could have used knives or bit the enemy with their teeth."   137

The worst thing about death is its *concentration*. It draws everything into its own final stricture. Religions don't want the final passage to be that constricted. Once past those narrow straits they paint pictures of immense vistas. What a relief!

What if those vistas were shifted so as to occur *before* those narrow straits?

Certainly, the cleverest thing Goethe did was to simply avoid the topic of death. He had enough equipoise to do so, but who else does?

Whoever can say spiritual things about death, whoever can bring himself to do *that*, serves it in the end.

"The Egyptians embalmed their dead and preserved them in their homes. The Persians sealed them in wax before burial so that the body could last as long as possible. The Magi had the custom of not burying their loved ones but rather for animals to tear them to shreds. In Hycrania the people kept mongrels, splendid house dogs, and as we know, purebred dogs, and thus

everyone purchased the best dog he could find in order to later
be torn to pieces by it, and that is what they thought made for
138   the best funeral!"   *Chrysippus of Soli*

1988

Pensées against death.

They must remain fragments: the only form possible. You cannot publish them yourself. You must not edit them. You must not *unify* them.

The Egyptian Idea of Revivification
Two brothers: Anup and Bata.

"Then he found a berry. He took it with him, because it was his younger brother Anup's heart. He brought along a pitcher of fresh water and laid it inside it and went about his daily activities.

"When night had fallen, Anup's heart soaked up all the water. Bata's limbs trembled all over and he looked at his older brother, grabbed the pitcher of fresh water in which the heart of his younger brother lay and he let him drink it down so that the heart found its rightful place. He was again as he once was. Each embraced the other, and each chatted with his comrade." 139

A scandal! He's alive again!

"The blood will flow ... The earth will burn from north to south, from east to west, and there will be mountains of dead from every land that wishes to enslave us. It will be the greatest slaughter in history. The dead will pile up as high as the Himalayas."

President Duvalier, at the start of the U.S. invasion of Haiti

God is the strangest concept ever created by humans, a genuine fantasy resulting from their desire for power. Our notion of what power is derives from Him alone. Yet it is clear to no one, for we are still dazzled by His aura and refuse to coldly dissect Him. He is easily disavowed, but not easily embraced. He can be dead, but no autopsy is allowed. This pompous figure has always disgusted me. Meanwhile, He has taken on an abstract-explosive honor: he *is* the atom bomb.

Everything is at stake in the book about death. Which will come first: the book or death?

It is important that I soon separate the diaries from the notes. The notes need to be accessible, for perhaps there is something within them that is still of value, which would justify publication. The diaries, however, in which the story of our love in all its wonderfulness and awfulness is laid out, are not meant for others. Perhaps I can allow them, or at least some of her lovely *letters*, to be made public fifty years after my death. Her letters are in some cases the most wonderful works of all, and nothing that I have written about us, or could write about us, even comes close. As a result of these letters, Hera will become immortal. However, they can only appear in a world that *deserves* them, and, if at all possible, *independent* from me later on.

No death ever ends.

1989

The *tone* of the Egyptians is like your own, one like no other. *Animals* considered as sacred as *writing*. Justice and its scales. The dismembered dead restored to life. The lament for the dead.

The lament for the dead that holds nothing against the dead.

To find one's way back to what the dead once loved about us. To relinquish what we hate, for the sake of the deceased. To purify oneself for the dead. The deceased as the ultimate authority. Nothing hidden from him.

To make use of the past as the time of the dead.

That which remains the same, the unalterable character, Don Quixote as well as Sancho Panza, the richness of their characters, despite the severest limitations. How fuzzy, how pale in comparison are all later novels.

Rhetoric of the highest level, but within the limits of their characters. The rhetoric of the knights rather than rhetoric of the proverbs.

The amicable fat man is by no means always wrong.

Lofty speeches are tolerable because they continually alternate with the fat man's speech.

If I could find the right kind of speaker to counter such speech, it would then be possible to rescue *Death's Enemy*.

Death's Enemy can be no less noble than the knight-errant. The only difficulty, one that perhaps makes it impossible, is that the knight-errant is an *ultimate* character, one who looks back on what had long existed. Death's Enemy concerns himself with nothing that already has been, but instead must win us over, even though to him everything is new.

Even when I read something boring of Goethe's (and there are endless examples of that), I never regret doing so.

One has the feeling that it has to do with the strength of an elder, or better yet, his ability to age. That which is boring is a necessary protection, for he is never reckless with his genius, meaning reckless with it as are others. He buries it in dull customs, in service to his and other princes, in possessions, in collecting, in conversation as a form of legacy. Although his genius is so immense, he treads carefully with it, like a paterfamilias.

Your *convictions* have not changed in the slightest. But how will you justify them? Your *repudiation* of death is no more absurd than the belief in resurrection that Christianity has put forth for two thousand years. The difference is that your repudiation has not found any form. How can you live with it when in fact people continuously die? What does the hater of death say when victims succumb all around him? He cannot ignore them, as they throw death in his face. He is more fascinated with death than other people. He *feeds* his hatred with the continuous experience of death. Confrontation with it becomes his only subject, the constant of his existence. What can he say, how can he maintain the relentlessness of his convictions when he looks on endlessly and sees how they are vanquished?

He sees that he is compelled to witness a constantly committed crime, observing it with outrage again and again, unable to stop it. This leads to the danger that he will *become inured to* this crime. He finds himself in a *war* without end. Any peaceful conclusion is to him suspect; it can only lead to the acknowledgment of defeat. But since he battles entirely alone, he alone carries the responsibility. A death conceded—and all deaths are conceded.

In a world *bursting* with the implements and administration of death, one person alone will stand up to it and therefore be taken seriously. Bemused smiles everywhere. The fool will soon see. When it's his turn, that will be the end of his recalcitrance.

As if he didn't know it! As if it would be possible for him to yield because of some practical, useful reason! How often beliefs have caused people to lose all sense of themselves! For which were they not ready to die! Can no one submit themselves to the declaration of a higher law that *forbids* death? It's amazing to think that it has hardly happened until now. It's amazing that humankind—and not just in *this* religion— could allow themselves to be duped by the expectation of an approaching Last Judgment.

The "modest" rulers of Islam, who think of the penalty of death as natural. This is the easiest path for them to God, for through the death decree they become God, but without succumbing to what they otherwise consider the worst blasphemy of all—equating oneself with God.

"In regard to the fear of death, not a drop of your blood must flow through my veins, if it meant holding me back. Also as a result of certain individual views that you in no way can share with me, an indifference to life has arisen, which to you will seem paradoxical, because you do not entirely know me. I am completely convinced that one can lose more than one's life in the world, and that life only holds its attraction for us as a means rather than a goal, and that one often loses very little when one has to shuffle off this planet."

Novalis in a letter to his father, February 1793   140

Novalis, my purest counterpart:
"Death is a self-conquering—one which, like any self-overcoming, opens up a new, easier existence."

"Life is the beginning of death. Life is at the beck and call of death. Death is equally an end and a beginning."

The Stoic: Set your heart on no one. He could die.
The Lover: Set your heart most deeply on the one who could die.
The Stoic: How are you doing, now that you've been abandoned? What do you love?
The Lover: Of all that I have lost, the lost one I love the most.
The Stoic: And what do you get out of it?
The Lover: Pain, pain.
The Stoic: Wouldn't it be easier to cut off an arm?
The Lover: Easier, but devoid of love.
The Stoic: That word. A delusion. A ludicrous word.
The Lover: But not unfeeling.
The Stoic: But even this feeling dies.
The Lover: It's your lack of feeling that dies.

The return of my dead ones, the only thing remaining to complete, but the desire for it that I feel inside is as strong within me as it ever was, and thus can I say: I am *entirely* alive.

1990

He interprets death.

It is said: "If a person suddenly recalls an earlier life and speaks of it, then that means he will die."   *Somadeva*   141
    And what if that person keeps it a secret?

When it comes to the dead and what happened to them, my anger makes me merciless.
    But they have to be my dead. As for the others, I only look on in pity or am shocked.

Today I encountered the most horrible story in the memoirs of a woman named Misia Sert. I call it *The Agony of the Flies*, and am here copying it out word for word:
    "One of my roommates was a master at catching flies. Patient study of these creatures had made it possible for her to find precisely the right point at which to stick them with a needle in order to string them together without killing them. In this way she made necklaces of living flies and reported with great excitement about the heavenly feel of her skin abuzz with desperate little legs and fluttering wings."   142

He who will not be dissuaded from facing death has the most religion of all.

"Sometime in the last decade of the second millennium, according to the estimates of cultural anthropologists, the day will come when for the first time the number of actual living humans will be larger than all who have previously lived put together since humankind first existed."

What nonsense! The plain fact is that they have none of them been alive at the same time.

It is a completely meaningless calculation.

What's important is the number of dead *still to come*.

With every person that dies the entire world dies with them.

That is the meaning of Christ on the Cross.

For some time, I have loved nothing better than to read the lives of the saints. They are figures in the truest sense, with nothing modern about them, forever unchanged, contorted with pain, but not corrupted, single-minded, immortal in their defiance.

Since they no longer believe in the devil, people have become dangerous.

Man no longer sees the devil: he has swallowed him whole.

"Death is a well into which garbage is thrown."

The only sentence of Lenin's that interests me. Where is it from?

Without flinching, he thrust the skewer through the body of the snail.

I used to love birds, now I love flowers. They hold still for eyes that are failing.

Might it also be right to close the eyes before death? No, three times over, no! Keep the eyes wide open to it, and curse it, curse it, and curse it again! Do not think of trying to appease it by dialing back your defiance or bestowing sporadic blessings.

For it does not matter that there are more and more people and creatures, such that one can avoid death through their *number*; what matters is that death is attacked by each individual, regardless of how many others it might also touch. The question of the *number* is irrelevant, for the individual, each individual, is confronted with death, and each individual must engage in battle with it.

The meaning of every death lament—the oldest human expression—used to be somewhat different.

People did not want it to be true. The deceased was feared because you could have protected him more. You called him back. You promised him everything that he might now need: help along his path forward, nourishment, courage, and perpetual remembrance. You visited him at the place where he asked you to. You invoked his spirit and swore to protect all his rights. No one has ever been handled more carefully, with more trepidation, and even if in life you hated the person— you still tried to hide it from the dead.

Earlier, when you destroyed everything that had belonged to him, that was more honest. Since you did not desire to rob the deceased, you were not prompted to keep anything from him. Later, with the *robbery* conducted by heirs, things became different, for nothing has changed our relationship with death more than this approved of and recommended thievery.

Imagine what our world would look like today if everything that belonged to someone who had died had to be destroyed.

The heirs would resort to necrophilia, a disgusting crime.

At least I don't carry any kind of grudge. Though I would still be happy to learn of Saddam's death.

I would love to have seen Prague again. Two weeks is not enough in one lifetime.

Werfel was also from Prague. One has to forgive Prague for that. His were the last works that the dying Kafka read. Werfel had sent him his novel about the opera. Since he could no longer speak, he should sing.

Werfel *literally* said to me, "Kafka was not a writer, he was a theologian."

Therefore, as a dead man Werfel was *baptized* and buried in evening dress. A. helped prepare this last toilette for the deceased.

A. despised Mahler because he was impotent. Werfel despised her, having happily let her deceive him. She shredded and destroyed his fame. Now he's nothing more than washed-up goods.

It's worth considering how the beliefs of the Jews branched off of those of the Egyptians. It's worth considering that in turning away from God I could have turned to Osiris.

I would have belonged to those who fled Egypt, but I would not have been on their side. In the land of Canaan, I would not have paid sacrifice to Baal, but rather Isis.

Under the Romans I would not have been Christian; I would have fallen for Isis. Not the Isis who carries a child, but the Isis who looked for and found Osiris's remains cut into pieces.

There are long, dark periods in my life during which I forget Isis. But then another person dies, and like her, I go in search of them.

Yet I have never found the pieces.

What I will leave behind nags at me. Thoughts are not possessions. Thoughts must spring up and they must be able to conceal themselves. Thoughts change their weight over time.

Thoughts burn bright and fade. Thoughts moan and are pummeled with silence. How can a thought be left behind?

If the Germans do not stop producing chemical and biological weapons, then they have made a mockery of all the trust they won through reunification.

They are not terrible for having weapons themselves, but a hundred times more terrible for the weaponry they manufacture for others. The hue and cry about it has not yet begun, but when it sweeps across the earth, one's eyes will suddenly be opened to what they were capable of earlier. How can they wait. They must preempt the storm which they have themselves ignited.

There is, strange as it sounds, more goodwill than anxiety in the world as a result of reunification, yet it is *tentative*, and through Saddam's threats with his weapons of mass destruction, which the Germans have provided him, this goodwill can very quickly turn into fear and hate. All renunciations and reassurances, which were once believed, will suddenly transform themselves into threats. Gas especially is the plague of the German nation. They must guard against having anything to do with gas, as if they were in the chamber themselves. Whoever does not see that is blind and is not fit to serve the Germans as a politician.

The Germans will not give up on gas. They produce it and continue to distribute it.

What do they think they are doing, given that they are doing so alone and under no pressure?

Do they *want* to see the weapons used?

Is the old hunger to kill rising in them again?

Will they hate Jews as long as they are confronted with them?

"In Buchenwald, in Buchenwald, we laid the Jews out cold."

If it were still possible to entirely disappear without a trace, really without a single trace—would you not opt for that?

What has there been that is more ridiculous than you?

Who has hated death so from his earliest youth?

Who has managed throughout his life, his long life, to lose the most precious and most devoted people he knew? Who lived on and continued to lose others? Who recognized, finally and irrefutably recognized, that survival is the core of every wretched power? Who has indeed deeply abhorred this kind of power, and nevertheless has grown older and older and is finally old? Who never once had a God before whom he could justify himself, and lived on without any such justification?

Who is convinced in his innermost self that because of his understanding of power he will live on, even when he is no longer alive, as a kind of Ixion lashed to a fiery wheel for all eternity?

An aged doctor who visits his surviving patients.

Despite the national bloodlust of the Germans, you can give thanks for the blessing of the birth of its purveyors. For every type of killing you can find someone to supply it.

You can't shake the feeling that many turn to this type of business, not just because it involves Jews.

When I first returned to Vienna after the war, I sat across from two grown men on a bus who scrutinized me. "G.C.L." said one of them, and the other nodded.

Later I asked a friend what it meant. "You don't know?" he replied, completely astounded. "That means Gas-Chamber Layabout, which means Jewish pig."

There, they ask each person first for his permission before he is slain. Whoever doesn't want to die is kept warm in a bread oven. After some time, he is again asked to give his permission.

I have slain no one. I am a virgin, as D. said to me on horse-back. But how many animals have I eaten. I am nevertheless a virgin, or just a baser kind of murderer.

Knowledge *orphaned*—how unspeakably sad.

The order cherished by a salesman lies in addition. The world ends. He tallies it up. Children starve. He tallies it up. Friends choke to death. He tallies it up.

The doctors boycotted him; he recovered and thanked them in effusive letters.

The "childish" thing about you is that seventy-eight years after the death of your father, when you were seven, you still have not accepted it. This childishness, precisely this kind of child-ishness, is what the world really needs.

I am completely conflicted within and have no answer.

I am also divided on the question of what's going on in the Gulf. We cannot let Saddam do as he wishes. For many it's about oil. But it's also about something else, something more important.

Removing Saddam means war, and with every means, even those that have been banned. With new means, which once used will exist in the world. I am against any kind of murder. The only solution in the Gulf is the murder of Saddam. I am in favor of this murder.

"It was the custom when searching for the drowned to bring along some roosters in the boat, which—supposedly—would begin to crow when the boat was above the body." *Bokushi* 144

Thomas Hürlimann introduced himself to me and then stood

by quietly. I like his work, and he himself pleases me too. He said he once carried only two books in his suitcase: Musil and *Kafka's Other Trial*. Naturally I was pleased at being made a neighbor of Musil, and even if he only wanted to say something pleasant to me, nevertheless he did at least understand *how* he might make me happy. I said to him that I had sensed a kinship between us when I first read him, and that it was true. "The Ticino Woman," a short story of his, I really enjoyed. He is the most talented among the young writers of Switzerland. The central event of his life was the death of his younger brother, at a very young age, of cancer. He *knows* death, like I do, and he has not accepted it. In that lies our kinship. Meeting him was the loveliest thing that happened to me this evening.

145

The immense, clear glass monster, and its shattering. The music of its destruction.

In sparing animals, a person grows younger. It's the hunt that makes him old.

The most beautiful thing about *longing* is the word for it.

A machine gun capable of firing as many shots as there are people who are still alive.

Enough. Once again it has happened. Whisked away by death on two consecutive days: Ott-Heinrich Keller in Halle, Dürrenmatt here. At my age there are always more, more, more. Will there from now on be at least one a day whom I knew?

146

I think of Dante's characters, who are rendered so clearly that you are entirely taken with them. You cannot pull yourself away, they are in a certain sense simplified, they who are burdened with the most important matters. Or is it he who captures you, *his* vision of their importance being the point. Their palpability is attained through their death. They are so monstrously alive *because* they are dead. It is the most astonishing conquest of death one can think of. One seeks out the dead precisely where they cannot escape. Perhaps they are the more present because *neither wants anything from the other*. Their desire for the earthly realm is greater than ours to know them. Both are insatiable, and that they cannot be dislodged is the greatest, the only real truth of the world, which we push at more and more, but without their budging a single millimeter.

Humankind will have given up entirely should it ever cease this hopeless pushing.

The notion of Celan as a martyr fills me with disgust. The way he panders to Lenz is nonsense. Celan was so shrewd—his country a kind of cocoon, and therefore all the more ambitious the creation that finally sprang from it. How clumsy, how hopelessly clumsy was Lenz. No suicide can take anything away from him, Lenz's situation being nothing but disgraceful, Celan's nothing but honorable.

Even so, there's nothing to be done about the ruthless murderer Claire Goll. 147

The stringency and the *demand* of Celan's work are to me unbearable. In reality it's not about the crimes, but rather his renown despite the criminals, a renown forged in the same language that he shares with them.

A completely new constellation of fame, for which he sacrificed himself. The suicide of a Jew as a German writer, one following immediately the murder of his brethren.

It is not surprising to find that I have no mercy for beasts like this Saddam.

Whoever scrupulously employs death to serve his own ends is completely beyond any mercy on my part.

I *remain* an unshakable enemy of all despots (those who fall under the narrow and genuine sense of power that I have depicted). Whether I would tolerate the use of power to kill them, if it came to pass in my own day, is another question. Then I might very well for a moment fall on their side, simply because of my hatred of any supreme power. But this moment would be brief, and I would feel ashamed because of it, and in any case, I would do everything possible to prevent their escaping and successfully continuing their power games. I would sentence them to *lifelong imprisonment* at a minimum.

1991

Death as a means of power cannot *suddenly* be stopped. But it is possible to think of a process that can prevent it from eventually happening. A year ago, one could still imagine that this path forward would be traveled. But this year, this wonderful year, is over, and we are right back where we were.

This desire to remain, a type of bookkeeping.

Wouldn't it be more appropriate if nothing remained of a life, nothing at all? If death would mean that everything connected to the image we have of someone would disappear on the spot? Would it not be more dignified for those of us who will follow? For perhaps everything of us that remains behind is a burdensome demand upon them. Perhaps humankind is therefore not free, namely because too much of the dead remains within us, and many refuse to ever let go of any of it.

There are some who are dead whom you *never* long for. Among these are some of your nearest and dearest.

When he says that he believes in nothing but transformation, he means that he works at nothing but the chance to escape death, knowing full well that he has not yet done so, but that someday others will.

The estimates being made in America today of how many deaths the Gulf War will lead to are somewhat scandalous.

And yet there is something better than what one was used to in earlier wars, namely a sense of the value of each individual life. None should be lost, not a single one. The tally of such individuals is horrific.

Everyone can count.

High numbers of casualties used to be thought of as intrinsic to the good fortune and glory of those who survived. Today it has turned into the horrific tally of the dead—those who are not free to decide whether they are for or against the war.

That one nitpicks about this number shows how meaningful it has become. However, it is also used by those who indiscriminately and heartlessly wish to rummage among the dead.

After the rain he went out in search of snails. He talked to them; they did not creep away from him. He held them in his hand, observed them and laid them to the side where no bird could see them.

When he died, all the snails from the neighborhood came together to form his funeral cortege.

"Creation," we say, and everyone is seen as creative, if one warrants it. And then we let that person be creative, and he creatively destroys everything.

Couldn't the Americans start the war in such a way that their planes only go after Saddam? They don't have to attack anything else, nor destroy anything, if it were only clear that his capture or death would end the war.

No threats should be made against collaborators and accomplices, but only against him, and everyone should be aware of that.

Has anything like this ever *seriously* been attempted?

Yesterday half the Iraqi air force was destroyed. Today they have eleven fighter jets left among seven hundred planes.

At the last moment, we have prevailed. In a year's time he might become unconquerable. Marches for peace throughout the world. "Peace in our time."

And if your loathing of death convulses you? The only possible outcome is that he must be annihilated.

What if that had happened in 1938—how the world would look today!

It will get worse. It looks like the son of a bitch was a much greater danger than we knew. If he is not brought down, everything will be different across the entire Earth.

The most contagious fanaticism which existed somewhere or other *continually* for more than a millennium has found its most dangerous leader.

It would be an abominable self-delusion to underestimate him—much like that of twenty-five years ago in Munich.

Islam, potentially the greatest mass that ever existed, will be activated by Saddam to swift action, i.e., *really* becoming a crowd. With every day that he prevails, the danger increases. It is completely senseless to bet on his giving in. He will never give in. *Three to six million dead*, just as he said, *he will see it through*. That means he will see everything through. He is calculating that America will not stand for ten thousand casualties. He is right about that, to America's credit, let it be said. It all comes down to one casualty: *him*. He will make the rest happen.

The Germans, who demonstrate for peace *before* they have hung their purveyors of poison gas.

Their peace demonstrations should also *insist* that these new war criminals are brought to justice.

Why doesn't anyone say something? Can no one teach them anything?

I have been overjoyed about their reunification without reservation. It was right, it was just that they came together. But now for the first time I feel something rising within me against the Germans. Eighty percent of them are against the Gulf War. They know who Saddam is. They know what he's planning to do. Unashamedly, albeit reproachfully, they call him the new Hitler. They know that their businessmen have enabled him through the production of poison gas and with the building of nuclear facilities. But they are for peace. He should be spared. Some of the Arabs will be grateful to them if he is. The world will not forget it. *Neither will I.*

Not even a week has passed since it started. I can't think about anything else. Perhaps that was the last chance the Earth had of escaping. But *has* it escaped? The prospects are uncertain, and I am full of doubt. Is the coalition, which means the Americans, really strong enough? Will it keep going until no one wishes to fight anymore? Will Kuwait be completely incinerated? I have a lot of confidence in Israel, especially after the third attack. It will certainly pull through. But will someone be able to kill the son of a bitch before his own country is laid waste? Who wants anything more to be burned to the ground? So much will be destroyed before he is destroyed. They waited too long. They fed him for too long. They begged him to spare the lives of the hostages. Everyone who was there only pumped up his delusion of omnipotence. And who wasn't there! Even venerable figures made the pilgrimage, and when he freed ten he felt ten thousand times stronger. People of this century do not know, they do not know what power is. They believe that they are the ones who allow it to be *supported*. When he begged those from whom he learned about omnipotence, they believed that they could bargain with him, haggling with him as if in a cheap marketplace.

I notice how biased I am and ask myself if I would be less so if the fate of the Jews in Israel was also not in question.

No, not in any way, and no matter how many times I go over what is happening: not in any way, no way could I be any less partial. I am the mortal enemy of Saddam, the dictator, a survivor in the worst sense of the word, the despot who wields his power in order to kill others en masse. For thirty years I have presented the image of this kind of survivor to the world, clearly and unmistakably anticipating the portrait of Saddam while thinking: once I forge this profile, it will no longer be possible for such a character to exist in the world. But there he is, yet again, not only possible, but fervently adored. Less fervently is he *hated*, though luckily there are always those who have decided to hunt him down.

He cannot succeed, he cannot prevail. It does not matter that the last of his predecessors, H., met the worst of ends: *Before* he died, he was able to unleash a world war. That alone amounts to a contagion which has led to Saddam, and he must be denied the chance to spark *his* world war. Whoever thinks it is entirely possible to do so without a war is marching for "peace," or what he thinks of as that.

During these times I feel close to death. It doesn't have anything to do with feeling weak, for my mind is as strong and clear as it ever was. But it could involve the recognition that my "survivor" will *never* disappear, that he is immortal, that he always returns, and *this* eternal return can't help but mean that humanity is lost and nothing can save it.

I feel in my gut how this realization is eating me up. It

doesn't yet have complete control of me, but it continues to threaten unabated.

What should one think about all those who will be mauled to death? What should one think when there is nothing to be done for them?

You have always recoiled from *grub* as life's innermost need. Has something changed? Can any of it change? You live by eating grub. Everyone does. Your eyes may lower, but still you see grub everywhere. How can humankind escape the force of grub, off of which it lives?

Humankind is trying to save the last specimens of an animal that is by now almost completely wiped out. Perhaps we will have no success in saving the few last specimens. But humankind reproduces rapidly, and there is nothing that will save the Earth from it. Will humankind ultimately choke on itself, on its own numbers?

This war is a daily, an hourly spectacle. What will they come up with once it ends?

I don't watch any of it, but I *hear* about it and I *read* constantly, news of it perhaps being the last thing my eyes will ever read.

That would certainly be an uncomfortable end to my reading life—but is there anything else that will occur in this lifetime?

Whatever I do always seems to me despicable because I never manage to finish anything, nor will that ever really change. A despicable life, and even if there could not have been any other life that was more sensible, it remains *despicable*.

It is one o'clock in the morning. I am feeling uncertain and sometimes think that I will not live to see the outcome of this war. That is a bitter pill to swallow, though I do not doubt the outcome of the war. But I deeply doubt it can be anything different. I am mortified by the weakness of the "Left," of which I always counted myself a member. Today I heard a discussion with a completely moderate writer, but one who was happy to forward the Left's central tenet: he is afraid of Bush and never even mentions Saddam, as if there was no such Saddam in the entire world, and claims that the Americans are warmongers, even though Saddam appears again to threaten all with gas and make good on his threats. Six times the writer said he was afraid, and without feeling at all ashamed of himself in regard to those who, day to day, live in the most pressing fear of all. I always thought him an idiot. Today he filled me with disgust.

The German politicians know what they have set in motion. *All* parties are suddenly ready to fork out money. The sudden outbreak of peace has cost them more than if they had hatched a new war. They wanted to look so good, so nice, so harmless, so innocent, and now stand pitifully before the world as peaceful purveyors of poison. If they do not come down heavily on these diabolical criminals, they will never outlive their shame. Auschwitz, which many Germans believed was behind them (as if such a thing could ever be left behind) has been surreptitiously reincarnated by their peddlers of poison, and now everyone tells them that over and over. The blindness and recklessness of these peddlers toward their own people (not to mention the malice directed toward those who they want to murder again) is unfathomable. I cannot wait for the demonstrations in German cities against the peddlers of poison. Something could really come of it.

This month ends with the world's misfortune. It brought it down upon itself, and still I continue to feel distraught and cling to it and wrestle with its fate.

All who missed out on life. All who were never loved. All who could not love. All who could not watch over a child. All who never traveled to other countries. All who never knew the many different kinds of animals. All who never heard a foreign language. All who were never astonished by faith. All who did not wrestle with death. All who were not overcome by the need to know. All who were not allowed to forget how much they knew. All who never swayed. All who never said no. All whose stomach never made them feel ashamed. All who did not dream of the end of murder. All who let their memories be stolen. All who never succumbed to their pride. All not ashamed of the honors conferred. All who did not shrink away, who could not disappear. All who could not lie unless it was for a good cause. All who did not tremble before the lightning bolt of truth. All who did not hunger for dead gods. All who were not comfortable with those whose talk they could not understand a word of. All who did not free any slaves. All who did not drown in compassion, who were ashamed that they had never killed anyone. All who did not allow themselves to be located out of gratitude. All who refused to vacate the Earth. All who could never forget what an enemy is. All who could never be freed from their honest ways. All who never gave too little. All who never let themselves be deceived, and all who let themselves forget how badly they were deceived. All who were not beheaded by their own hubris, all who did not smile knowingly. All who did not laugh magnanimously. All the lives missed out on.

It again looks as bad as it has in the most recent years, only the monstrous depth of the deadly danger to both sides prevents war from breaking out. But this time the danger appears to be coming from the Arab side, through the public threats made, the cruder weapons, and the abandoning of all self-restraint. There has never been this kind of calculation of the number of days before war breaks out. Is a war that is announced in this way at all possible? All the powers of prevention still have time to be implemented. But what will be achieved through such prevention? The process of disarmament, which was the great hope set in motion by the powers that be, was undercut by the open market for weapons. While the super powers negotiated with one another, they armed other, smaller nations, until suddenly they became bigger, overweaponized entities in their own right. Now these very same weapons need to be confiscated. How can that happen without a war? The attempt to do it through threats is not dishonorable, *because there is no other choice available*. But what happens when the threats are not taken seriously? That indeed now seems to be the case.

One thing is clear above all: The concentrated power of "survivors" (in my sense of the word), those who hardly sneeze at the death of another, but also actively wish it, these people must be stopped at all costs. Wherever this power exists, it must be destroyed. The survivors remain *the* number one danger to humankind, having reached the highest level through the availability of new types of weapons.

Saddam's every sentence is an illustration of this danger. He says nothing that does not speak to it. He ridicules others because they do not consider killing openly as an option. He knows exactly what power is, and says it and practices it. All of his dodges and tricks are calculations based on death. That others want to *avoid* death is what sets his killing game in motion. Everything that is about to happen is being willed to avoid his own death. That is why he is even prepared to forego—for a little while—the death of others.

Increasingly it appears that the only solution to this monstrous danger is the death of Saddam. It is not out of the realm of possibility that one of his officers might be convinced to do the deed.

Indeed, the greatest irony would be the death of Saddam at the hands of a *Palestinian*.

Honor and power do not stand for one another. Honor needs mouths that *speak* it, and therefore has no desire that those mouths should die, though this is the only reason why. Power needs death, because its foundational urge is survival.

The cemetery that for many years he has had his eye on is getting bigger. To whom will he leave himself, where will he be put?

The only interesting thing about Saddam is his *candor*. He is the clearest of his sort. Not a single duplicitous word about death. A bunker strong as stone.

Maybe they will tear him to pieces. Maybe he will not become a saint.

Wisdom saps his strength, banalities keep him alive.

What hope can this person still have? Is it suicide? Is he trying to turn himself into a martyr? Does his downfall require a million dead?

Is there no one who can depose him? Are *all* his generals pathetic creatures? Do none of them realize that the greatest, the only chance for Iraq is for Saddam to go?

No one at all seems to know who the people around him are. There must indeed be one or two among them who are *not* from his family.

If life were incapable of being destroyed, what would then set us off?

My Saturday begins at two o'clock in the morning. In Israel it is Purim, everyone in the street and wearing masks. Never before have I felt so close to them. Six weeks in the gas chambers with kith and kin, and they are still alive.

It will go so far that I will die a simple Jew.

The time of my long marriage with the Germans is over.

He persists most of all in this *most vulgar* of feelings, namely To-Want-To-Remain-Alive. Why is he so proud of it? He persists most of all, yes, most of all in what the most disgusting of worms wants, and wanting it just as much as the worm who, having been cut in two, will regenerate itself completely. He proclaims it, just like a German proclaims that he is a German, a Jew that he is a Jew, and a Swiss that he is Swiss. Is there anything more random? Unimportant, fleeting, emptier, more absurd, not even having anything to do with language? Is there nothing more senseless than feeling that you are an enemy of someone because he is a German, a Jew, a Swiss?

Powerful, overwhelming, raging stories, or rare visitations one is relentlessly forced to bear, these are nothing but dry runs for the final incantations that await us. Nothing is for naught, it all gathers weight.

Whip away at your horse! Don't give up, never, never give in to sadness. You still *see* it coming, and even if you have gone blind—you will still see it coming.

Everything depends on this unshakable stance, which does not blind us.

Slowly he loses one after another, the letters of the alphabet. Which remain? Which does he slur? Which is the last that he slurs?

Max Frisch died this morning. I heard it this afternoon from von Jacobi, who called from the *Zürcher Zeitung*. I have been asked to contribute two or three sentences about what he means to me.

I'm a little reluctant to do so, for I have not seen him for more than ten years. But I will think about it and see if anything occurs to me. Tomorrow at 9 a.m., Jacobi will call back, and I will read the following sentences to him:

"I can't believe that Max Frisch is no longer alive. His art was an art of doubt. I would call it a doubt built out of unceasing small steps, in essence a doubt opposed to storytelling, which thus turned against itself. Since it was the opposite of storytelling, he could utilize it in such a way as to keep his doubt ever alive. One thought of him as the original founder of a completely unheroic yet insistent form of authenticity. I wish that I could turn the kind of doubt, of which he was a master, against the last point of his life, namely his death."

That is very short. I normally would never write something this short for official purposes. I did it in this case because of a deep estrangement between Frisch and myself, because he resented me for several reasons, and I resented him for the same. It's true that I only know a part of his work, but what I have said is true, and the fact that I wished he were not dead is even more true. I don't think there is any reason to feel pangs of conscience about this little obituary.

Metastases: today the Greek word cited more than any other.
Metamorphoses should replace it.

Realpolitik! The politics of implications and charges tied to killing. All the more real as a result.

Be careful when it comes to mourning. It has a tendency to eat you Jews up.

Much that he wrote decades ago and never read again now invigorates him. These notes are his own years reversed. He pulls years out of his pockets and grazes upon them. They are never confused, remain separate, and will radiate new meaning for another fifty years.

With what will they be confronted? With what sort of creatures? Wrenched, twisted, scattered, stretched? Will his sentences be afraid amid such creatures? Will they be drowned, hung, choked to death? Which sentence has the strength to look the future in the eye? Marx lies in pieces, Freud as well, computers are everywhere. Millions of them? In my eyes the stars crumble. No image survives. What Hera restored is now hidden in Japan. There it will probably end up on the woodpile of the purchaser about to light a fire. Those wonderful Van Goghs. Who could buy them back now?

The most hated thing of all has won. Money buys everything. The screaming souls of the past can be had for a price, before they put a bullet in their head.

Now I am waiting for a call from Johanna tomorrow, just as earlier I waited for a call from Hera. It's as if the mother buried herself inside the daughter and secretly listens while my daughter talks to me. Or at least that's how it feels to me. Someday she won't be able to help herself and will say two words, and I, out of happiness, will fall to the earth dead.

I have said something about Max Frisch and need to call myself to account for it.

I have not said anything that I did not mean. He was made up of small doubts. He was really a master of them. That he meant nothing to *me* as a writer, nothing at all, was not important, because many, to my astonishment, thought him *essential*.

But I also said that I did not want to believe he was dead, and that I wished I could turn his doubt against his death. That was a way of grieving for him. It was grief. We knew each other quite well and had not seen each other for many years. I never cared for him very much. Hera and I, we joked about him. Hera never believed that I took him seriously. It's true, I never took him seriously—as opposed to Dürrenmatt. But he took great pains for my sake, even though I didn't mean much to him either. The external estrangement began when he sent me *Man in the Holocene* with a pompous dedication. I was nauseated by this book. It reminded me of Thomas Bernhard, but it was *calculated*. I didn't even thank him for it. It would have required extreme indecency to say *anything* about this sorry effort. He heard nothing from me. We never met by chance again. Then came the Nobel Prize. I never expected it at all. He had been waiting for it, one could even say for decades. He never forgave me for it. He then continued to wait for nine long years. He had a petty way of wishing for big things. He never wrote me about my receiving it, and thus revealed a lot in not doing so. I heard from others how deeply he resented me for having won the prize. With each passing year his disappointment increased his resentment. He didn't say a thing when Hera died, not a single word, though he knew her well. That seemed to me the pinnacle of pettiness, and for that I hated him. He would have sensed it, for he knew well what death means to me.

Then I heard six months ago that he had the same horrible disease. From this moment on I sensed something like love for him. I would have loved to see him and convince him that the "Prize" means nothing *whatsoever*. Only when one does *not* have it does it appear desirable, otherwise it's a kind of leprosy, much more than other kinds of fame. He had certainly not wished to see me again. Most likely right up until the end he still resented me because of this same matter.

I was asked to say something about him by people who really were his enemies. I could not say no, because in this moment I was something *more* in the eyes of the world, mainly because of being a living winner of the "Prize." I tried to say something about what he had accomplished as a writer, specifically his doubt, and I am not ashamed to have said that his death affected me very much because he died still unhappy with me, and because I despair over the death of anyone, although he had indeed known Hera.

This summation for his obituary, which no one who knew our relationship would have expected from me, is so true that I do not wish to add anything to it.

The Depletion of the Animals, the first title for the new book, which I'm really considering.

Maybe it sounds quite trivial, but not to me. I really do need to have something in the book that is immediately captivating. Up to now only the report about apes being used as salespeople in West Africa has anything to do with it.

Added to the alarm over the increasingly successful extermination of animals is the distressing news today of their artificial alteration by us. Now comes the time of *monstrosities*. There is no end in sight to what kind of random, horrid forms will appear on Earth. One cannot call them metamorphoses, for they are calculated and enforced. In our hands will lie the creation of an annual fair of monstrosities. Nothing more will appear that we do not want to appear. Whatever goal is deemed not agreeable will be canceled. There is no animal that will be able to protect itself. Slaughterhouses make a quick job of it, so will they be seen as the most humane? Supposedly through gene manipulation humankind will protect itself. Perhaps it will only succeed in hindering its own protection. But the more we succeed, the more animals will be used to protect us. What should have continued uninterrupted for the foreseeable future, namely the continuance and expansion of animals, will through our own arbitrary despotism be cut off and stifled.

Maybe it will be possible to create animals who neither eat nor shit. They can still be called animals and we can be proud of them. There is no end to humankind's madness, for such madness is bound to bring about our own downfall.

The only thing that Musil has in common with Proust is that both are *absolute* writers. Each person is shaped by *his* story, not that of *history*. Each person is beyond compare. Each is meant to be seen as if there were no other person in the world. Each person belongs amid all his complexity. To each belongs his complete metamorphosis. (Localized details are deceptive, for they are only a sideshow, they alter nothing.)

Those who are *absolute* do not frivolously engage with destruction, for it is hard for them to separate themselves from their audience, although they have thousands looking on. But when they must finally be destroyed, that's when they are finished. But that does not matter, for they allow much else to go on that is indestructible. We can say that the only ones to whom death can do little are the absolute writers, because their figures are *indestructible.*

Bury your dead. They will contact you in their own good time. Don't keep poking at them. They hate being at your mercy.

Dying doesn't mean being rendered completely under someone else's power.

Suddenly all the myths that he has read in the last eighty years crawl out of him like worms.

Again Herodotus: sublime delight. My true teacher? The same kind of curiosity, the contempt for "facts." Freewheeling and therefore valid, *uninterrupted* storytelling.

To read every syllable of his again in order to completely retain him. To die with such stories upon one's lips.

He plucks people from his meditations, in which he constantly carries them around. At all times he has these people inside him. He could populate a city with them. He chooses to keep them in the dungeons of his memory. Sometimes he would like to see one, so he yanks him out and cooks him like a fish.

To your health! Someday he will choke on one bone or another.

Mistrust of submitting to anything, anything that smacks of obedience, especially if it were to mean obeying death.

There, you dream of fire and flee and flee, continuing to burn, until you wake up.

1992

It is possible that the rigidity of your hatred of death has denied you certain experiences of the times. There could be times that you simply don't wish to be true and thus you suppressed them.

When there is no reason for hopelessness, it disguises itself as disappointment, meaning disappointment over a life that supposedly was a not a life at all.

Yet it was more than a life, it was a life for many, fear for many, expectation for many, and, even if very rarely, success. Not once did this life entirely lack radiance. With her with whom you breathed as one, you were in Stockholm, and of all the prizewinners' wives, she was the most beautiful. If since then there has been no more pomp, that's the way you wanted it, having fended it off, your pride coming to the fore instead. And then two years ago the *loveliest* thing of all: Veza's name on her books—Veza, who now carries your name and will be forever linked to you—is that not the most wonderful thing of all, this resurrection twenty-seven years after her death?

Harder than the renunciation of Paradise is, I find, the renunciation of the underworld. Ah, the shadows, if only the shadows were what my death will be!

That I want something more does not mean that I renounce what little there might be.

As tough as any killing is, the rejection of death must be just as tough.

If it *must* occur, then let it happen in the middle of a word that is split in two by dying.

He is looking to retrieve the lives of the suicides he has known. How happy they are to come along, and how surprised they are for the company. He talks to them, each talks back to him. None understands what they did, none would do it again.

Together they thank him, this chorus of suicides.

Devotion grows with the number of years that have lapsed since someone's death. Anyone who grows very old ends up ossified with devotion.

He *knows* too little to die. Perhaps in the very next moment he might come to know the most important thing of all.

It doesn't have to be the last book. You don't want a swan song.

However, you don't wish to die quietly at all.

Indeed, you experienced a death very young and a birth very late. That is what has *made* you what you are, the space between the two events amounting to some sixty years.

I can no longer handle such feelings. I felt too much grief to deal with the dead. There was too much delight in me, namely love.

One loves the dead for their failings. That's why there are no dead angels.

Ignoble views of death even among the Chinese—especially in contrast to its overpowering meaning in their *rites*.

There is a ferocity in you that you have always underestimated. It's the ferocity of your consciousness of death.

Nothing more outrageous than the idea of a *last* person. For whom would that person die?

The *word* genocide must be done away with. It has become the most dangerous word of all. It is the most *alluring* word of all.
   Everything that has ever served killing, every word, every opinion, every conviction, all of it returns.
   That is the *only* eternal return.

What have you ever done except *reclaim* immortality from the gods.

Someone turns one hundred and converts to the religion of death.

The man who, fifty-five years after her death named his mother on every page of his book, has freed me from her.
   Since I read his book, for the first time she is *gone for good.*

What effect do millions of years of Earth's history have on modern humankind's sense of itself?
   Modern humankind is the result of more time than ever before. Everything happens faster and faster, yet how long was the run-up to it! The relation of its short span of life (even when it is extended) to the unspeakably long prehistory has something tantalizing and intoxicating about it, making it capable of all the more. Prohibitions, which might seem to affect life for more and more people, have less and less weight. They mean nothing more to anyone than a shake of the head. It is also true that—during such extended periods—countless more have died. The survivors look back at ever more dead. They begin to despise them. There are too many of them. Among them are entire generations of animals, assassinated.

Both are apparent victims, animals as well as humans. There are so many that one despises them. That could also mean *all* of them. The difference between many and all narrows. A complete extinction begins to be more coolly contemplated. Once it is perceived, you separate yourself from it—the exception.

It ends up either fun or a game to latch on to the extinction of others and examine it.

Not only are ever greater numbers of dead possible, they will also be *wished for* in order to increase survival.

A manuscript, half of which you gradually end up striking. Suddenly you discover that it has no more bones. It quivers and flutters, and before it shrivels up, you hear yet another wail from it, which opens your ears and eyes.

Really I have not accomplished anything that turned out as it should. *One* novel instead of the eight that were planned. *One* volume of *Crowds and Power* instead of the two that were planned. Three plays instead of a lifetime's worth of dramas written. The only thing that I have consistently pursued over fifty years are the notes, and only then because of their inconsequence.

I am gradually learning to appreciate that there is nothing more vulgar, banal, trivial, or full of demagoguery than my battle against death.

I have begun to feel ashamed of it, and yet I continue to forward it undeterred.

Man-eating Tiger
"When a tiger kills a human being, he eats the thigh, the belly and the breast, after which follows the shoulders, the back,

the limbs, and the head. Sometimes he leaves the head undisturbed, sometimes he gnaws on it like a nut. He rips off the clothes with his teeth and completely strips the person before

he eats him." *F. Mayer*

Daniel Bodmer has written me. Today we are going to the Fluntern cemetery. There I shall see what kind of grave might be available.

He is the first to take seriously my wish to *remain* in Zürich, even when I am no longer alive. His own love for this city corresponds with mine.

Why is it not immaterial where one's grave is?
Because later people will come to see where one "lies."

Should what he has done with his life really mean something, his name will be bound up with the city which he loved the most. For me, without a doubt, that city is Zürich. Countless people have lived in Vienna, and it doesn't matter whatsoever if one is counted among them. In Zürich, the only one who mattered to me in German literature (since Goethe) is Büchner. He only lived here a few months, but how it would have pleased him to remain here. Also because of him do I wish to

be buried in Zürich.

Yesterday a visit to the wonderful Fluntern Cemetery. On a hot summer day it could not have looked any more beautiful or luminous.

My thoughts were put at ease at the site of the grave near the edge of the forest, not far from Joyce. Would it bother him to be so close? Would it bother me? There will be no monument, but rather just a modest stone plate with my name on it, as well as those of Veza and Hera.

I, who never want to die, am happy about the fact the *three names* will be together in this place.

I know that this will happen; perhaps later on my views will be of use to people. It's a wonder that I have been here this long. Also a wonder that I could live this long in the city of my heart. I showed it to Veza. In summer 1961, on our way back from Greece, I spent ten days with Veza in Zürich. We lived in the old Dolder Forest Inn, which she loved. I took her through the old city, and she was enchanted by the old Petersplatz. We sailed on the lake to Rapperswil. Greece had been terrible for her, for she suffered from the mosquitoes and flies, and really only visited it because I wanted to. In Zürich she felt good and recovered from Greece. She also had a visitor here, a granddaughter of her stepfather, Erna Alkalay, who lived in Belgrade and was married to an architect. She traveled with us on the steamboat. Gerti Spitz, a childhood friend, also came from America. I pursued Hera, whose name I didn't even know, in the Kunsthaus Zürich, and told Veza about her. During these days my earlier life was knotted up with my later life, and no one was anyone's enemy.

Which is why it is okay that both names will be united with mine on the stone.

Less legitimate is the nearness of Joyce. I have complete respect for him, but really I don't like him. The only time that we met was in January 1935, at the reading of my play *The Comedy of Vanity* in Zürich. He didn't like me either. It will be hard to find anything that we have in common. Perhaps most of all the love we both have for Svevo, which perhaps was demonstrated by Joyce (his encouragement of *Zeno*) and with more decisive consequences (the invitation to Paris, which led to Svevo's later fame).

Very different kinds of people will visit him and me, and it is not clear which of us will receive more appreciation. We were both stateless, but I had the good fortune to find a city that I felt to be my *home above all others*, he died in this same city as an exile.

150

These days I am somewhat heartbroken by people from *very small* countries. Their death is a greater burden to others.

The Earth as The Titanic. The last musician.

Back then with Selimović, I thought to myself: this mighty, proud person! Like a Scottish Highlander. Naturally, he was a partisan. He happily fought. I respected that, for he had fought against some of the worst.

And now? Are they all like that? Serbs, Muslims, and Croats? Are they all equally murderous? Are they happy to be that?

They step on each other's heads with their boots. The leader of the Serbs during the shelling of Sarajevo is a *doctor* who worked at a hospital. A doctor.

A doctor. The word *groans* and will from now on always groan.

151

"Spiders are animals that are very much prized in Ethiopia. That's why children are admonished not to kill one, for people say: 'That is my aunt.'

"In Tigre they don't kill spiders, because their stomach supposedly reminds them of a pregnant woman."

In the book that someone brought to me today from Paris, I find the following sentence, which could have been written by myself:

"The responsibility for his next of kin certainly underlies his fear of his own death."

I know nothing of Lévinas, for I know nothing other than

what he looks like. Still today his descent from Heidegger depresses me a great deal. Then in the last conversation in the book I found the above quote.

152

Whom have I *not* shown Zürich from the Sonnenberg overlook? Everyone is always enchanted, just as I was when I was eight.

No one, not even I, knew back then that my grave would end up very close by.

To have died yesterday, his latest trick.

Total loneliness: the presence of those who are no longer there.

The eerie celebrations of the Sephardic Jews in Sarajevo. From their own graveyard, the oldest in the city, they are shot at by snipers who use dug-up gravestones as cover.

All the guests arrive in bulletproof vests, which they drop off for the party as they are searched for weapons.

There are still thousands of them in Sarajevo.

Before the World War there were 12,500. Then 8,000 were killed.

I was in this cemetery when I visited Sarajevo twenty years ago. I had forgotten it. Yesterday, I read the report about the snipers who dug in behind huge gravestones. Today was the first time I recalled this cemetery, which I was proudly shown by a young pair of German scholars, both Bosnian Serbs. They were dedicated followers of Tito, themselves Communists, the young man trying to stick his party's pin on me, a gesture of hospitality which with some effort I managed to fend off.

He no longer breathed and kept on reading.

A skylark flew in through the open window and rose toward the heavens.

This November is now coming to an end, as well as this year. Something keeps us going. No one knows how long this cursed world will continue. Using three pigs, they are shown how to slit someone's throat. All of it was ordered. People gladly obeyed. Women were raped, carried off, and shot. A child in a little red dress, ten years old, tried to hide behind her grandmother. All of them were shot to death. Towns were being "cleansed." What remains is nothing but blood.

And now if only *they* could be cleansed—because the world must punish them, each one who ordered it and each who carried it out must die—especially given the fact of all those who disappeared from the face of the earth. What remains is *us*, and we are capable of it all ourselves, ready to grab the pig by its ears and pull its head back.

We have these ears and a knife in our own hands, and in slitting the throats of others, we slit our own throat as well.

Think of the dinosaurs that disappeared. Will *ants* be the ones to expose the remains of the humans who disappeared?

1993

Oh if I only knew whether a single word counts! How I would hold on to it and stroke it and caress it: a single word.

I cannot renounce words. I could, if need be, lay down naked to die. But I cannot do it without words.

To confront the murder of animals and the murder of the incapacitated. Are they the same thing?

The love of death among the Romantics raises my hackles. They act as if *their* death was something special.

He's looking for the place where everyone remains alive.

Kill whom? By whom are they murdered? Bosnians.

The dead impose a barrier. They also provide an opening.
  The first is awful and has led to nothing but misfortune.
  The second will save the world through pity.

What is more bitter: death itself or the time afterward that is free of pain? And why are all doctrines so keen to involve even worse pains after death?
  I see nothing. I have reached that point. Who sees more? Who is capable of calming me with what he sees?

While there are more and more of them, causing more despair, he continues to preach: not one, not a single one should be lost, each should live, forever.

Is there not a single one worthy of living forever?

About this he says nothing. He has no opinion on it what-soever.

Despots worry the most about their immortality.

That's why there is nothing left but to be ashamed of what you want for yourself.

Whenever the subject of despots comes up, he feels as if he's been murdered.

Büchner's grave, which he finally found, is obsolete: it reminds one of *Danton's Death*.

Now, after *Woyzeck* and *Lenz*, the entire Zürichberg would not suffice for Büchner's grave.

One should not be surprised about the cult of those who died too young. We are all *guilty* of the years swindled away from them.

Ridiculous humankind: death has set its teeth into us, and you want to free your spirit from it?

But it is essential that one also *remains*, even if you are a hundred years old. It is essential that one never *deceives* others, as well as himself, about death, nor stands weak before it or even *morally* abhors it while suffering his own pain.

The wretched relatives, who try to hog the view of the dead one, their eager but ineffectual masquerade.

Let it go, and don't preach to D. anymore.

I'll start just calling it D. By shortening it, it takes up less space. Absent the "eath," it loses the empty sigh of futility.

He died, if only not to complain anymore.

On a bench the old woman reads the obituaries.

Will humankind ever be thought to have reached its end? Will it disappear before everything ends? Must it disappear so not to be seen as having reached its end?

For some time he has been catching himself saying in conversation: "When I am a hundred years old." He therefore entertains the possibility, he holds it as plausible, he mentions people that he knew, *respectable* people who were ninety-eight, ninety-six, ninety-four, and he knew them at their liveliest. Maybe this should be the speech directed against death which one can make while alive?

The Bible, through its incomparable power, has contributed to the misfortune of the Jews.
    Who condones someone else being chosen?

It's now like it was in Vienna eighty years ago. Bloodlust everywhere. What kind of neutral Switzerland does one have to inhabit to come to one's senses? If I had thought that my life would end amid the same conditions that gave rise to the First World War, once again all of it unfolding in Sarajevo, and again among the Serbs—would I have wanted to live on to see it?

Goldoni died on February 6, 1793, poor and blind in Paris at eighty-six years of age.
    On the same day Chénier gave a beautiful speech about him at the Convention. One should think of him as the Voltaire, the Molière of Italy, and again award him a (small) royal pension, which he had lost in recent years, as did all of the

royal pensioners. The Convention agreed with Chénier and adopted this well-intentioned resolution. Goldoni died, without learning of it, that same day.

Could there be a sadder end?

Shed skins, empty.
    No longer stuffed. The straw has run out.

This grandfather of yours, this person who gave off the greatest, most devilish feeling of vitality, which would have done him no good at all.

He would have been shoved into the cattle car, he would have been selected on the ramp, he would have screamed while choking on the gas.

If you had experienced that, you would have become an entirely different person.

If that had happened to your mother, to Veza, you would have killed *yourself*. It is not possible to know something like that and do *nothing*.

Your *charitable* statements (in your notes) during the last years of the war had nothing to do with how little you knew of what was going on. They sprang from the knowledge of destroyed German cities, of defeat and the terrible revenge that threatened the Germans. Back then people really thought Germany would become a wasteland. The fate of these "guinea pigs sacrificed to a faith," as I called them then, concerned me more and more the closer the war got to the complete destruction of the Germans.

It was worse than if Caesar's Rome, which I have always hated, had been physically snuffed out along *with him*. I have otherwise never thought much of historical parallels, which in themselves never *really* exist, but back then I saw Germany as Carthage, as completely laid to waste before my very eyes.

The ninety-year-old develops his plan to become the new Proust. He plans to begin tomorrow.

This is the draft of the letter that I will dictate to Johanna tomorrow, my reply to Herr Rainer Böhlke in Neustadt, who three weeks ago sent me the following letter:

> Gartenstraße 35
> 3057 Neustadt
> March 24, 1993

To the Very Honorable Herr Canetti,

As a single man, one does not think just about the past. No, one's thoughts also radiate out from one's own existence.

To that point, I possess a not inconsiderable estate and wish to leave it to you in my will.

It would be a great honor for me, for in this way I would like to use my fortune to express my admiration for your work.

It would be a great joy to me if you would accept my inheritance after my departure from this life. I deeply hope that with this assistance you will be able to attend even more intensely to your meaningful literary work.

> Your benefactor,

My reply will be:

> C./ c/o Carl Hanser Verlag
> April 15, 1993

Most Honored Herr Böhlke,

Your letter reached me just after Easter. I am sorry that I could not reply earlier.

Your offer astounds me. I beg you not to think badly of me when I say that I cannot accept it.

I will soon be 88 years old. There really is not a lot more that one can expect from me. The books themselves provide enough for me to live on.

But let me not ignore the fact that in earlier, more difficult times, I would never have thought to live off an inheritance from someone which I did not have coming to me otherwise.

I thank you for your proposition and hope for you many more years than he to whom you have directed your good graces.

With best wishes,
Elias Canetti

I mean no condescension whatsoever when I say that I respect and admire Weizsäcker, the German president, and can almost say that I revere him.

He does not let someone like Kohl dissuade him from what he thinks is essential. He has courage. Soon murder threats will *rain* down upon him.

Hatred against the Turks and Romany has *balkanized* Germany. The river of blood that the Englander Enoch Powell predicted could really come to pass there. The animosity of the Germans against the Turks, their truest admirers, is absurd. Needless to say, it is outrageous that the descendants of the murderers of the Armenians should suffer the same fate as the Jews. Turning the other cheek means nothing to the Turks. Since very small children are being targeted, they will *never* forgive.

He lives with the perception that he does not exist, but he cannot tell anyone. If others knew, he would disappear entirely. However, if he manages to keep it a secret, he can grow old without anyone ever noticing.

Darwinism, which turns death into something *progressive*.

We leave nothing behind. We leave sentences that are falsely written and even more falsely understood.

However, if it is all pointless, if eighty-eight years really comes to nothing worthwhile, when every hour of every day, every month, and every year comes to absolutely nothing— then why do you constantly keep writing about what vexes you? Are not these sentences meant to be read by someone who through them comes to his senses, takes them in hand, considers them, thinks about them, and is done with them?

God—only the word is not entirely dead to me. I still need it at unexpected moments, never out of resignation, never out of faith, but separate from any kind of gratitude, angry, existing for the sake of this anger, like a wasp banging against the windowpane for the seven-hundredth time, until I—who is that?—set it free.

1994

The escape to Dante, in Italian. His teachings seeming your very own.

It was very early on, when you were seven, that your father gave you a version of Dante made for children.

Now in my ninetieth year, he has become essential.

There, it is burning fiercely and cannot be extinguished soon enough.

They have schools there for people a hundred years old, but not for younger people.

There, their teeth grow until they choke on them.

It is time for me to sort matters out again within myself. Without writing I come undone. I sense how my life dissolves into dead, dull speculation when I no longer write down what is on my mind. I will try to change that.

Afterword

The Book Against Death is the lifelong project that, by definition, Elias Canetti could never live to complete. Having in
1937 systematically begun to collect notes about the meaning,
nature, and consequence of death, in 1942 Canetti began to
compose his own aphorisms, musings, tirades, notes, and
commentaries on and against death, right up until 1994, the
year of his own passing, his hope being that he would one day
complete and publish an entire book on the subject.

And yet, as Peter von Matt observes in the afterword to
the German edition, just as Robert Musil could never manage to write the last sentence of *The Man Without Qualities*,
Canetti could never write the first sentence to what he thought
would be his most vital work and lasting legacy. Despite having finally completed his monumental 1960 study *Crowds and
Power* (perhaps *the* seminal work needed to understand the
machinations of twentieth-century history and beyond), despite having written a novel, three plays, and several volumes
of celebrated memoirs, all of which landed him the 1981 Nobel
Prize in Literature, Canetti was overwhelmed by the "reckoning" with death he felt chosen to complete, especially after
having been shattered by the death of his father in 1912 when
he was seven, and the loss of his beloved mother in 1937, the
very year he set out to write *The Book Against Death*. However,
though Canetti may have felt that "[as] long as I have not formulated clearly and wholeheartedly what death means, I will
not have lived," he nevertheless did not succumb to defeat,
but instead remained driven by the very life force he wished to
celebrate, ennoble, inspire, and most of all plant with defiance

in the face of the forces of death that he felt "infected" modern humankind.

The result is not a book *about* death, but the extended action of a mind obsessed and churning with the power and poignancy of life. Instead of "accepting" death, Canetti's eye remains ever trained on it as an adversary. Against it he pits the daily urge to write, and thus to live, filling notepad after notepad with the notes and aphorisms he worked at each morning. Because the central impetus behind the project was Canetti's burning desire to "defeat death," only by continuing to live and to write could he maintain that battle. "The greatest struggle in life is not to become inured to death," he writes. Canetti also admits, "As long as I write I feel (absolutely) safe," for only then is his mind quiet and strong, the formulation of his thoughts against death equal to "the constant pacing of the tiger behind its bars in order not to miss the single brief instant of its release." The reader experiences that same release in witnessing the mercurial energy at the heart of Canetti's most potent observations, whether it be the early experience of death leaving "a wound that turns into a lung through which you breathe," or the sad realization that "[t]he souls of the dead are in others, namely those left behind, and they slowly die out entirely."

Canetti completed some two thousand pages of notes and aphorisms over the course of sixty-five years, the earliest note incorporated here being from a 1929 notebook when Canetti was twenty-four, while the latest was composed close to the time of his own death in 1994. While roughly one third of the entries gathered here were published in the collections of notes and aphorisms that brought him fame, *The Book Against Death* is the most thematically unified of his books, two-thirds of this one's contents appearing in German for the first time in 2014. Part notebook, part catalogue of meditations, part diary, part musings on current events and writers dead and alive, part personal wrestling with the loss of his parents, his two wives, a younger brother, and numerous friends, along with reflections on the birth of his daughter late in life, *The Book Against Death* is Canetti's most personal work, spanning more than half a century of his life and thought via the most comprehensive collection of his notes and aphorisms ever published.

Canetti's "notes" are not mere jottings randomly scribbled down, but rather a conscious art form that demands the active work of the reader to complete their meaning. Whether it be the observation that "Death is born of God and has gobbled up its Father," or the lament, "We do not die of sadness—out of sadness we live on," his aphorisms are gems we contemplate to sharpen the facets of our own thinking. Within each lies the significance of the whole, and within the whole we witness the warp and woof of a mind in constant thought. Like fireworks, they erupt from the small to the large, illuminating the dark through their explosive yet ordered, connective pulse. We may be told that "[t]he dead are nourished on judgment, the living on love," but what that actually *means* for our lives is something to be pondered at length. Meanwhile, buried within the observation that "[t]he worst crime did not deserve death, and without the *acceptance* of death, the worst crime would not even exist" lies a revolutionary rethinking of human justice and culpability.

Canetti's notes are neither morose nor gloomy. Sardonic, melancholy, aghast, enigmatic, passionate—they are fueled by the fire of a man writing *for* life *against* death in a century and locale suffused with the latter. Begun amid the rise of fascism in the 1930s, they find an urgent impetus in the cataclysm of the 1940s. "I cannot let this war pass without hammering out a weapon within my heart that will conquer death," notes Canetti in 1942 while also lamenting the many friends already lost. And yet *The Book Against Death* takes on more than the Second World War and the Holocaust, for Canetti muses upon the role that death has always played in history, and how our response to death shapes who we are. Thus, besides his own thoughts, Canetti includes quotes by other writers and thinkers, including Goethe, Franz Grillparzer, Robert Walser, Walter Benjamin, and Arno Schmidt, as well as newspaper and scholarly accounts of different practices and beliefs about death, ranging from ancient Egypt to Native America, China, India, Latin America, and Greece. The result is an encyclopedic overview of death as filtered through a mind gifted with an astounding power to both synthesize and parse the topic in a way that does not exhaust it, but explores it anew.

There is also a clear political stance that runs throughout Canetti's thinking on the subject, for he is not only obsessed with somehow finding a way to defeat death, but more pointedly with defeating the employment of death as a means to power, most of all through the willingness to kill others. "The first human would be the one who never killed and never wished for death," he observes, while elsewhere he muses that "the *one* virtue" of manifesting a powerful hatred of death could be "that human beings will no longer wish to kill." For, as Canetti makes clear, despots do not hate death, but rather embrace it as a means to their own ends, the most important of which is self-preservation. "Out of the efforts of a single individual to stave off death the monstrous edifice of power is created," Canetti observes, having experienced an extreme form of tyranny under Hitler, but also recognizing what he felt to be the return of the "survivor," he who stops at nothing to perpetuate his hold on power, in a figure such as Saddam Hussein, or what he surely would have seen in Vladimir Putin were he writing today. Indeed, despite having spent his life presenting "the image of this kind of survivor to the world,"

Canetti cannot help but fear that "my 'survivor' will *never* disappear, that he is immortal, that he always returns, and *this* eternal return can't help but mean that humanity is lost and nothing can save it."

Related to this is the threat of nuclear annihilation that arose out of the Second World War, leading the man who wrote so perceptively about the mysterious and terrifying power of crowds to admit to himself, "You are no longer obsessed with crowds ... Mass death has replaced your concerns with the masses." For Canetti, as for many others, the detonations at Hiroshima and Nagasaki meant that "[i]n a single monstrous leap [death] has attained the power of contagion like never before. Now it is really all-powerful, now it is the true God." Should one sense a religious ring to this sentiment, one would not be mistaken, even though throughout his notes Canetti condemns "the religion of death" at the heart of any professed faith in immortality. Instead, he insists that "there are *two* different kinds of life, the immortal and the mortal, yet the lesser one is the immortal, and not the other way around." For Canetti, all such intimations of immortality are not only invitations to delusion, but also sinister ploys aimed at convincing human beings to trade their own humanity for the false, controlling ideals propagated by church and state alike. Against this Canetti poses "the beginning of the true Enlightenment: one that establishes the right of *every* individual to live on," a right that in his view is not only inalienable, but a moral necessity.

"I accept *no* death," Canetti declares while underscoring "the sanctity of each person, but also really the sanctity of each life." While understanding perfectly well that death is inevitable, the distinction he insists upon lies in there being no need to live *as if* death were inevitable and all-controlling. Thus, Canetti's focus is not so much on the fact that we die, but rather the consequences of not only how we think about death, but also the effect of averting our eyes from it. "He who will not be dissuaded from facing death has the most religion of all," he notes, and while this again may seem to be about facing one's own death, Canetti makes very clear that it would be "awful if my own tough-minded, fearless stance is in the end 'explained away' as psychological, as if it only springs from special circumstances in my life, and thus means something to me alone." Instead, the consequences of his recalcitrance are much broader and deeper in arguing for a complete and radical transformation of our entire conception of death, as he explains:

> As soon as matters look hopeless for someone mortally ill, everything beyond what is happening to him seems a senseless waste that only matters to the living. Many think that this is the battlefield on which death is fought. But that is not what I am talking about at all. I am talking about a false *attitude* which is found particularly among the healthy, a division, namely between life and death, as if both were two equal entities. It is this attitude which grants death the same standing as life. To equate them is a distortion, one nourished by every kind of faith that ascribes more and more to death.

This is Canetti's central position in a nutshell, but it does not encapsulate the full dynamic of his imagination in grappling with death. In addition to defiance, feelings of tenderness, regret, guilt, and whimsy populate Canetti's consciousness and serve as a humanizing tonic to his obsession. Though on the one hand he may feel that "death is my lead weight, and I take desperate measures not to shed it," on the other he records the very strangeness of death as event and entity when noting without further explanation, "He died in his sleep. In which dream?" or simply observes the poignancy of "The hundred-year-old woman who knows all the names of her dogs," or hauntingly imagines snails forming a funeral cortege for the man who gathers them after a rainstorm and moves them to where no bird can find them. "Adam strangles God; Eve looks on," reads another entire entry, one which contains a depth charge of religious implications, but another single note evokes the pedestrian absurdity of our passing in proclaiming, "His last wish: One last sneeze." In other words, to "[t]ake apart death, its inner workings," Canetti feels compelled to employ any tool available to him, be it anger, personal loss, historical atrocity, or even the mordant and absurd: "A people made up of individuals who have kangaroo-like pouches, into which they stuff their shriveled dead and carry them around with them."

"I hate death, therefore I am," Canetti makes clear, declaring his own "Cogito ergo sum" to be *Mortem odi ergo sum*." Behind this rage, however, beats the heart of the "one possibility: until you draw your last breath, to hope for a way out not yet known to us." Though this may seem the most futile of all hopes, it is also the most nobly quixotic, for as Canetti notes, "It does not matter what one calls this hope, so long as it exists." In an era of calculated demonization and brazen despotism, one can only hope that such a hope still exists. *The Book Against Death* argues that it does.

PETER FILKINS

Acknowledgments

Elias Canetti, *Das Buch gegen den Tod, mit einem Nachwort von Peter Matt* (Carl Hanser Verlag, 2010) is the source text for this translation. Throughout the translation I have included titles, authors, and citations as noted by Canetti for various quotes he includes from other writers, scholars, and sources, though I have not tracked down the editions which he cites to verify page or volume numbers. I have also provided further biographical information on the people and sources mentioned in his notes, except in cases where the figure is already well known to the general reader (Goethe, Kafka, Michelangelo, etc.). For texts that clearly seem quoted from news reports or historical accounts, or where a text has no clear attribution, I state as such in the endnotes to distinguish those entries from ones that Canetti wrote, or attached a heading to, or for which he provided a general attribution. For the few quotes Canetti writes down in English or French, I have translated the German translation included in the Hanser edition. Otherwise all quotes from likely non-German texts that do not list a different source language in the notes should be considered to have been quoted by Canetti in German. Therefore it helps to remember that these are Canetti's notebooks, full of unattributed and unsourced quotes, and entries made in several different languages. I have tried to preserve the nature of the ad hoc conversation Canetti maintained throughout decades of thought and reading, rather than opt for an archaeological rendering of his sources.

For the original inspiration to translate this book, I am deeply indebted to Joshua Cohen, as well as for his inclusion of a selection from these notes and aphorisms in *I Want to Keep Smashing Myself until I Am Whole: An Elias Canetti Reader* (Picador, 2022), which he edited. I am also grateful to the National Endowment for the Humanities for an NEH Summer Stipend, as well as to Peter Thompson for an Ezra Translation Residency, which provided valuable time and focus to complete the rough draft. Selections have also appeared in *Ezra: An Online Journal of Translation, Salmagundi, The Paris Review Daily,* and *Harper's Magazine.* I am grateful to the editors of each for their interest and support.

Endnotes

1 Quoted in English and followed by a German translation. No attribution provided.

2 Quoted in English and followed by a German translation. No attribution provided.

3 Quoted in English and followed by a German translation. No attribution provided.

4 Antoinette Bourignon (1616–1680), French-Flemish mystic who predicted the arrival of the end times in her lifetime, followed by the onset of the Last Judgment, after which she would restore Christianity on earth.

5 Antoinette Bourignon (1616–1680), French-Flemish mystic who predicted the arrival of the end times in her lifetime, followed by the onset of the Last Judgment, after which she would restore Christianity on earth.

6 Quoted in English and followed by a German translation. No attribution provided.

7 Quoted in English and followed by a German translation. No attribution provided.

8 Quoted in English and followed by a German translation. No attribution provided

9 La Bruyère: Jean de La Bruyère (1645–1696), French philosopher known for his satire. Quoted in French and followed by a German translation.

10 Daisy Bates. *The Passing of the Aborigines: A Lifetime Spent Among the Natives of Australia* (London: John Murray, 1938). Quoted in English and followed by a German translation.

11 Thomas More (1478–1535), Catholic philosopher, author, and humanist beheaded by Henry VIII. The quote is taken from William Roper's *The Life of Thomas More*, first published in 1626. Quoted in English and followed by a German translation.

12 Marco Polo, *The Description of the World*, vol. I, trans. A.
    C. Moule and Paul Pelliot (London: Routledge, 1938), 50.
    Quoted in English and followed by a German translation.
13 Franz Grillparzer (1791–1872), Austrian playwright and
    diarist.
14 Quoted in English and followed by a German translation.
    No attribution provided.
15 Quoted in English and followed by a German translation.
16 No attribution provided.
17 François Rabelais (1494–1553), French writer and priest.
18 "The Vision of Tnugdalus" is a twelfth-century religious
    text, written by Brother Marcus of Regensburg, which sets
    out the otherworldly vision of the Irish knight Tnugdalus,
    later known as Tundalus.
19 Ananda was one of Buddha's ten principal disciples. On
    several occasions the Buddha hinted that his life could be
    prolonged a full eon, but that he would have to be asked to
    do so. Ananda never took the hint, and therefore never made
    the request, thus resulting in Buddha's death.
20 Quoted in English and followed by a German translation.
21 Georg Canetti (1911–1971), Elias Canetti's younger brother.
22 Heinrich Wilhelm von Kleist (1777–1811), German poet,
    dramatist, novelist, and short story writer who murdered his
    terminally ill companion, Henriette Vogel, before turning
    the gun on himself.
23 *Les Bambara du Ségou* was published in Paris in 1924 and is a
    historical, ethnographic, and literary study of the people of
    the French Sudan written by Charles Monteil (1870–1949).
24 Quoted in English and followed by a German translation.
25 Leo Perutz (1882–1957), Austrian novelist born in Prague
    and who later lived in Vienna.
26 The Kanaimà is the spirit of vengeance who kills at night
    while disguised as jaguars, boas, and other animals.
27 The Taulipang and Arecuna are tribes living in the border
    region between Venezuela, Guyana, and Brazil. The Pis-
    chaukó were a legendary tribe of Kanaimà, who were their

mortal enemies. See Neil L. Whitehead, *Dark Shamans: Kanaimà and the Poetics of Violent Death* (Durham, NC: Duke University Press, 2002) 80.

28 Cesare Pavese (1908–1950), Italian writer.

29 Sanskrit epic written between the seventh and fourth centuries BCE.

30 Mozi (470–391 BCE), Chinese philosopher and founder of Mohism, which argued against Confucianism and Taoism in advocating universal love and equality, along with modest funeral rites in order to devote wealth to social good instead. See Stanford Encyclopedia of Philosophy (https://plato. stanford.edu/entries/mohism/), accessed 15 July 2023.

31 The quotation can be translated as "Now I am going to kill Laurica!" and the incident is recounted in Canetti's memoir *The Tongue Set Free*.

32 Quoted in French and followed by a German translation.

33 Jean Améry (1912–1978), born Hanns Chaim Mayer, Austrian essayist and Holocaust survivor.

34 Also known as the *Pirkei Avot*, a compilation of teachings and maxims from the Rabbinic Jewish tradition.

35 Robert Walser (1878–1956), German-speaking Swiss writer and author of the short story "Frau Scheer." Robert Walser, *Berlin Stories*, trans. Susan Bernofsky (New York: New York Review of Books Classics, 2012).

36 *Der Ackermann aus Böhmen* (*The Plowman from Bohemia*) is a Medieval text written in 1401 by Johannes von Tepl (ca. 1315–ca. 1415).

37 Simon Wiesenthal (1908–2005), Jewish Austrian Holocaust survivor, Nazi hunter, and writer. Michael Kohlhaas is the titular character of an 1808 novella written by Heinrich von Kleist.

38 The Zohar, also known as Kabbalah, is a foundational text of Jewish mysticism.

39 Robert Musil (1880–1942), Austrian writer best known for his unfinished novel *The Man Without Qualities*.

40 Gerhard Fritsch (1924–1969), Austrian writer.

Thomas Bernhard (1931–1989), Austrian writer.

Herbert Zand (1923–1970), Austrian writer.

Friedrich Heer (1916–1983), Austrian historian.

Jeannie Ebner (1918–2004), Austrian writer.

Franz Nabl (1883–1974), Austrian writer.

41 Rudolf Höss (1900–1947), longest-serving commandant of Auschwitz. Quoted in English in and followed by a German translation. The quote is taken from the affidavit Höss gave at the Nuremberg War Crimes Trial.

42 Canetti is referring here to such incidents as the My Lai massacre, committed by American troops in a Vietnamese village on March 16, 1968.

43 Alexander Herzen (1812–1870), Russian writer and thinker. In The "Influence of the Belles Lettres," Herder writes: "The frivolous has triumphed over the weighty, the imagination has usurped the understanding, and the more external stimuli and inducements there are to promote these excrescences of the human mind and of belles lettres, the more they flourish, choking what is dry and serious with their exuberant growth." Alexander Herzen, *Selected Writings on Aesthetics*, trans. Gregory Moore (Princeton: Princeton UP, 2006) 335–36.

44 Iris Murdoch (1919–1999), Irish and British novelist and philosopher.

45 "N." refers to Friedrich Nietzsche (1844–1900), German philosopher.

46 Ivan Bunin (1870–1953), Russian writer who wrote a memoir of Tolstoy titled *The Liberation of Tolstoy: A Tale of Two Writers*, trans Thomas Gaiton Marullo (Evanston: Northwestern University Press, 2001).

47 Canetti means here the Vietnam War.

48 The birth referred to is that of Canetti's daughter, Johanna, his only child.

49 Stendhal's *De l'Amour* (*On Love*) is a philosophical treatise that he published in 1822.

50 *New Scientist* 25, no. 428 (Jan. 28, 1965): 205; quoted in Vitus B. Dröscher, *Die freundliche Bestie*, 89–90.

51   Lorna Marshall (1898–2002), American anthropologist who studied the Kung people of the Kalahari Desert.
52   Johann Gottfried von Herder (1744–1803), German philosopher, theologian, and poet.
Jean Paul (1763–1825), German novelist and short-story writer.
53   Verrier Elwin, *Myths of Middle India* (London: Oxford University Press, 1949), 413. Quoted in English and followed by a German translation.
54   Verrier Elwin, *Maria Murder and Suicide* (London: Oxford University Press, 1950), 58.
55   Walter Benjamin. "The Storyteller: Reflections on the Works of Nikolai Leskov," in *Illuminations: Essays and Reflections.* Trans. Harry Zohn. Ed. Hannah Arendt (New York: Harcourt, 1968).
56   No attribution provided.
57   Hans Mayer (1907–2001), German literary scholar.
Ulrich Becher (1910–1990), German author and playwright.
Alfred Döblin (1878–1957), German novelist and essayist; Peter Huchel (1903–1981), German poet and editor; Hans Fallada (1893–1947), German novelist.
58   Pythagoras of Samos (c. 570–c. 495 BCE), Greek philosopher. No attribution provided.
59   No author or source is given for this note.
60   Arnaldo Momigliano (1908–1987), Italian historian.
61   Samuel Beckett, "First Love," in *First Love and Other Novellas* (New York and London: Penguin 1994).
62   Arno Schmidt (1914–1979), German writer and translator. The quotation appears in his novella *Leviathan*, published in 1949. Courtesy of the Arno Schmidt Foundation, Bargfeld (Germany).
63   No attribution provided.
64   Felipe Huamán Poma de Ayala (1534–1615), Quecha nobleman who chronicled the mistreatment of the Incas by the Spanish. The Aya Marcay Quilla is the twelfth month of the Incan calendar and the title of one of Poma de Ayala's

chronicles. Quoted in English and followed by Canetti's German translation.

65 No attribution provided.

66 *Hyperion* is an epistolary novel written by Friedrich Hölderlin (1770–1843), published in two volumes in 1797 and 1799.

67 Nikephoros I (750–811) served as Byzantine Emperor from 802 to 811. Theophanes the Confessor (758/760–817/818), Byzantine monk and chronicler.

68 Quoted in English and followed by a German translation.

69 Sofia Fedorechenko, *Ivan Speaks*, trans. Thomas Whittemore (Boston: Houghton Mifflin, 1919). The book compiles accounts given in 1915–1916 by Russian soldiers fighting in the First World War. Canetti quotes from the German translation, published as *Der Russe redet*.

70 Sophie Scholl (1921–1943), German student and anti-Nazi activist.

71 Shimen Shmuel Frug (1860–1916), Russian-Yiddish poet.

72 Elisabeth Brock-Sulzer (1903–1981), Swiss theater critic.

73 No attribution provided.

74 No attribution provided.

75 No attribution provided.

76 No attribution provided.

77 Curt Nimuendajú, *The Tikuna*, ed. Robert H. Lowie, trans. William D. Hohenthal (Berkeley: University of California Press, 1952), 135.

78 Horst Günther, *Insel Almanach auf das Jahr 1981: Karl Philip Moritz, wer ist das?* (Frankfurt am Main: Insel Verlag, 1980), 80–81.

79 No attribution provided.

80 Johann George Adam Forster (1754–1794), German naturalist, ethnologist, and travel writer.

81 Johann Peter Eckermann (1792–1854), author of *Gespräche mit Goethe* (*Conversations with Goethe*), first published in 1836.

82 No attribution provided.

83 Wolfram Eberhard, *Volksmärchen aus Sudost-China*, No. 67 (Helsinki: Suoolamainen Tiedeakatemia, 1941), 112–13.

84 Jean-Paul Sartre (1905–1980), French author and playwright.

85 Gabriel Marcel (1889–1973), French philosopher and playwright.

86 No attribution provided.

87 No attribution provided.

88 No attribution provided.

89 Carl Ludwig Siegel (1896–1981), German mathematician. No attribution provided.

90 Hermann Broch (1886–1951), Austrian writer.

91 Juan Rulfo (1917–1986), Mexican writer.

92 Luis Buñuel (1900–1983), Spanish filmmaker.

93 Odilio of Cluny (962–1049), fifth Benedictine Abbot of Cluny. No source attribution for the quote.

94 Jürgen Stroop (1895–1952), German SS commander. No attribution provided.

95 Max Horkheimer (1895–1973), German philosopher and sociologist.
    Theoder W. Adorno (1903–1969), German sociologist, critic, and composer.
    Gershom Scholem (1897–1982), German-born Israeli philosopher and historian.

96 Eduard von Bauernfeld (1802–1890), Austrian playwright.

97 No attribution provided.

98 Julie de Krüdener (1764–1824), Russian writer, traveler, evangelist, and mystic.
    Johann Heinrich Jung-Schilling (1740–1817), German writer. No attribution provided.

99 No attribution provided.

100 Quoted in English and followed by a German translation.

101 No attribution is provided for this quotation in English. which is followed by a German translation.

102 No attribution provided.

103 The Bajau Laut are maritime nomads who have lived for

centuries almost entirely at sea in the ocean between Malaysia, the Philippines, and Indonesia.

104 Antonio Canova (1757–1822), Italian sculptor.

105 Johann Schiltberger (1380– c. 1440), German writer who wrote accounts of his travels through Europe, Asia, and Africa.

106 Fritz Wotruba (1902–1975), Austrian sculptor.
"D.S." is Dieter Sulzer (1943–1983), German art historian.

107 Alexandra David-Néel (1868–1969), Belgian-French explorer and writer.

108 Quoted in English and followed by a German translation.

109 Gottfried Benn (1886–1956), German poet.

110 Marie von Thurn und Taxis (1855–1934), German patron of Rainer Maria Rilke (1875–1926), the German poet.

111 Quoted in English and followed by a German translation.

112 Ferdinand Hodler (1853–1918), Swiss painter.

113 Hartmut Fähndrich (b. 1944), German translator of Arabic literature.

114 No attribution provided.

115 Josef Mengele (1911–1979), SS officer and physician at Auschwitz.

116 Telford Taylor (1908–1998), American lawyer who was Counsel for the Prosecution at the Nuremburg Trials after the Second World War.

117 Heinrich Böll (1917–1985), German writer.
"G.G. " refers to Günter Grass (1927–2015), German writer.

118 Jules Renard (1864–1910), French writer. Quoted in French and followed by a German translation.

119 Karlheinz Stockhausen (1928–2007), German composer.

120 No attribution provided.

121 Lucius Anneaus Seneca (c. 4 BCE–65 CE), Roman philosopher.
Francis Bacon (1561–1626) English philosopher and statesman. His essay "Of Death" was first published in 1612, then in enlarged form in 1625. Quoted in Latin and followed by a German translation.

122 The Ojibwa are an indigenous people of the northern

midwest of the U.S. and south-central Canada.

123 Walther Rehm (1901–1963), German literary scholar.

124 Friedrich Wilhelm Joseph Schelling (1775–1854), German philosopher.

Eberhard Friedrich von Georgii (1757–1830), German jurist.

125 Al-Ghazali (1058–1111), Persian philosopher and theologian.

Erwin Gräf (1914–1936), German scholar and translator.

126 Abu Hasan al-Ash'ari (c. 874–976), Muslim theologian.

127 Moritz Heimann (1868–1925), German writer.

128 No attribution provided.

129 No attribution provided.

130 No attribution provided.

131 Yantou Quanhuo (828–887), Chinese Zen master.

No attribution provided.

132 Jesus, son of Sirach, was the father of Ben Sira, who wrote the *Book of Sirach*, or *Ecclesiaticus*, between 200 and 175 BCE.

133 Quoted in English and followed by a German translation.

134 Jakob Michael Reinhold Lenz (1751–1792), German writer.

135 Hans Saner (1934–2017), Swiss philosopher.

136 Reinhart Koselleck (1923–2006), German historian.

137 No attribution provided.

138 Chrysippus of Soli (d. 206 BCE), Greek Stoic philosopher.

139 No attribution provided.

140 Novalis (1772–1801), born Georg Philipp Friedrich Freiherr, German aristocrat and writer.

141 Somadeva, eleventh-century writer from Kashmir.

142 Misia Sert (1872–1950), Polish pianist and host of a Paris salon.

143 Franz Werfel (1890–1945), Austrian-Czech novelist.

"A." is Alma Mahler (1879–1964), composer, author, and socialite whose first husband was Gustav Mahler (1860–1911), Austrian-Czech composer and conductor.

144 Susuki Bokushi (1770–1842), Japanese writer.

145 Thomas Hürlimann (b. 1950), Swiss playwright.

146 Ott-Heinrich Keller (1906–1990), German mathematician.

Friedrich Dürrenmatt (1921–1990), Swiss author and dramatist.

147 Paul Celan (1920–1970), Romanian-born German-language poet. "Lenz" refers to the titular character of a story by Georg Büchner written in 1836.
Claire Goll (1890–1977), German-French writer, whose accusation of plagiarism against Celan contributed to the depression that led to his suicide.

148 The identity of the author and source for this quote remain unknown.

149 Georg Büchner (1813–1837), German dramatist.

150 Italo Svevo, pseudonym of Aron Hector Schmitz (1861–1928), Italian writer.

151 Mehmed "Meša" Selimović (1910–1982), Yugoslav writer.

152 Emmanuel Lévinas (1906–1995), French philosopher.

153 Carlo Goldoni (1707–1793), Italian dramatist.
André Marie Chénier (1762–1794), French poet.

154 Several famous writers and artists, including Amy Tan, Isabel Allende, Matt Groening, and Frank Zappa, also received the same letter in 1993 from Rainer Böhlke of Neustadt, Germany.
Https://www.latimes.com/archives/la-xpm-1993-09-27-vw-39618-story.html, accessed 15 July 2023.

155 Richard Karl von Weizsäcker (1920–2015), German politician and president of Germany from 1984 to 1994.
Helmut Kohl (1930–2017), chancellor of Germany from 1982 to 1998.
Enoch Powell (1912–1998), British politician.
Canetti refers here to the 1993 attack in the German village of Sollingen by far-right extremists in which three girls and two women died in a fire, and fourteen others were wounded, among them several children.

New Directions Paperbooks — a partial listing

Adonis, Songs of Mihyar the Damascene
César Aira, Ghosts
  An Episode in the Life of a Landscape Painter
Ryanosuke Akutagawa, Kappa
Will Alexander, Refractive Africa
Osama Alomar, The Teeth of the Comb
Guillaume Apollinaire, Selected Writings
Jessica Au, Cold Enough for Snow
Paul Auster, The Red Notebook
Ingeborg Bachmann, Malina
Honoré de Balzac, Colonel Chabert
Djuna Barnes, Nightwood
Charles Baudelaire, The Flowers of Evil*
Bei Dao, City Gate, Open Up
Yevgenia Belorusets, Lucky Breaks
Rafael Bernal, His Name Was Death
Mei-Mei Berssenbrugge, Empathy
Max Blecher, Adventures in Immediate Irreality
Jorge Luis Borges, Labyrinths
  Seven Nights
Coral Bracho, Firefly Under the Tongue*
Kamau Brathwaite, Ancestors
Anne Carson, Glass, Irony & God
  Wrong Norma
Horacio Castellanos Moya, Senselessness
Camilo José Cela, Mazurka for Two Dead Men
Louis-Ferdinand Céline
  Death on the Installment Plan
  Journey to the End of the Night
Inger Christensen, alphabet
Julio Cortázar, Cronopios and Famas
Jonathan Creasy (ed.), Black Mountain Poems
Robert Creeley, If I Were Writing This
H.D., Selected Poems
Guy Davenport, 7 Greeks
Amparo Dávila, The Houseguest
Osamu Dazai, The Flowers of Buffoonery
  No Longer Human
  The Setting Sun
Anne de Marcken
  It Lasts Forever and Then It's Over
Helen DeWitt, The Last Samurai
  Some Trick
José Donoso, The Obscene Bird of Night
Robert Duncan, Selected Poems
Eça de Queirós, The Maias
Juan Emar, Yesterday

William Empson, 7 Types of Ambiguity
Mathias Énard, Compass
Shusaku Endo, Deep River
Jenny Erpenbeck, Go, Went, Gone
  Kairos
Lawrence Ferlinghetti
  A Coney Island of the Mind
Thalia Field, Personhood
F. Scott Fitzgerald, The Crack-Up
Rivka Galchen, Little Labors
Forrest Gander, Be With
Romain Gary, The Kites
Natalia Ginzburg, The Dry Heart
Henry Green, Concluding
Marlen Haushofer, The Wall
Victor Heringer, The Love of Singular Men
Felisberto Hernández, Piano Stories
Hermann Hesse, Siddhartha
Takashi Hiraide, The Guest Cat
Yoel Hoffmann, Moods
Susan Howe, My Emily Dickinson
  Concordance
Bohumil Hrabal, I Served the King of England
Qurratulain Hyder, River of Fire
Sonallah Ibrahim, That Smell
Rachel Ingalls, Mrs. Caliban
Christopher Isherwood, The Berlin Stories
Fleur Jaeggy, Sweet Days of Discipline
Alfred Jarry, Ubu Roi
B.S. Johnson, House Mother Normal
James Joyce, Stephen Hero
Franz Kafka, Amerika: The Man Who Disappeared
Yasunari Kawabata, Dandelions
Mieko Kanai, Mild Vertigo
John Keene, Counternarratives
Kim Hyesoon, Autobiography of Death
Heinrich von Kleist, Michael Kohlhaas
Taeko Kono, Toddler-Hunting
László Krasznahorkai, Satantango
  Seiobo There Below
Ágota Kristóf, The Illiterate
Eka Kurniawan, Beauty Is a Wound
Mme. de Lafayette, The Princess of Clèves
Lautréamont, Maldoror
Siegfried Lenz, The German Lesson
Alexander Lernet-Holenia, Count Luna

Denise Levertov, Selected Poems
Li Po, Selected Poems
Clarice Lispector, An Apprenticeship
   The Hour of the Star
   The Passion According to G.H.
Federico García Lorca, Selected Poems*
Nathaniel Mackey, Splay Anthem
Xavier de Maistre, Voyage Around My Room
Stéphane Mallarmé, Selected Poetry and Prose*
Javier Marías, Your Face Tomorrow (3 volumes)
Bernadette Mayer, Midwinter Day
Carson McCullers, The Member of the Wedding
Fernando Melchor, Hurricane Season
   Paradais
Thomas Merton, New Seeds of Contemplation
   The Way of Chuang Tzu
Henri Michaux, A Barbarian in Asia
Henry Miller, The Colossus of Maroussi
   Big Sur & the Oranges of Hieronymus Bosch
Yukio Mishima, Confessions of a Mask
   Death in Midsummer
Eugenio Montale, Selected Poems*
Vladimir Nabokov, Laughter in the Dark
Pablo Neruda, The Captain's Verses*
   Love Poems*
Charles Olson, Selected Writings
George Oppen, New Collected Poems
Wilfred Owen, Collected Poems
Hiroko Oyamada, The Hole
José Emilio Pacheco, Battles in the Desert
Michael Palmer, Little Elegies for Sister Satan
Nicanor Parra, Antipoems*
Boris Pasternak, Safe Conduct
Octavio Paz, Poems of Octavio Paz
Victor Pelevin, Omon Ra
Fernando Pessoa
   The Complete Works of Alberto Caeiro
Alejandra Pizarnik
   Extracting the Stone of Madness
Robert Plunket, My Search for Warren Harding
Ezra Pound, The Cantos
   New Selected Poems and Translations
Qian Zhongshu, Fortress Besieged
Raymond Queneau, Exercises in Style
Olga Ravn, The Employees
Herbert Read, The Green Child
Kenneth Rexroth, Selected Poems
Keith Ridgway, A Shock

Rainer Maria Rilke
   Poems from the Book of Hours
Arthur Rimbaud, Illuminations*
   A Season in Hell and The Drunken Boat*
Evelio Rosero, The Armies
Fran Ross, Oreo
Joseph Roth, The Emperor's Tomb
Raymond Roussel, Locus Solus
Ihara Saikaku, The Life of an Amorous Woman
Nathalie Sarraute, Tropisms
Jean-Paul Sartre, Nausea
Kathryn Scanlan, Kick the Latch
Delmore Schwartz
   In Dreams Begin Responsibilities
W.G. Sebald, The Emigrants
   The Rings of Saturn
Anne Serre, The Governesses
Patti Smith, Woolgathering
Stevie Smith, Best Poems
   Novel on Yellow Paper
Gary Snyder, Turtle Island
Muriel Spark, The Driver's Seat
   The Public Image
Maria Stepanova, In Memory of Memory
Wislawa Szymborska, How to Start Writing
Antonio Tabucchi, Pereira Maintains
Junichiro Tanizaki, The Maids
Yoko Tawada, The Emissary
   Scattered All over the Earth
Dylan Thomas, A Child's Christmas in Wales
   Collected Poems
Thuan, Chinatown
Rosemary Tonks, The Bloater
Tomas Tranströmer, The Great Enigma
Leonid Tsypkin, Summer in Baden-Baden
Tu Fu, Selected Poems
Elio Vittorini, Conversations in Sicily
Rosmarie Waldrop, The Nick of Time
Robert Walser, The Tanners
Eliot Weinberger, An Elemental Thing
   Nineteen Ways of Looking at Wang Wei
Nathanael West, The Day of the Locust
   Miss Lonelyhearts
Tennessee Williams, The Glass Menagerie
   A Streetcar Named Desire
William Carlos Williams, Selected Poems
Alexis Wright, Praiseworthy
Louis Zukofsky, "A"

*BILINGUAL EDITION

For a complete listing, request a free catalog from New Directions, 80 8th Avenue, New York, NY 10011
or visit us online at ndbooks.com